Get the eBook FREE!

(PDF, ePub, Kindle, and liveBook all included)

We believe that once you buy a book from us, you should be able to read it in any format we have available. To get electronic versions of this book at no additional cost to you, purchase and then register this book at the Manning website.

Go to https://www.manning.com/freebook and follow the instructions to complete your pBook registration.

That's it!
Thanks from Manning!

Transfer Learning for Natural Language Processing

PAUL AZUNRE

MANNING

SHELTER ISLAND

For online information and ordering of this and other Manning books, please visit
www.manning.com. The publisher offers discounts on this book when ordered in quantity.
For more information, please contact

> Special Sales Department
> Manning Publications Co.
> 20 Baldwin Road
> PO Box 761
> Shelter Island, NY 11964
> Email: orders@manning.com

Manning Publications Co.   Development editor: Susan Ethridge
20 Baldwin Road   Technical development editor: Al Krinker
PO Box 761   Review editor: Aleksandar Dragosavljević
Shelter Island, NY 11964   Production editor: Keri Hales
                                     Copy editor: Pamela Hunt
                                     Proofreader: Melody Dolab
                          Technical proofreader: Ariel Gamiño
                                      Typesetter: Dennis Dalinnik
                                  Cover designer: Marija Tudor

ISBN: 9781617297267
Printed in the United States of America

This book is dedicated to my wife, Diana, son, Khaya, and puppy, Lana, who shared the journey of writing it with me.

contents

v

preface

Over the past couple of years, it has become increasingly difficult to ignore the break-neck speed at which the field of natural language processing (NLP) has been progressing. Over this period, you have likely been bombarded with news articles about trending NLP models such as ELMo, BERT, and more recently GPT-3. The excitement around this technology is warranted, because these models have enabled NLP applications we couldn't imagine would be practical just three years prior, such as writing production code from a mere description of it, or the automatic generation of believable poetry and blogging.

A large driver behind this advance has been the focus on increasingly sophisticated transfer learning techniques for NLP models. Transfer learning is an increasingly popular and exciting paradigm in NLP because it enables you to adapt or transfer the knowledge acquired from one scenario to a different scenario, such as a different language or task. It is a big step forward for the democratization of NLP and, more widely, artificial intelligence (AI), allowing knowledge to be reused in new settings at a fraction of the previously required resources.

As a citizen of the West African nation of Ghana, where many budding entrepreneurs and inventors do not have access to vast computing resources and where so many fundamental NLP problems remain to be solved, this topic is particularly personal to me. This paradigm empowers engineers in such settings to build potentially life-saving NLP technologies, which would simply not be possible otherwise.

I first encountered these ideas in 2017, while working on open source automatic machine learning technologies within the US Defense Advanced Research Projects

Agency (DARPA) ecosystem. We used transfer learning to reduce the requirement for labeled data by training NLP systems on simulated data first and then transferring the model to a small set of real labeled data. The breakthrough model ELMo emerged shortly after and inspired me to learn more about the topic and explore how I could leverage these ideas further in my software projects.

Naturally, I discovered that a comprehensive practical introduction to the topic did not exist, due to the sheer novelty of these ideas and the speed at which the field is moving. When an opportunity to write a practical introduction to the topic presented itself in 2019, I didn't think twice. You are holding in your hands the product of approximately two years of effort toward this purpose. This book will quickly bring you up to speed on key recent NLP models in the space and provide executable code you will be able to modify and reuse directly in your own projects. Although it would be impossible to cover every single architecture and use case, we strategically cover architectures and examples that we believe will arm you with fundamental skills for further exploration and staying up-to-date in this burgeoning field on your own.

You made a good decision when you decided to learn more about this topic. Opportunities for novel theories, algorithmic methodologies, and breakthrough applications abound. I look forward to hearing about the transformational positive impact you make on the society around you with it.

acknowledgments

I am grateful to members of the NLP Ghana open source community, where I have had the privilege to learn more about this important topic. The feedback from members of the group and users of our tools has served to underscore my understanding of how transformational this technology truly is. This has inspired and motivated me to push this book across the finish line.

I would like to thank my Manning development editor, Susan Ethridge, for the uncountable hours spent reading the manuscript, providing feedback, and guiding me through the many challenges. I am thankful for all the time and effort my technical development editor, Al Krinker, put in to help me improve the technical dimension of my writing.

I am grateful to all members of the editorial board, the marketing professionals, and other members of the production team that worked hard to make this book a reality. In no particular order, these include Rebecca Rinehart, Bert Bates, Nicole Butterfield, Rejhana Markanovic, Aleksandar Dragosavljević, Melissa Ice, Branko Latincic, Christopher Kaufmann, Candace Gillhoolley, Becky Whitney, Pamela Hunt, and Radmila Ercegovac.

The technical peer reviewers provided invaluable feedback at several junctures during this project, and the book would not be nearly as good without them. I am very grateful for their input. These include Andres Sacco, Angelo Simone Scotto, Ariel Gamiño, Austin Poor, Clifford Thurber, Jaume López, Marc-Anthony Taylor, Mathijs Affourtit, Matthew Sarmiento, Michael Wall, Nikos Kanakaris, Ninoslav Cerkez, Or Golan, Rani Sharim, Sayak Paul, Sebastián Palma, Sergio Govoni, Todd Cook, and

Vamsi Sistla. I am thankful to the technical proofreader, Ariel Gamiño, for catching many typos and other errors during the proofreading process. I am grateful to all the excellent comments from book forum participants that further helped improve the book.

I am extremely grateful to my wife, Diana, for supporting and encouraging this work. I am grateful to my Mom and my siblings—Richard, Gideon, and Gifty—for continuing to motivate me.

about this book

This book is an attempt to produce a comprehensive practical introduction to the important topic of transfer learning for NLP. Rather than focusing on theory, we stress building intuition via representative code and examples. Our code is written to facilitate quickly modifying and repurposing it to solve your own practical problems and challenges.

Who should read this book?

To get the most out of this book, you should have some experience with Python, as well as some intermediate machine learning skills, such as an understanding of basic classification and regression concepts. It would also help to have some basic data manipulation and preprocessing skills with libraries such as Pandas and NumPy.

That said, I wrote the book in a way that allows you to pick up these skills with a bit of extra work. The first three chapters will rapidly bring you up to speed on everything you need to know to grasp the transfer learning for NLP concepts sufficiently to apply in your own projects. Subsequently, following the included curated references on your own will solidify your prerequisite background skills, if that is something you feel that you need.

Road map

The book is divided into three parts. You will get the most out of it by progressing through them in the order of appearance.

Part 1 reviews key concepts in machine learning, presents a historical overview of advances in machine learning that have enabled the recent progress in transfer learning for NLP, and provides the motivation for studying the subject. It also walks through a pair of examples that serve to both review your knowledge of more traditional NLP methods and get your hands dirty with some key modern transfer learning for NLP approaches. A chapter-level breakdown of covered concepts in this part of the book follows:

- Chapter 1 covers what exactly transfer learning is, both generally in AI and in the context of NLP. It also looks at the historical progression of technological advances that enabled it.
- Chapter 2 introduces a pair of representative example natural language processing (NLP) problems and shows how to obtain and preprocess data for them. It also establishes baselines for them using the traditional linear machine learning methods of logistic regression and support vector machines.
- Chapter 3 continues baselining the pair of problems from chapter 2 with the traditional tree-based machine learning methods—random forests and gradient boosting machines. It also baselines them using key modern transfer learning techniques, ELMo and BERT.

Part 2 dives deeper into some important transfer learning NLP approaches based on shallow neural networks, that is, neural networks with relatively few layers. It also begins to explore deep transfer learning in more detail via representative techniques, such as ELMo, that employ recurrent neural networks (RNNs) for key functions. A chapter-level breakdown of covered concepts in this part of the book follows:

- Chapter 4 applies shallow word and sentence embedding techniques, such as word2vec and sent2vec, to further explore some of our illustrative examples from part 1 of the book. It also introduces the important transfer learning concepts of domain adaptation and multitask learning.
- Chapter 5 introduces a set of deep transfer learning NLP methods that rely on RNNs, as well as a fresh pair of illustrative example datasets that will be used to study them.
- Chapter 6 discusses the methods introduced in chapter 5 in more detail and applies them to the datasets introduced in the same chapter.

Part 3 covers arguably the most important subfield in this space, namely, deep transfer learning techniques relying on transformer neural networks for key functions, such as BERT and GPT. This model architecture class is proving to be the most influential on recent applications, partly due to better scalability on parallel computing architectures than equivalent prior methods. This part also digs deeper into various adaptation strategies for making the transfer learning process more efficient. A chapter-level breakdown of covered concepts in this part of the book follows:

- Chapter 7 describes the fundamental transformer architecture and uses an important variant of it—GPT—for some text generation and a basic chatbot.

- Chapter 8 covers the important transformer architecture BERT and applies it to a number of use cases, including question answering, filling in the blanks, and cross-lingual transfer to a low-resource language.
- Chapter 9 introduces some adaptation strategies meant to make the transfer learning process more efficient. This includes the strategies of discriminative fine-tuning and gradual unfreezing from the method ULMFiT, as well as knowledge distillation.
- Chapter 10 introduces additional adaptation strategies, including embedding factorization and parameter sharing—strategies behind the ALBERT method. The chapter also covers adapters and sequential multitask adaptation.
- Chapter 11 concludes the book by reviewing important topics and briefly discussing emerging research topics and directions, such as the need to think about and mitigate potential negative impacts of the technology. These include biased predictions on different parts of the population and the environmental impact of training these large models.

Software requirements

Kaggle notebooks are the recommended way of executing these methods, because they allow you to get moving right away without any setup delays. Moreover, the free GPU resources provided by this service at the time of writing expand the accessibility of all these methods to people who may not have access to powerful GPUs locally, which is consistent with the "democratization of AI" agenda that excites so many people about NLP transfer learning. Appendix A provides a Kaggle quick start guide and a number of the author's personal tips on how to maximize the platform's usefulness. However, we anticipate that most readers should find it pretty self-explanatory to get started. We have hosted all notebooks publicly on Kaggle with all required data attached to enable you to start executing code in a few clicks. However, please remember to "copy and edit" (fork) notebooks—instead of copying and pasting into a new Kaggle notebook—because this will ensure that the resulting libraries in the environment match those that we wrote the code for.

About the code

This book contains many examples of source code both in numbered listings and in line with normal text. In both cases, source code is formatted in a `fixed-width font like this` to separate it from ordinary text. Sometimes code is also **in bold** to highlight code that has changed from previous steps in the chapter, such as when a new feature adds to an existing line of code.

In many cases, the original source code has been reformatted; we've added line breaks and reworked indentation to accommodate the available page space in the book. In rare cases, even this was not enough, and listings include line-continuation markers (➥). Additionally, comments in the source code have often been removed from the listings when the code is described in the text. Code annotations accompany many of the listings, highlighting important concepts.

The code for the examples in this book is available for download from the Manning website at http://www.manning.com/downloads/2116 and from GitHub at https://github.com/azunre/transfer-learning-for-nlp.

liveBook discussion forum

Purchase of *Transfer Learning for Natural Language Processing* includes free access to a private web forum run by Manning Publications where you can make comments about the book, ask technical questions, and receive help from the author and from other users. To access the forum, go to https://livebook.manning.com/#!/book/transfer-learning-for-natural-language-processing/discussion. You can also learn more about Manning's forums and the rules of conduct at https://livebook.manning.com/#!/discussion.

Manning's commitment to our readers is to provide a venue where a meaningful dialogue between individual readers and between readers and the author can take place. It is not a commitment to any specific amount of participation on the part of the author, whose contribution to the forum remains voluntary (and unpaid). We suggest you try asking the author some challenging questions lest his interest stray! The forum and the archives of previous discussions will be accessible from the publisher's website as long as the book is in print.

about the author

PAUL AZUNRE holds a PhD in Computer Science from MIT and has served as a principal investigator on several DARPA research programs. He founded Algorine Inc., a research lab dedicated to advancing AI/ML and identifying scenarios where they can have a significant social impact. Paul also co-founded Ghana NLP, an open source initiative focused on using NLP and Transfer Learning with Ghanaian and other low-resource languages.

about the cover illustration

The figure on the cover of *Transfer Learning for Natural Language Processing* is captioned "Moluquoise," or Moluccan woman. The illustration is taken from a collection of dress costumes from various countries by Jacques Grasset de Saint-Sauveur (1757–1810), titled *Costumes civils actuels de tous les peuples connus*, published in France in 1788. Each illustration is finely drawn and colored by hand. The rich variety of Grasset de Saint-Sauveur's collection reminds us vividly of how culturally apart the world's towns and regions were just 200 years ago. Isolated from each other, people spoke different dialects and languages. In the streets or in the countryside, it was easy to identify where they lived and what their trade or station in life was just by their dress.

The way we dress has changed since then and the diversity by region, so rich at the time, has faded away. It is now hard to tell apart the inhabitants of different continents, let alone different towns, regions, or countries. Perhaps we have traded cultural diversity for a more varied personal life—certainly for a more varied and fast-paced technological life.

At a time when it is hard to tell one computer book from another, Manning celebrates the inventiveness and initiative of the computer business with book covers based on the rich diversity of regional life of two centuries ago, brought back to life by Grasset de Saint-Sauveur's pictures.

Part 1

Introduction and overview

Chapters 1, 2, and 3 review key concepts in machine learning, present a historical overview of advances in machine learning enabling recent progress in transfer learning for NLP, and stress the importance of studying the subject. They also walk through a pair of relevant examples that serve to both review your knowledge of more traditional NLP methods and get your hands dirty with some key modern transfer learning for NLP approaches.

What is transfer learning?

This chapter covers

- What exactly transfer learning is, both generally in artificial intelligence (AI) and in the context of natural language processing (NLP)
- Typical NLP tasks and the related chronology of NLP transfer learning advances
- An overview of transfer learning in computer vision
- The reason for the recent popularity of NLP transfer learning techniques

Artificial intelligence (AI) has transformed modern society in a dramatic way. Machines now perform tasks that human used to do, and they do them faster, cheaper, and, in some cases, more effectively. Popular examples include computer vision applications, which teach computers how to understand images and videos, such as for the detection of criminals in closed-circuit television camera feeds. Other computer vision applications include the detection of diseases from images of patients' organs and the defining of plant species from plant leaves. Another important branch of AI, natural language processing (NLP), deals particularly with the analysis and processing of human natural language data. Examples of

3

NLP applications include speech-to-text transcription and translation between various languages.

The most recent incarnation of the technical revolution in AI robotics and automation—which some refer to as the Fourth Industrial Revolution[1]—was sparked by the intersection of algorithmic advances for training large neural networks, the availability of vast amounts of data via the internet, and the ready availability of massively parallel capabilities via graphical processing units (GPUs), which were initially developed for the personal gaming market. The recent rapid advances in the automation of tasks relying on human perception, specifically computer vision and NLP, required these strides in neural network theory and practice to happen. The growth of this area enabled the development of sophisticated representations of input data and desired output signals to handle these difficult problems.

At the same time, projections of what AI will be able to accomplish have significantly exceeded what has been achieved in practice. We are warned of an apocalyptic future that will erase most human jobs and replace us all, potentially even posing an existential threat to us. NLP is not excluded from this speculation, as it is today one of the most active research areas within AI. It is my hope that reading this book will contribute to helping you gain a better understanding of what is realistically possible to expect from AI, machine learning, and NLP in the near future. However, the main purpose of this book is to arm readers with a set of actionable skills related to a recent paradigm that has become important in NLP—transfer learning.

Transfer learning aims to leverage prior knowledge from different settings—be it a different task, language, or domain—to help solve a problem at hand. It is inspired by the way in which humans learn, because we typically do not learn things from scratch for any given problem but rather build on prior knowledge that may be related. For instance, learning to play a musical instrument is considered easier when one already knows how to play another instrument. Obviously, the more similar the instruments—an organ versus a piano, for example—the more useful prior knowledge is and the easier learning the new instrument will be. However, even if the instruments are vastly different—such as the drum versus the piano—some prior knowledge can still be useful, even if less so, such as the practice of adhering to a rhythm.

Large research laboratories, such as Lawrence Livermore National Laboratories or Sandia National Laboratories, and large internet companies, such as Google and Facebook, are able to learn large sophisticated models by training deep neural networks on billions of words and millions of images. For instance, Google's NLP model BERT (Bidirectional Encoder Representations from Transformers), which will be introduced in the next chapter, was pretrained on the English version of Wikipedia (2.5 billion words) and the BookCorpus (0.8 billion words).[2] Similarly, deep convolutional neural networks (CNNs) have been trained on more than 14 million images of

---

[1] K. Schwab, *The Fourth Industrial Revolution* (Geneva: World Economic Forum, 2016).

[2] J. Devlin et al., "BERT: Pre-Training of Deep Bidirectional Transformers for Language Understanding," *arXiv* (2018).

the ImageNet dataset, and the learned parameters have been widely outsourced by a number of organizations. The amounts of resources required to train such models from scratch are not typically available to the average practitioner of neural networks today, such as NLP engineers working at smaller businesses or students at smaller schools. Does this mean that the smaller players are locked out of being able to achieve state-of-the-art results on their problems? Most definitely not—thankfully, the concept of transfer learning promises to alleviate this concern if applied correctly.

WHY IS TRANSFER LEARNING IMPORTANT?

Transfer learning enables you to adapt or transfer the knowledge acquired from one set of tasks and/or domains to a different set of tasks and/or domains. What this means is that a model trained with massive resources—including data, computing power, time, and cost—which were once open sourced can be fine-tuned and reused in new settings by the wider engineering community at a fraction of the original resource requirements. This represents a big step forward for the democratization of NLP and, more widely, AI. This paradigm is illustrated in figure 1.1, using the act of learning how to play a musical instrument as an example. It can be observed from the figure that information sharing between the different tasks/domains can lead to a reduction in data required to achieve the same performance for the later, or *downstream*, task B.

1.1 Overview of representative NLP tasks

The goal of NLP is to enable computers to understand natural human language. You can think of it as a process of systematically encoding natural language text into numerical representations that accurately portray its meaning. Although various taxonomies of typical NLP tasks exist, the following nonexhaustive list provides a framework for thinking about the scope of the problem and framing appropriately the various examples that will be addressed by this book. Note that some of these tasks may (or may not, depending on the specific algorithm selected) be required by other, more difficult, tasks on the list:

- *Part-of-speech (POS) tagging*—Tagging a word in text with its part of speech; potential tags include verb, adjective, and noun.
- *Named entity recognition (NER)*—Detecting entities in unstructured text, such as PERSON, ORGANIZATION, and LOCATION. Note that POS tagging could be part of an NER pipeline.
- *Sentence/document classification*—Tagging sentences or documents with predefined categories, such as sentiments {"positive," "negative"}, various topics {"entertainment," "science," "history"}, or some other predefined set of categories.
- *Sentiment analysis*—Assigning to a sentence or document the sentiment expressed in it, for example, {"positive," "negative"}. Indeed, you can arguably view this as a special case of sentence/document classification.
- *Automatic summarization*—Summarizing the content of a collection of sentences or documents, usually in a few sentences or keywords.

Traditional paradigm: Parallel training for different tasks/domains

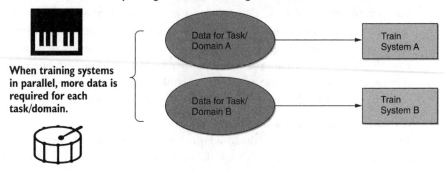

Transfer learning paradigm: Knowledge is shared between different tasks/domains.

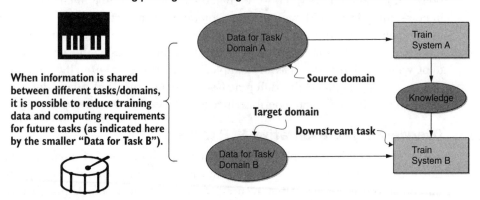

Figure 1.1 An illustration of the advantages of the transfer learning paradigm—shown in the bottom panel—where information is shared between systems trained for different tasks/domains, versus the traditional paradigm—shown in the top panel—where training occurs in parallel between tasks/domains. In the transfer learning paradigm, reduction in data and computing requirements can be achieved via the information/knowledge sharing. For instance, we expect a person to learn to play the drums more easily if they know how to play the piano first.

- *Machine translation*—Translating sentences/documents from one language into another language or a collection of languages.
- *Question answering*—Determining an appropriate answer to a question posed by a human; for example, Question: What is the capital of Ghana? Answer: Accra.
- *Chatterbot/chatbot*—Carrying out a conversation with a human convincingly, potentially aiming to accomplish some goal, such as maximizing the length of the conversation or extracting some specific information from the human. Note that a chatbot can be formulated as a question-answering system.
- *Speech recognition*—Converting the audio of human speech into its text representation. Although a lot of effort has been and continues to be spent making speech recognition systems more reliable, in this book it is assumed that a text representation of the language of interest is already available.

- *Language modeling*—Determining the probability distribution of a sequence of words in human language, where knowing the most likely next word in a sequence is particularly important for language generation—predicting the next word or sentence.
- *Dependency parsing*—Splitting a sentence into a *dependency tree* that represents its grammatical structure and the relationships between its words. Note that POS tagging can be important here.

1.2 Understanding NLP in the context of AI

Before proceeding with the rest of this book, it is important to understand the term natural language processing and to correctly situate it with respect to other commonly encountered terms, such as artificial intelligence, machine learning, and deep learning. The popular media often assign meanings to these terms that do not match their use by machine learning scientists and engineers. As such, it is important to kick off our journey by defining precisely what we mean when we use these terms, as shown in the Venn diagram in figure 1.2.

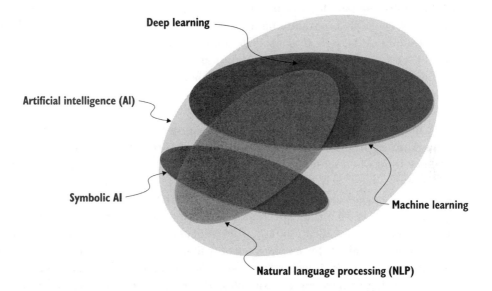

Figure 1.2 **A Venn diagram visualization of the terms natural language processing (NLP), artificial intelligence (AI), machine learning, and deep learning relative to each other. Symbolic AI is also shown.**

As you can see, deep learning is a subset of machine learning, which in turn is a subset of AI. NLP is a subset of AI as well, with a nonempty intersection with deep learning and machine learning. This figure expands on the one presented by François Chollet.[3]

---

[3] F. Chollet, *Deep Learning with Python* (New York: Manning Publications, 2018).

Please see chapter 6 and section 8.1 of his book for a good overview of the application of neural nets to text. Symbolic AI is also shown in the figure and will be described in the next subsection.

1.2.1 Artificial intelligence (AI)

Artificial intelligence as a field came about in the middle of the 20th century, as a broad effort to make computers mimic and perform tasks typically carried out by human beings. Initial approaches focused on manually deriving and hard-coding explicit rules for manipulating input data for each circumstance of interest. This paradigm is typically referred to as *symbolic AI*. It worked for well-defined problems such as chess but notably stumbled when encountering problems from the perception category, such as vision and speech recognition. A new paradigm was needed, one where the computer could learn new rules from data, rather than having a human supervisor specify them explicitly. This led to the rise of machine learning.

1.2.2 Machine learning

In the 1990s, the paradigm of machine learning became the dominant trend in AI. Instead of explicitly programming a computer for every possible scenario, the computer would now be *trained* to associate input to output signals by seeing many examples of such corresponding input-output pairs. Machine learning employs heavy mathematical and statistical machinery, but because it tends to deal with large and complex datasets, the field relies more on experimentation, empirical observations, and engineering than mathematical theory.

A machine learning algorithm learns a representation of input data that transforms it into appropriate output. For that, it needs a collection of data, such as a set of sentence inputs in a sentence classification task, and a set of corresponding outputs, for example, tags such as {"positive," "negative"} for sentence classification. Also needed is a *loss function*, which measures how far the current output of the machine learning model is from the expected output of the dataset. To aid in understanding, consider a binary classification task, where the goal of machine learning might be to pick a function called the *decision boundary* that will cleanly separate data points of the different types, as shown in figure 1.3. This decision boundary should *generalize* beyond training data to unseen examples. To make this boundary easier to find, you

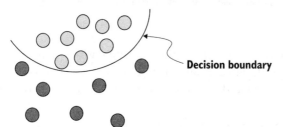

Decision boundary

Figure 1.3   An illustrative example of a major motivating task in machine learning: finding a decision boundary in the hypothesis set to effectively separate different types of points from each other. In the case shown in this figure, the hypothesis set may be the set of arcs.

might want to first preprocess or transform the data into a form more amenable for separation. We seek such transformations from the allowable set of functions called the *hypothesis set*. Automatically determining such a transformation, which makes the machine learning end goal easier to accomplish, is specifically what is referred to as *learning*.

Machine learning automates this process of searching for the best input-output transformation inside some predefined hypothesis set, using guidance from some feedback signal embodied by the loss function. The nature of the hypothesis set determines the class of algorithms under consideration, as we outline next.

Classical machine learning is initiated with probabilistic modeling approaches such as *naive Bayes*. Here, we make a *naive* assumption that the input data features are all independent. *Logistic regression* is a related method and typically the first one a data scientist will try on a dataset to baseline it. The hypothesis sets for both of these classes of methods are sets of linear functions.

Neural networks were initially developed in the 1950s, but it was not until the 1980s that an efficient way to train large networks was discovered—backpropagation coupled with the stochastic gradient descent algorithm. While backpropagation provides a way to compute gradients for the network, stochastic gradient descent uses these gradients to train the network. We review these concepts briefly in appendix B. The first successful practical application occurred in 1989, when Yann LeCun of Bell Labs built a system for recognizing handwritten digits, which was then used heavily by the US Postal Service.

Kernel methods rose in popularity in the 1990s. These methods attempt to solve classification problems by finding good decision boundaries between sets of points, as was conceptualized in figure 1.3. The most popular such method is the *support vector machine* (SVM). Attempts to find a good decision boundary proceed by mapping the data to a new high-dimensional representation where hyperplanes are valid boundaries. The distance between the hyperplane and the closest data points in each class is then maximized. The high computational cost of operating in the high-dimensional space is alleviated using the *kernel trick*. Instead of computing high-dimensional data representations explicitly, a *kernel function* is used to compute distances between points at a fraction of the computing cost. This class of methods is backed by solid theory and is amenable to mathematical analysis, which is linear when the kernel is a linear function—attributes that made these methods extremely popular. However, performance on perceptual machine learning problems left much to be desired, because these methods first required a manual *feature engineering* step, which was brittle and prone to error.

Decision trees and related methods are another class of algorithms that is still widely used. A decision tree is a decision support aid that models decisions and their consequences as *trees*, that is, a graph where any two nodes are connected by exactly one path. Alternatively, a tree can be defined as a flowchart that transforms input values into output categories. The popularity of decision trees rose in the 2010s, when methods relying on them began to be preferred over kernel methods. This popularity benefited from their ease of visualization, comprehension, and explainability. To aid in understanding, figure 1.4 shows an example decision tree structure that classifies the input {A,B} in category 1 if A<10, category 2 if A>=10 while B<25, and category 3 otherwise.

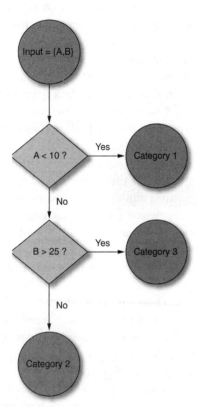

Figure 1.4   Example decision tree structure that classifies the input {A,B} in category 1 if A<10, category 2 if A>=10 while B<25, and category 3 otherwise

Random forests provide a practical machine learning method for applying decision trees. This method involves generating a large number of specialized trees and combining their outputs. Random forests are extremely flexible and widely applicable, making them often the second algorithm to try after logistic regression for baselining. When the Kaggle open competition platform started out in 2010, random forests quickly became the most widely used algorithm on the platform. In 2014, *gradient-boosting machines* took over. They iteratively learn new decision-tree-based models that address weak points of models from the previous iterations. At the time of this writing, they are widely considered to be the best class of methods for addressing nonperceptual machine learning problems. They are still extremely popular on Kaggle.

Around 2012, GPU-trained deep convolutional neural networks (CNNs) began to win the yearly ImageNet competition, marking the beginning of the current deep learning "golden age." CNNs started to dominate all major image-processing tasks, such as object recognition and object detection. Similarly, we can find applications in the processing of human natural language, that is, NLP. Neural networks learn via a succession of increasingly meaningful, layered representations of the input data. The number of these *layers* specifies the *depth* of the model. This is where the term *deep learning*—the process of training deep neural networks—comes from. To distinguish them from deep learning, all aforementioned machine learning methods are often referred to as *shallow* or *traditional* learning methods. Note that neural networks with a small depth would also be classified as shallow but not traditional. Deep learning has come to dominate the field of machine learning, being a clear favorite for perceptual problems and sparking a revolution in the complexity of problems that can be handled.

Although neural networks were inspired by neurobiology, they are not direct models of how our nervous system works. Every layer of a neural network is parameterized by a set of numbers, referred to as the layer's weights, specifying exactly how it transforms the input data. In deep neural networks, the total number of parameters can easily reach into the millions. The already-mentioned backpropagation algorithm is the algorithmic engine used to find the right set of parameters, that is, to *learn* the network. A visualization of a simple neural network with two fully connected hidden layers is shown in figure 1.5. Also shown on the right is a summarized visualization of the same, which we will often employ. A deep neural network would have many such layers. A notable neural network architecture that does not conform to such a *feedforward* nature is the *long short-term memory* (LSTM) recurrent neural network (RNN) architecture. Unlike the feedforward architecture in figure 1.5, which accepts a fixed-length input of length 2, LSTMs can process input sequences with arbitrary lengths.

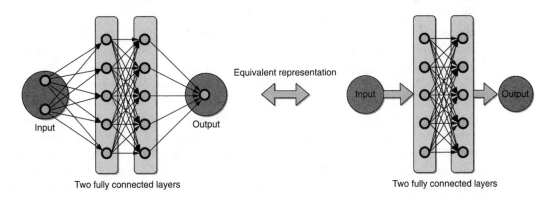

Figure 1.5 **Visualization of a simple feedforward neural network with two fully connected hidden layers (left). On the right is a summarized equivalent representation, which we will often employ to simplify diagrams.**

As previously touched on, what sparked the most recent interest in deep learning was spanned hardware, the availability of vast amounts of data, and algorithmic progress. GPUs had been developed for the video gaming market, and the internet matured to begin providing the field with unprecedented quality and quantity of data. Wikipedia, YouTube, and ImageNet are specific examples of data sources, the availability of which has driven many advances in computer vision and NLP. The ability of neural networks to eliminate the need for expensive manual feature engineering—which is needed to apply shallow learning methods to perceptual data successfully—is arguably the factor that influenced the ease of adoption of deep learning. Because NLP is a perceptual problem, it will also be the most important class of machine learning algorithms addressed in this book, albeit not the only one.

Next, we aim to get some insight into the history and progression of advances in NLP.

1.2.3   *Natural language processing (NLP)*

Language is one of the most important aspects of human cognition. It stands to reason that in order to create true artificial intelligence, a machine needs to be taught how to interpret, understand, process, and act on human language. This underlines the importance of NLP to the fields of AI and machine learning.

Just like the other subfields of AI, initial approaches to handling NLP problems, such as sentence classification and sentiment analysis, were based on explicit rules, or symbolic AI. Such systems typically could not generalize to new tasks and would break down easily. Since the advent of kernel methods in the 1990s, human effort has been channeled toward feature engineering—transforming the input data manually into a form that the shallow learning methods could use to produce useful predictions. This method is extremely time-consuming, task-specific, and inaccessible to a nonexpert. The advent of deep learning, around 2012, sparked a true revolution in NLP. The ability of neural networks to automatically engineer appropriate features in some of their layers lowered the bar for the applicability of these methods to new tasks and problems. Human effort then focused on designing the appropriate neural network architecture for any given task, as well as tuning various hyperparameter settings during training.

The standard way to train NLP systems involves collecting a large set of data points, each reliably annotated with output labels, such as "positive" or "negative," in a sentiment analysis task of sentences or documents. These data points are then supplied to the machine learning algorithm to learn the best representation or transformation of input to output signals that could potentially generalize to new data points. Both within NLP and in other subfields of machine learning, this process is often referred to as the paradigm of *supervised learning*. The labeling process, which is typically done manually, provides the "supervision signal" for learning the representative transformation. Learning representations from unlabeled data, on the other hand, is referred to as *unsupervised learning*.

Although today's machine learning algorithms and systems are not a direct replica of biological learning systems and should not be considered models of such systems, some of their aspects are inspired by evolutionary biology, and, in the past, inspirations drawn from biology have guided significant advances. Based on this, it seems flawed that for each new task, language, or application domain, the supervised learning process has traditionally been repeated from scratch. This process is somewhat antithetical to the way natural systems learn—building on and reusing previously acquired knowledge. Despite this, significant advances have been achieved in learning for perceptual tasks from scratch, notably in machine translation, question-answering systems, and chatbots, although some drawbacks remain. In particular, today's systems are not robust in handling significant changes in the sample distribution from which the input signals are drawn. In other words, the systems learn how to perform well on inputs of a certain kind or type. If we change the input type, it can lead to a significant degradation in performance and sometimes absolute failure. Moreover, to fully democratize AI and make NLP accessible to the average engineer at a small business—or to anyone without the resources possessed by major internet companies—it would be extremely helpful to be able to download and reuse knowledge acquired elsewhere. This is also important to anyone living in a country where the lingua franca may differ from English or other popular languages for which pretrained models exist, as well as anyone working on tasks that may be unique to their part of the world or tasks that no one has ever explored. Transfer learning provides a way to address some of these issues.

Transfer learning enables one to literally transfer knowledge from one *setting*—which we define as a combination of a particular task, domain, and language—to a different setting. The original setting is naturally referred to as the *source setting*, and the final setting is referred to as the *target setting*. The ease and success of the transfer process hinges on the similarity of the source and target settings. Quite naturally, a target setting that is "similar" to the source in some sense, which we will define later on in this book, leads to an easier and more successful transfer.

Transfer learning has been in implicit use in NLP for much longer than most practitioners realize, because it is a common practice to vectorize words using pretrained embeddings such as *word2vec* or *sent2vec* (more on these in the next section). Shallow learning methods have typically been applied to these vectors as features. We cover both of these techniques in more detail in the next section and in chapter 4 and apply them in various ways throughout the book. This popular approach relies on an unsupervised preprocessing step, which is used to first train these embeddings without any labels. Knowledge from this step is then transferred to the specific application in a supervised setting, where the said knowledge is refined and specialized to the problem at hand using a shallow learning algorithm on a smaller set of labeled examples. Traditionally, this paradigm of combining unsupervised and supervised learning steps has been referred to as *semisupervised learning*.

We next expand on the historical progression of advances in NLP, with a particular focus on the role transfer learning has played recently in this important subfield of AI and machine learning.

1.3 *A brief history of NLP advances*

To frame your understanding of the state and importance of transfer learning in NLP, it can be helpful to first gain a better sense of the kinds of tasks and techniques that have historically been important for this subfield of AI. This section covers these tasks and techniques and culminates in a brief overview of recent advances in NLP transfer learning. This overview will help you appropriately contextualize the impact of transfer learning in NLP and understand why it is more important now than ever before.

1.3.1 *General overview*

NLP was born in the middle of the 20th century, alongside AI. A major historical NLP landmark was the Georgetown Experiment of 1954, in which a set of approximately 60 Russian sentences was translated into English. In the 1960s, the Massachusetts Institute of Technology (MIT) NLP system ELIZA convincingly simulated a psychotherapist. Also in the 1960s, the vector space model for information representation was developed, where words came to be represented by vectors of real numbers, which were amenable to computation. The 1970s saw the development of a number of chatterbot/chatbot concepts based on sophisticated sets of handcrafted rules for processing the input information.

In the 1980s and 1990s, we saw the advent of the application of systematic machine learning methodologies to NLP, where rules were discovered by the computer versus being crafted by humans. This advance coincided with the explosion in the wider popularity of machine learning during that time, as we have already discussed earlier in this chapter. The late 1980s witnessed the application of *singular value decomposition* (SVD) to the vector space model, leading to *latent semantic analysis*—an unsupervised technique for determining the relationship between words in language.

In the early 2010s, the rise of neural networks and deep learning in the field dramatically transformed NLP. Such techniques were shown to achieve state-of-the-art results for the most difficult NLP tasks, such as machine translation and text classification. The mid-2010s witnessed the development of the word2vec model,[4] and its variants sent2vec,[5] doc2vec,[6] and so on. These neural-network-based techniques vectorize words, sentences, and documents (respectively) in a way that ensures the distance between vectors in the generated vector space is representative of the difference in meaning between the corresponding entities, that is, words, sentences, and documents. Indeed, some interesting properties of such embeddings allowed analogies to be handled—the distance between the words *Man* and *King* are approximately equal to the distance between the words *Woman* and *Queen* in the induced vector space, for instance. The metric used to train these neural-network-based models was derived from the field of linguistics, more specifically *distributional semantics*, and did not

---

[4] T. Mikolov et al., "Efficient Estimation of Word Representations in Vector Space," *arXiv* (2013).

[5] M. Pagliardini et al., "Unsupervised Learning of Sentence Embeddings Using Compositional n-Gram Features," Proc. of NAACL-HLT (2018).

[6] Q. V. Le et al., "Distributed Representations of Sentences and Documents," *arXiv* (2014).

require labeled data. The meaning of a word was assumed to be tied to its context, that is, the words surrounding it.

The variety of methods for embedding various units of text, such as words, sentences, paragraphs, and documents, became a key cornerstone of modern NLP. Once text samples are embedded into an appropriate vector space, analysis can often be reduced to the application of a well-known shallow statistical/machine learning technique for real vector manipulation, including clustering and classification. This can be viewed as a form of *implicit transfer learning*, and a semisupervised machine learning pipeline—the embedding step is unsupervised and the learning step is typically supervised. The unsupervised pretraining step essentially reduces the requirements for labeled data and, thereby, computing resources required to achieve a given performance—something we will learn to leverage transfer learning to do for us for a broader range of scenarios in this book.

Around 2014, *sequence-to-sequence* models[7] were developed and achieved a significant improvement in difficult tasks such as machine translation and automatic summarization. In particular, whereas pre–neural network NLP pipelines consist of several explicit steps, such as POS tagging, dependency parsing, and language modeling, it was shown that machine translation could be carried out "sequence to sequence." Here the various layers of a deep neural network automate all of these intermediate steps. These models learn to associate an input sequence, such as a source sentence in one language, with an output sequence—for example, that sentence's translation into another language—via an encoder that converts inputs into a context vector and a decoder that converts it into the target sequence. Both the encoder and decoder were typically designed to be *recurrent neural networks* (RNNs). These are able to encode order information in the input sentence, something earlier models, such as the bag-of-words model, couldn't do, leading to significant improvements in performance.

It was discovered, however, that long input sequences were harder to deal with, which motivated the development of the technique known as *attention*. This technique significantly improved the performance of machine translation sequence-to-sequence models by allowing the model to focus on the parts of the input sequence that were most relevant for the output. A model called *the transformer*[8] took this a step further by defining a *self-attention layer* for both the encoder and decoder, allowing both to build better context for text segments with respect to other text segments in the input sequence. Significant improvements in machine translation were achieved with this architecture, and it was observed to be better suited for training on massively parallel hardware than prior models, speeding up training by up to an order of magnitude.

Up until about 2015, most practical methods for NLP focused on the *word level*, which means that the whole word was treated as an indivisible atomic entity and assigned a feature vector. This approach has several disadvantages, notably how to treat never-before-seen or *out-of-vocabulary* words. When the model encountered such

---

[7] I. Sutskever et al., "Sequence to Sequence Learning with Neural Networks," NeurIPS Proceedings (2014).
[8] A. Vaswani et al., "Attention Is All You Need," NeurIPS Proceedings (2017).

words—for instance, if a word was misspelled—the method would fail because it could not vectorize it. In addition, the rise of social media changed the definition of what was considered natural language. Now, billions of people express themselves online using emoticons, newly invented slang, and deliberately misspelled words. It was not long until it was realized that the solution to many of these issues came naturally from treating language at the character level. In this paradigm, every character would be vectorized, and as long as the human was expressing themself with allowable characters, vector features could be generated successfully, and the algorithm could be successfully applied. Zhang et al.[9] showed this in the context of character-level CNNs for text classification and demonstrated a remarkable robustness to misspellings.

1.3.2   Recent transfer learning advances

Traditionally, learning has proceeded in either a fully supervised or fully unsupervised fashion for any given problem setting—a particular combination of task, domain, and language—from scratch. As previously alluded to, semisupervised learning was recognized as early as 1999, in the context of SVMs, as a way to address potentially limited labeled data availability. An initial unsupervised pretraining step on larger collections of unlabeled data made downstream supervised learning easier. Variants of this were studied to address potentially noisy—possibly incorrect—labels, which is an approach sometimes referred to as *weakly supervised learning*. However, it was often assumed that the same sampling distribution held for both the labeled and unlabeled datasets.

Transfer learning relaxes these assumptions. In 1995, at the Conference on Neural Information Processing Systems (NeurIPS), one of the biggest conferences on machine learning, transfer learning was popularly recognized as "learning to learn." Essentially, it was stipulated that intelligent machines need to possess lifelong learning capabilities that reuse learned knowledge for new tasks. This has since been studied under a few different names, including *learning to learn, knowledge transfer, inductive bias*, and *multitask learning*. In multitask learning, an algorithm is trained to perform well on multiple tasks simultaneously, thereby uncovering features that may be more generally useful. However, it wasn't until around 2018 that practical and scalable methods were developed to achieve it in NLP for the hardest perceptual problems.

The year 2018 saw nothing short of a revolution in the field of NLP. The understanding in the field of how to best represent collections of text as vectors evolved dramatically. Moreover, it became widely recognized that open source models could be fine-tuned or transferred to different tasks, languages, and domains. At the same time, several of the big internet companies released even more and bigger NLP models for computing such representations and also specified well-defined procedures for fine-tuning them. All of a sudden, the ability to attain state-of-the-art results in NLP became accessible to the average practitioner, even an independent one. Some called it NLP's "ImageNet moment," referencing the explosion in computer vision applications

---

[9] X. Zhang et al., "Character-Level Convolutional Networks for Text Classification," NeurIPS Proceedings (2015).

witnessed post-2012, when a GPU-trained neural network won the ImageNet computer vision competition. Just as was the case for the original ImageNet moment, for the first time, a library of pretrained models became available for a large subset of NLP data, together with well-defined techniques for fine-tuning them to particular tasks at hand with labeled datasets of a size significantly smaller than would be needed otherwise. This book's purpose is to describe, elucidate, evaluate, demonstrably apply, compare, and contrast the various techniques that fall into this category. We briefly overview these techniques next.

Early explorations of transfer learning for NLP focused on analogies to computer vision, where it has been used successfully for over a decade. One such model—Semantic Inference for the Modeling of Ontologies (SIMOn)[10]—employed character-level convolutional neural networks (CNNs) combined with bidirectional LSTMs for structural semantic text classification. The SIMOn approach demonstrated NLP transfer learning methods directly analogous to those that have been used in computer vision. The rich body of knowledge on transfer learning for computer vision applications motivated this approach. The features learned by this model were shown to be useful for unsupervised learning tasks and to work well on social media language data, which can be somewhat idiosyncratic and very different from the kind of language on Wikipedia and other large book-based datasets.

One notable weakness of the original formulation of word2vec was disambiguation. There was no way to distinguish between various uses of a word that may have different meanings depending on context, such as the case of homographs—duck (posture) versus duck (bird) or fair (a gathering) versus fair (just). In some sense, the original word2vec formulation represents each such word by the average vector of the vectors representing each of these distinct meanings of the homograph. *Embeddings from Language Models*[11]—abbreviated ELMo after the popular *Sesame Street* character—is an attempt to develop contextualized embeddings of words using bidirectional LSTMs. The embedding of a word in this model depends very much on its context, with the corresponding numerical representation being different for each such context. ELMo did this by being trained to predict the next word in a sequence of words, which is very much related to the concept of language modeling that was introduced at the beginning of the chapter. Huge datasets, like Wikipedia and various datasets of books, are readily available for training in this framework.

The Universal Language Model Fine-Tuning[12] (ULMFiT) method was proposed to fine-tune any neural-network-based language model for any particular task and was initially demonstrated in the context of text classification. A key concept behind this method is *discriminative fine-tuning*, where the different layers of the network are

---

[10] P. Azunre et al., "Semantic Classification of Tabular Datasets via Character-Level Convolutional Neural Networks," *arXiv* (2019).

[11] M. E. Peters et al., "Deep Contextualized Word Representations," Proc. of NAACL-HLT (2018).

[12] J. Howard et al., "Universal Language Model Fine-Tuning for Text Classification," Proc. of the 56th Annual Meeting of the Association for Computational Linguistics (2018).

trained at different rates. The OpenAI *Generative Pretrained Transformer* (GPT) modified the encoder-decoder architecture of the transformer to achieve a fine-tunable language model for NLP. It discarded the encoders and retained the decoders and their self-attention sublayers. Bidirectional Encoder Representations from Transformers[13] (BERT) did the opposite, modifying the transformer architecture by preserving the encoders and discarding the decoders and also relying on *masking* of words, which would then need to be predicted accurately as the training metric. These concepts will be discussed in detail in the upcoming chapters.

In all of these language-model-based methods—ELMo, ULMFiT, GPT, and BERT—it was shown that generated embeddings could be fine-tuned for specific downstream NLP tasks with relatively few labeled data points. The focus on language models was deliberate: it was hypothesized that the hypothesis set induced by them would be generally useful, and the data for massive training was known to be readily available.

Next, we highlight key aspects of transfer learning in computer vision to even better frame transfer learning in NLP and to see if anything can be learned and borrowed for our purposes. This knowledge will become a rich source of analogies that will be used to drive our exploration of NLP transfer learning in the remainder of the book.

1.4   *Transfer learning in computer vision*

Although the target of this book is NLP, it is helpful to frame NLP transfer learning in the context of computer vision transfer learning. One reason for doing this is that neural network architectures from the two subfields of AI may share some similar features, so techniques from computer vision can be borrowed, or, at the very least, be used to inform, techniques for NLP. Indeed, the availability of such techniques in computer vision is arguably a large driver behind recent NLP transfer learning research. Researchers can access a library of well-defined computer vision methods to experiment with in the relatively unexplored domain of NLP. The extent to which such techniques are directly transferable is, however, an open question, and it is important to remain mindful of a number of important differences. One such difference is that NLP neural networks tend to be shallower than those used in computer vision.

1.4.1   *General overview*

The goal of computer vision or machine vision is to enable computers to understand digital images and/or videos, including methods for acquiring, processing, and analyzing image data and making decisions based on their derived representation. Video analysis can typically be carried out by splitting videos into frames, which can then be

---

[13] J. Devlin et al., "BERT: Pre-Training of Deep Bidirectional Transformers for Language Understanding," Proc. of NAACL-HLT (2019).

viewed as an image analysis problem. Thus, computer vision can be posed as an image analysis problem theoretically without the loss of generality.

Computer vision was born along with AI in the middle of the 20th century. Vision, obviously, is an important part of cognition, so researchers seeking to build intelligent robots recognized it as being important early on. Initial methods in the 1960s attempted to mimic the human visual system, whereas focus on extracting edges and modeling of shapes in scenes rose in popularity in the 1970s. The 1980s witnessed more mathematically robust methods developed for various aspects of computer vision, notably facial recognition and image segmentation, with mathematically rigorous treatments emerging by the 1990s. This move coincided with the rise in popularity of machine learning during that time, as we already touched on. The following couple of decades saw focus and effort spent on developing better feature-extraction methods for images, prior to the application of a shallow machine learning technique. The "ImageNet moment" of 2012, when GPU-accelerated neural networks won the prominent ImageNet competition by a wide margin for the very first time, marked a revolution in the field.

ImageNet[14] was originally published in 2009 and rapidly became the basis of a competition for testing the best methods for object recognition. The famed 2012 neural network entry pointed to deep learning as the way forward for computer vision in particular and perceptual problems in machine learning in general. Importantly for us, a number of researchers quickly realized that neural network weights from pretrained ImageNet models could be used to initialize neural network models for other, sometimes seemingly unrelated, tasks and achieve a significant improvement in performance.

1.4.2 Pretrained ImageNet models

The various teams that have won the hallmark ImageNet yearly competition have been very generous with sharing their pretrained models. Notable examples of such CNN models follow.

The VGG architecture was initially introduced in 2014, with variants VGG16 (a depth of 16) and VGG19 (a depth of 19 layers). To make the deeper network converge during training, the shallower network needed to be trained until convergence first and its parameters used to initialize the deeper network. This architecture has been found to be somewhat slow to train and relatively large in terms of overall number of parameters—130 million to 150 million parameters in size.

Some of these issues were addressed by the ResNet architecture in 2015. Despite being substantially deeper, the number of parameters was significantly reduced—the smallest variant, ResNet50, is 50 layers deep with approximately 50 million parameters. A key to achieving this reduction was regularization via a technique called *max pooling* and a modular design out of subbuilding blocks.

---

[14] J. Deng et al., "ImageNet: A Large-Scale Hierarchical Image Database," Proc. of NAACL-HLT (2019).

Other notable examples include Inception and its extension Xception, proposed in 2015 and 2016, respectively, which aim to create multiple levels of extracted features by stacking multiple convolutions within the same network module. Both of these models achieved further significant reduction in model size.

1.4.3   *Fine-tuning pretrained ImageNet models*

Due to the existence of the pretrained CNN ImageNet models that have been presented, it is uncommon for practitioners to train computer vision models from scratch. By far the more common approach is to download one of these open source models and either use it to initialize a similar architecture prior to learning on limited labeled data, such as *fine-tuning* a subset of the layers, or to use it as a fixed feature extractor.

A visualization of how a subset of layers to be fine-tuned is typically selected in a feed-forward neural network is shown in figure 1.6. A threshold is moved away from the output (and toward the input) as more data becomes available in the target domain, with layers between the threshold and output retrained. This change occurs because the increased amount of data can be used to train more parameters effectively than could be done otherwise. Additionally, movement of the threshold must happen in the right-to-left direction, that is, away from the output and toward the input. This movement direction allows us to retain layers encoding general features that are close to the input, while retraining layers closer to the output, which encode features specific to the source domain. Moreover, when the source and target are highly dissimilar, some of the more specific parameters/layers to the right of the threshold can be discarded.

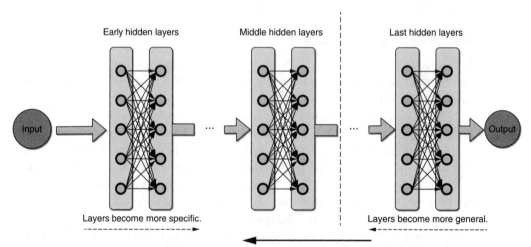

Figure 1.6   Visualization of the various transfer learning heuristics applicable in computer vision for feedforward neural network architectures, which we will draw on in NLP whenever possible. A threshold is moved to the left, with more availability of training data in the target domain, and all parameters to the right of it are retrained, with the exception of those that are discarded due to increasing dissimilarity between source and target domains.

Feature extraction, on the other hand, involves removing only the last layer of the network, which, instead of producing data labels, will now produce a set of numerical vectors on which a shallow machine learning method, such as the support vector machine (SVM), can be trained as before.

In the retraining or *fine-tuning* approach, the prior pretrained weights do not all stay fixed, but a subset of them can be allowed to change based on the new labeled data. However, it is important to make sure that the number of parameters being trained does not lead to overfitting on limited new data, which motivates us to freeze some to reduce the number of parameters being trained. Picking the number of layers to freeze has typically been done empirically, with the heuristics in figure 1.6 guiding it.

It has been established in CNNs that the early layers—those closer to the input layer—perform functions more general to the task of image processing, such as detecting any edges in the image. Later layers—those closer to the output layer—perform functions more specific to the task at hand, such as mapping final numerical outputs to specific labels. This arrangement leads us to unfreeze and fine-tune layers closer to the output layer first and then incrementally unfreeze and fine-tune layers closer to the input layer if performance is found to be unsatisfactory. This process can continue as long as the available labeled dataset for the target task can support the increase in training parameters.

A corollary of this process is that if the labeled dataset for the target task is very large, the whole network should probably be fine-tuned. If the target dataset is small, on the other hand, one needs to think carefully about how similar the target dataset is to the source dataset. If it is very similar, the model architecture can be directly initialized to pretrained weights when fine-tuning. If very different, it may be beneficial to discard the pretrained weights in some of the later layers of the network when initializing, because they may not have any relevance to the target task. Moreover, because the dataset is not large, only a small set of the remaining later layers should be unfrozen while fine-tuning.

We will conduct computational experiments to explore these heuristics further in the subsequent chapters.

1.5 Why is NLP transfer learning an exciting topic to study now?

Now that we have framed the current state of NLP in the context of the general artificial intelligence and machine learning landscapes, we are in a good position to summarize why the key theme of this book is important and why you, the reader, should care very much about it.

By now it should be clear that recent years have seen a rapid acceleration in advances in this field. A number of pretrained language models have been made available, along with well-defined procedures, for the very first time, for fine-tuning them to more specific tasks or domains. It was discovered that analogies could be made to the way transfer learning had been conducted in computer vision for a decade, and a number of research groups were able to rapidly draw on a body of existing computer vision techniques to push forward the state of our understanding of NLP transfer learning. This work has achieved the important advantage of reducing computing and training time requirements for these problems for the average practitioner without access to massive resources.

A lot of excitement exists in the field right now, and droves of researchers are working on this problem area. A lot of outstanding questions in a subject this novel present an opportunity for machine learning researchers to make a name for themselves by helping move the state of knowledge forward. Simultaneously, social media, which has become an increasingly significant factor in human interaction, presents new challenges not seen in NLP before. These challenges include slang/jargon and emoticon use, which may not be found in the more formal language that is typically used to train language models. A demonstrative example is the severe vulnerabilities discovered with the social media natural language ecosystem—notably with regard to election interference claims by sovereign democracies against other foreign governments, such as the Cambridge Analytica scandal.[15] In addition, the general sense of the worsening of the "fake news" problem has increased interest in the field and has driven discussions of the ethical considerations that should be made when building these systems. All this, coupled with the proliferation of increasingly sophisticated chatbots in a variety of domains, and associated cybersecurity threats, implies that the problem of transfer learning in NLP is poised to continue growing in significance.

Summary

- Artificial intelligence (AI) holds the promise of fundamentally transforming our society. To democratize the benefits of this transformation, we must ensure that state-of-the-art advances are accessible to everyone, regardless of language, access to massive computing resources, and country of origin.

- Machine learning is the dominant modern paradigm in AI, which, rather than explicitly programming a computer for every possible scenario, *trains* it to associate input to output signals by seeing many examples of such corresponding input-output pairs.

- Natural language processing (NLP), the subfield of AI we will be discussing in this book, deals with the analysis and processing of human natural language data and is one of the most active areas of AI research today.

- A recently popularized paradigm in NLP, transfer learning, enables you to adapt or transfer the knowledge acquired from one set of tasks or domains to a different set of tasks or domains. This is a big step forward for the democratization of NLP and, more widely, AI, allowing knowledge to be reused in new

---

[15] K. Schaffer, Data versus Democracy:- How Big Data Algorithms Shape Opinions and Alter the Course of History (New York: Apress, 2019).

settings at a fraction of the previously required resources, which may not be available to everyone.

- Key modeling frameworks enabling transfer learning in NLP include ELMo and BERT.
- The recent rise in the importance of social media has changed the definition of what is considered natural language. Now, billions of people express themselves online using emoticons, newly invented slang, and deliberately misspelled words. All these present new challenges, which we must take into account when developing new transfer learning techniques for NLP.
- Transfer learning is relatively well understood in computer vision, and whenever possible, we should draw on this body of knowledge when experimenting with new transfer techniques for NLP.

Getting started
with baselines:
Data preprocessing

This chapter covers

- Introducing a pair of natural language processing (NLP) problems
- Obtaining and preprocessing NLP data for such problems
- Establishing baselines for these problems using key *generalized linear methods*

In this chapter, we dive directly into solving NLP problems. This will be a two-part exercise, spanning this chapter and the next. Our goal will be to establish a set of baselines for a pair of concrete NLP problems, which we will later be able to use to measure progressive improvements gained from leveraging increasingly sophisticated transfer learning approaches. In the process of doing this, we aim to advance your general NLP instincts and refresh your understanding of typical procedures involved in setting up problem-solving pipelines for such problems. You will review techniques ranging from tokenization to data structure and model selection. We first train some traditional machine learning models from scratch to establish some preliminary baselines for these problems. We complete the exercise in chapter 3, where we apply the simplest form of transfer learning to a pair of recently popularized deep pretrained language models. This involves fine-tuning only a handful of the final layers of each network on a target dataset. This activity will serve as a form of an applied hands-on introduction to the main theme of the book—transfer learning for NLP.

We will focus on a pair of important representative example NLP problems: spam classification of email and sentiment classification of movie reviews. This exercise will arm you with a number of important skills, including some tips for obtaining, visualizing, and preprocessing data. We will cover three major model classes: generalized linear models such as logistic regression, decision tree–based models such as random forests, and neural network-based models such as ELMo. These classes are additionally represented by support vector machines (SVMs) with linear kernels, gradient-boosting machines (GBMs), and BERT, respectively. The different types of models to be explored are shown in figure 2.1. Note that we do not explicitly address rule-based methods. A widely used example of these is a simple keyword-matching approach that would label all emails containing certain preselected phrases; for example, "free lottery tickets" as spam, and "amazing movie" as a positive review. Such methods are often implemented as the first attempt at solving NLP problems in many industrial applications but are quickly found to be brittle and difficult to scale. As such, we do not discuss rule-based approaches much further. We discuss data for the problems and its preprocessing, and introduce and apply generalized linear methods to the data in this chapter. In the next chapter, which serves as part two of the overall exercise, we apply decision-tree-based methods and neural-network-based methods to the data.

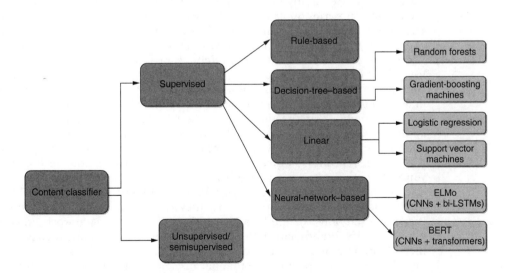

Figure 2.1 The different types of supervised models to be explored in the content classification examples in this and the next chapter.

We present code samples for every example and model class represented to enable you to quickly pick up the essence of these technologies, while also allowing you to develop coding skills that will directly transfer to your own problems. All code snippets are provided as rendered Jupyter notebooks in the companion GitHub repository to this book,[1] as well as Kaggle notebooks/kernels that you can begin running within a few minutes without dealing with any installation or dependency issues. Rendered Jupyter notebooks provide representative output that can be expected when they are executed correctly, and Kaggle provides a browser-based Jupyter execution environment, which also offers a limited amount of free GPU computing. A mostly equivalent alternative to this is Google Colab, but this is not the system we elected to employ here. Jupyter can also be easily installed locally with Anaconda, and you are welcome to convert the notebooks into .py scripts for local execution, if that is your preference. However, the Kaggle notebooks are the recommended way of executing these methods, because they will allow you to get moving right away without any setup delays. Moreover, the free GPU resources provided by this service at the time of writing expand the accessibility of all these methods to people who may not have access to powerful GPUs locally, which is consistent with the "democratization of AI" agenda that excites so many people about NLP transfer learning. Appendix A provides a Kaggle quick start guide and a number of the author's personal tips on how to maximize the platform's usefulness. However, we anticipate that most readers should find it pretty self-explanatory to get started. Please also note the important technical caveats in the note that follows.

> **NOTE** Kaggle frequently updates the dependencies, that is, the versions of the installed libraries on its Docker images. To ensure that you are using the same dependencies as we did when we wrote the code—to guarantee the code works with minimal changes out of the box—please make sure to select "Copy and Edit Kernel" for each notebook of interest, links to which are listed in the companion repository to the book. If you copy and paste the code into a new notebook and don't follow this recommended process, you may need to adapt the code slightly for the specific library versions installed for that notebook at the time you created it. This recommendation also applies if you elect to install a local environment. For local installation, pay attention to the frozen dependency requirement list we have shared in the companion repository, which will guide you on which versions of libraries you will need. Please note that this requirements file is for the purpose of documenting and exactly replicating the environment on Kaggle on which the results reported in the book were achieved; on a different infrastructure, it can be used only as a guide, and you shouldn't expect it to work straight out of the box due to many potential architecture-specific dependency conflicts. Moreover, most of the requirements will not be necessary for local installation. Finally, please note that because ELMo has not yet been ported

---

[1] https://github.com/azunre/transfer-learning-for-nlp

> to TensorFlow 2.x at the time of this writing, we are forced to use TensorFlow 1.x to compare it fairlyto BERT. In the companion repository, we do, however, provide an illustration of how to use BERT with TensorFlow 2.x for the spam classification example.[2] We transition in later chapters from TensorFlow and Keras to the Hugging Face transformers library, which uses TensorFlow 2.x. You could view the exercise in chapters 2 and 3 as a historical record of and experience with early packages that were developed for NLP transfer learning. This exercise simultaneously helps you juxtapose TensorFlow 1.x with 2.x.

2.1 Preprocessing email spam classification example data

In this section, we introduce the first example dataset we will look at in this chapter. Here, we are interested in developing an algorithm that can detect whether or not any given email is spam at scale. To do this, we will build a dataset from two separate sources: the popular Enron email corpus as a proxy for email that is not spam, and a collection of "419" fraudulent emails as a proxy for email that is spam.

We will view this as a supervised classification task, where we will first train a classifier on a collection of emails labeled as either spam or not spam. Although some labeled datasets exist online for training and testing that match this problem closely, we will instead take the route of creating our own dataset from some other well-known email data sources. The reason for doing this is to more closely represent how data collection and preprocessing often happen in practice, where datasets first have to be built and curated, versus the simplified manner in which these processes are often represented in the literature.

In particular, we will sample the Enron corpus—the largest public email collection, related to the notorious Enron financial scandal—as a proxy for email that are not spam, and sample "419" fraudulent emails, representing the best known type of spam, as a proxy for email that are spam. Both of these types of email are openly available on Kaggle,[3,4] the popular data science competition platform, which makes running the examples there particularly easy without too many local resources.

The Enron corpus contains about half a million emails written by employees of the Enron Corporation, as collected by the Federal Energy Commission for the purposes of investigating the collapse of the company. This corpus has been used extensively in the literature to study machine learning methods for email applications and is often the first data source researchers working with emails look to for initial experimentation with algorithm prototypes. On Kaggle, it is available as a single-column .csv file with one email per row. Note that this data is still cleaner than one can expect to typically find in many practical applications in the wild.

---

[2] https://www.kaggle.com/azunre/tlfornlp-chapters2-3-spam-bert-tf2
[3] https://www.kaggle.com/wcukierski/enron-email-dataset
[4] https://www.kaggle.com/rtatman/fraudulent-email-corpus

Figure 2.2 shows the sequence of steps that will be performed on each email in this example. The body of the email will first be separated from the headers of the email, some statistics about the dataset will be teased out to get a sense of the data, stopwords will be removed from the email, and it will then be classified as either spam or not spam.

Figure 2.2   Sequence of preprocessing tasks to be performed on input email data

2.1.1   Loading and visualizing the Enron corpus

The first thing we need to do is load the data with the popular Pandas library and take a peek at a slice of the data to make sure we have a good sense of what it looks like. Listing 2.1 shows the code to do that once the Enron corpus dataset has been obtained and placed in the location specified by the variable `filepath` (in this case, it is pointing to its location in our Kaggle notebook). Ensure all libraries are PIP-installed before importing via the following command:

```
pip install <package name>
```

Listing 2.1   Loading the Enron corpus

Linear algebra ⊳

```
import numpy as np
import pandas as pd            ◁─ Data processing, CSV file
                                  I/O (e.g., pd.read_csv)

filepath = "../input/enron-email-dataset/emails.csv"

emails = pd.read_csv(filepath)    ◁─ Reads the data into a Pandas
                                     DataFrame called emails

print("Successfully loaded {} rows and {} columns!".format(emails.shape[0],
    emails.shape[1]))         ◁─ Displays status and
print(emails.head(n=5))          some loaded emails
```

Successful execution of the code will confirm the number of columns and rows loaded, and display the first five rows of the loaded Pandas *DataFrame*, through an output that looks like this:

```
Successfully loaded 517401 rows and 2 columns!

                      file                                          message
0     allen-p/_sent_mail/1.    Message-ID: <18782981.1075855378110.JavaMail.e...
1    allen-p/_sent_mail/10.    Message-ID: <15464986.1075855378456.JavaMail.e...
2   allen-p/_sent_mail/100.    Message-ID: <24216240.1075855687451.JavaMail.e...
3  allen-p/_sent_mail/1000.    Message-ID: <13505866.1075863688222.JavaMail.e...
4  allen-p/_sent_mail/1001.    Message-ID:<30922949.1075863688243.JavaMail.e...
```

Although this exercise has allowed us to get a sense of the resulting DataFrame and get a good feel for its shape, it is not too clear what each individual email looks like. To achieve this, we take a closer look at the very first email via the next line of code

```
print(emails.loc[0]["message"])
```

to produce the following output:

```
Message-ID: <18782981.1075855378110.JavaMail.evans@thyme>
Date: Mon, 14 May 2001 16:39:00 -0700 (PDT)
From: phillip.allen@enron.com
To: tim.belden@enron.com
Subject:
Mime-Version: 1.0
Content-Type: text/plain; charset=us-ascii
Content-Transfer-Encoding: 7bit
X-From: Phillip K Allen
X-To: Tim Belden <Tim Belden/Enron@EnronXGate>
X-cc:
X-bcc:
X-Folder: \Phillip_Allen_Jan2002_1\Allen, Phillip K.\'Sent Mail
X-Origin: Allen-P
X-FileName: pallen (Non-Privileged).pst

Here is our forecast
```

We see that the messages are contained within the *message* column of the resulting DataFrame, with the extra fields at the beginning of each message—including *Message ID, To, From,* and so on—being referred to as the message's *header information* or simply *header*.

Traditional spam classification methods derive features from the header information for classifying the message as spam or not. Here, we would like to perform the same task based on the content of the message only. One possible motivation for this approach is the fact that email training data may often be de-identified in practice due to privacy concerns and regulations, thereby making header info unavailable. Thus, we need to separate the headers from the messages in our dataset. We do this via the function shown in the next listing. It employs the email package for processing email messages, which comes prepacked with Python (that is, it does not need to be PIP-installed).

Listing 2.2 Separating and extracting email bodies from header information

```
import email

def extract_messages(df):
    messages = []
    for item in df["message"]:
        e = email.message_from_string(item)    ◁──┐  Returns a message
        message_body = e.get_payload()    ◁────────┘  object structure
                                                        from a string

                                                      Gets the
                                                      message body
```

```
        messages.append(message_body)
    print("Successfully retrieved message body from emails!")
    return messages
```

We now execute the email-body-extracting code as follows:

```
bodies = extract_messages(emails)
```

which confirms success by printing the following text to screen:

```
Successfully retrieved message body from emails!
```

We then can display some processed emails via

```
bodies_df = pd.DataFrame(bodies)
print(bodies_df.head(n=5))
```

with the display confirming successful execution by resembling the following output:

```
                                    0
0                   Here is our forecast\n\n
1                   Traveling to have a business meeting takes the...
2                   test successful.  way to go!!!
3                   Randy,\n\n Can you send me a schedule of the s...
4                   Let's shoot for Tuesday at 11:45.
```

2.1.2 *Loading and visualizing the fraudulent email corpus*

Having loaded the Enron emails, let's do the same for the "419" fraudulent email corpus, so that we can have some example data in our training set representing the spam class. Obtain the dataset from the Kaggle link that was presented earlier, making sure to adjust the `filepath` variable accordingly (or just use our Kaggle notebooks that already have the data attached to them), and repeat the steps as shown in listing 2.3.

> NOTE Because this dataset comes as a .txt file, versus a .csv file, the preprocessing steps are slightly different. First of all, we have to specify the encoding when reading the file as Latin-1; otherwise the default encoding option of UTF-8 will fail. It is often the case in practice that one needs to experiment with a number of different encodings, with the aforementioned two being the most popular ones, to get some datasets to read correctly. Additionally, note that because this .txt file is one big column of emails (with headers) separated by line breaks and white space, and is not separated nicely into rows with one email per row—as was the case for the Enron corpus—we can't use Pandas to neatly load it as we did before. We will read all the emails into a single string and split the string on a code word that appears close to the beginning of each email's header, for example, "From r." Please see our rendered notebooks that visualize this data on either GitHub or Kaggle to verify that this unique code word appears close to the beginning of each fraudulent email in this dataset.

Listing 2.3   Loading the "419" fraudulent email corpus

```
filepath = "../input/fraudulent-email-corpus/fradulent_emails.txt"
with open(filepath, 'r',encoding="latin1") as file:
    data = file.read()

fraud_emails = data.split("From r")
```

> Split on a code word appearing close to the beginning of each email

```
print("Successfully loaded {} spam emails!".format(len(fraud_emails)))
```

The following output confirms the success of the loading process:

```
Successfully loaded 3978 spam emails!
```

Now that the fraudulent data is loaded as a list, we can convert it into a Pandas Data-
Frame in order to process it with the functions we have already defined, as follows:

```
fraud_bodies = extract_messages(pd.DataFrame(fraud_emails,columns=
    ["message"],dtype=str))
fraud_bodies_df = pd.DataFrame(fraud_bodies[1:])
print(fraud_bodies_df.head())
```

Successful execution of this code segment will lead to output that gives us a sense of
the first five emails that were loaded, as shown next:

```
Successfully retrieved message body from e-mails!
                                                  0
0   FROM:MR. JAMES NGOLA.\nCONFIDENTIAL TEL: 233-27-587908.\nE-MAIL:
    (james_ngola2002@maktoob.com).\n\nURGENT BUSINESS ASSISTANCE AND
    PARTNERSHIP.\n\nDEAR FRIEND,\n\nI AM ( DR.) JAMES NGOLA, THE PERSONAL
    ASSISTANCE TO THE LATE CONGOLESE (PRESIDENT LAURENT KABILA) WHO WAS
    ASSASSINATED BY HIS BODY G...
1   Dear Friend,\n\nI am Mr. Ben Suleman a custom officer and work as
    Assistant controller of the Customs and Excise department Of the Federal
    Ministry of Internal Affairs stationed at the Murtala Mohammed
    International Airport, Ikeja, Lagos-Nigeria.\n\nAfter the sudden death
    of the former Head of s...
2   FROM HIS ROYAL MAJESTY (HRM) CROWN RULER OF ELEME KINGDOM \nCHIEF DANIEL
    ELEME, PHD, EZE 1 OF ELEME.E-MAIL \nADDRESS:obong_715@epatra.com
    \n\nATTENTION:PRESIDENT,CEO Sir/ Madam. \n\nThis letter might surprise
    you because we have met\nneither in person nor by correspondence. But I
    believe\nit is...
3   FROM HIS ROYAL MAJESTY (HRM) CROWN RULER OF ELEME KINGDOM \nCHIEF DANIEL
    ELEME, PHD, EZE 1 OF ELEME.E-MAIL \nADDRESS:obong_715@epatra.com
    \n\nATTENTION:PRESIDENT,CEO Sir/ Madam. \n\nThis letter might surprise
    you because we have met\nneither in person nor by correspondence. But I
    believe\nit is...
4   Dear sir, \n \nIt is with a heart full of hope that I write to seek your
    help in respect of the context below. I am Mrs. Maryam Abacha the former
    first lady of the former Military Head of State of Nigeria General Sani
    Abacha whose sudden death occurred on 8th of June 1998 as a result of
    cardiac ...
```

Having loaded both datasets, we are now ready to sample emails from each one into a single DataFrame that will represent the overall dataset covering both classes of emails. Before doing this, we must decide how many samples to draw from each class. Ideally, the number of samples in each class will represent the natural distribution of emails in the wild—if we expect our classifier to encounter 60% spam emails and 40% nonspam emails when deployed, then a ratio such as 600 to 400, respectively, might make sense. Note that a severe imbalance in the data, such as 99% for nonspam and 1% for spam, may overfit to predict nonspam most of the time, an issue than needs to be considered when building datasets. Because this is an idealized experiment, and we do not have any information on the natural distributions of classes, we will assume a 50/50 split. We also need to give some thought to how we are going to tokenize the emails, that is, split emails into subunits of text—words, sentences, and so forth. To start off, we will tokenize into words, because this is the most common approach. We must also decide the maximum number of tokens per email and the maximum length of each token to ensure that the occasional extremely long email does not bog down the performance of our classifier. We do all this by specifying the following general hyperparameters, which will later be tuned experimentally to enhance performance as needed:

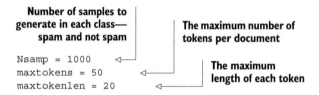

```
Nsamp = 1000
maxtokens = 50
maxtokenlen = 20
```

Number of samples to generate in each class—spam and not spam (Nsamp = 1000)

The maximum number of tokens per document (maxtokens = 50)

The maximum length of each token (maxtokenlen = 20)

With these hyperparameters specified, we can now create a single DataFrame for the overarching training dataset. Let's take the opportunity to also perform the remaining preprocessing tasks, namely, removing stop words, punctuations, and tokenizing.

Let's proceed by defining a function to tokenize emails by splitting them into words as shown in the following listing.

Listing 2.4   Tokenizing each email into words

```
def tokenize(row):
    if row in [None,'']:
        tokens = ""
    else:
        tokens = str(row).split(" ")[:maxtokens]
    return tokens
```

Split every email string on spaces to create a list of word tokens.

Taking another look at the emails on the previous two pages, we see that they contain a lot of punctuation characters, and the spam emails tend to be capitalized. In order to ensure that classification is done based on language content only, we define a function to remove punctuation marks and other non-word characters from the emails. We do this by employing *regular expressions* with the Python *regex* library. We also normalize words by turning them into lower case with the Python string function `.lower()`. The preprocessing function is shown in the next listing.

Listing 2.5   Removing punctuation and other nonword characters from emails

```
import re
def reg_expressions(row):
    tokens = []
    try:
        for token in row:
            token = token.lower()
            token = re.sub(r'[\W\d]', "", token)
            token = token[:maxtokenlen]
            tokens.append(token)
    except:
        token = ""
        tokens.append(token)
    return tokens
```

Match and remove any nonword characters.

Truncate token

Finally, let's define a function to remove *stop words*—words that occur so frequently in language that they offer no useful information for classification. This includes words such as "the" and "are," and the popular library NLTK provides a heavily used list that we will employ. The stop word removal function is shown in the next listing. Note that NLTK also has some methods for punctuation removal, as an alternative to what was done in listing 2.5.

Listing 2.6   Remove stop words

```
import nltk

nltk.download('stopwords')
from nltk.corpus import stopwords
stopwords = stopwords.words('english')

def stop_word_removal(row):
    token = [token for token in row if token not in stopwords]
    token = filter(None, token)
    return token
```

This is where stop words are actually removed from token list.

Removes empty strings—'', None, and so on—as well

We are now going to put all these functions together to build the single dataset representing both classes. The process is illustrated by the script in the next listing. In that script, we convert the combined result into a NumPy array, because this is the input data format expected by many of the libraries we will use.

Listing 2.7   Putting preprocessing steps together to build email dataset

```
import random

EnronEmails = bodies_df.iloc[:,0].apply(tokenize)
EnronEmails = EnronEmails.apply(stop_word_removal)
```

Applies predefined processing functions

```
EnronEmails = EnronEmails.apply(reg_expressions)
EnronEmails = EnronEmails.sample(Nsamp)

SpamEmails = fraud_bodies_df.iloc[:,0].apply(tokenize)
SpamEmails = SpamEmails.apply(stop_word_removal)
SpamEmails = SpamEmails.apply(reg_expressions)
SpamEmails = SpamEmails.sample(Nsamp)

raw_data = pd.concat([SpamEmails,EnronEmails], axis=0).values
```

> **Samples the right number of emails from each class**

> **Converts to NumPy array**

Now let's take a peek at the result to make sure things are proceeding as expected:

```
print("Shape of combined data represented as NumPy array is:")
print(raw_data.shape)
print("Data represented as NumPy array is:")
print(raw_data)
```

This yields the following output:

```
Shape of combined data represented as NumPy array is:
(2000, )
Data represented as NumPy array is:
[['dear', 'sir', 'i' 'got' ... ]
 ['dear', 'friend' ' my' ...]
 ['private', 'confidential' 'friend', 'i' ... ]
 ...
```

We see that the resulting array has divided the text into word units, as we intended.

Let's create the headers corresponding to these emails, consisting of `Nsamp`=1000 of spam emails followed by `Nsamp`=1000 of nonspam emails, as shown next:

```
Categories = ['spam','notspam']
header = ([1]*Nsamp)
header.extend(([0]*Nsamp))
```

We are now ready to convert this NumPy array into numerical features that can actually be fed to the algorithms for classification.

2.1.3   *Converting the email text into numbers*

In this chapter, we start by employing what is often considered the simplest method for *vectorizing* words, that is, converting them into numerical vectors—the *bag-of-words* model. This model simply counts the frequency of word tokens contained in each email and thereby represents it as a vector of such frequency counts. We present the function for assembling the bag-of-words model for emails in listing 2.8. Please note that in doing this, we retain only tokens that appear more than once, as captured by the variable `used_tokens`. This enables us to keep the vector dimensions significantly lower than they would be otherwise. Please also note that one can achieve this using various built-in vectorizers in the popular library scikit-learn (our Jupyter notebook shows how to do this). However, we focus on the approach shown in listing 2.8, because we find it to be more illustrative than a black box function achieving the same. We also note the scikit-learn vectorization methods include counting occurrences of sequences of any *n* words, or *n-grams*, as well as the *tf-idf* approach—important fundamental concepts you should brush up on if rusty. For the problems shown here, we did not notice an improvement when using these vectorization methods over the bag-of-words approach.

Listing 2.8 Assembling a bag-of-words representation

```
def assemble_bag(data):
    used_tokens = []
    all_tokens = []

    for item in data:
        for token in item:
            if token in all_tokens:              ◁─┐  If token has been seen
                if token not in used_tokens:         before, appends it to the
                    used_tokens.append(token)        output list used_tokens
            else:
                all_tokens.append(token)

    df = pd.DataFrame(0, index = np.arange(len(data)), columns = used_tokens)

    for i, item in enumerate(data):      ◁─┐  Creates a Pandas DataFrame counting
        for token in item:                   frequencies of vocabulary words—
            if token in used_tokens:         corresponding to columns, in each
                df.iloc[i][token] += 1       email—corresponding to rows
    return df
```

Having defined the `assemble_bag` function, let's use it to actually carry out the vectorization and visualize it as follows:

```
EnronSpamBag = assemble_bag(raw_data)
print(EnronSpamBag)
predictors = [column for column in EnronSpamBag.columns]
```

A slice of the output DataFrame looks as follows:

	fails	report s	events	may	compliance	stephanie
0	0	0	0	0	0	0
1	0	0	0	0	0	0
2	0	0	0	0	0	0
3	0	0	0	0	0	0
4	0	0	0	0	0	0
...	...	...	...	...	...	...
1995	1	2	1	1	1	0
1996	0	0	0	0	0	0
1997	0	0	0	0	0	0
1998	0	0	0	0	0	1
1999	0	0	0	0	0	0

```
[2000 rows x 5469 columns]
```

The column labels indicate words in the vocabulary of the bag-of-words model, and the numerical entries in each row correspond to the frequency counts of each such word for each of the 2,000 emails in our dataset. Notice that it is an extremely sparse DataFrame—it consists mostly of values of 0.

Having fully vectorized the dataset, we must remember that it is not shuffled with respect to classes; that is, it contains Nsamp = 1000 spam emails followed by an equal number of nonspam emails. Depending on how this dataset is split—in our case, by picking the first 70% for training and the remainder for testing—this could lead to a training set composed of spam only, which would obviously lead to failure. To create a randomized ordering of class samples in the dataset, we will need to shuffle the data in unison with the header/list of labels. The function for achieving this is shown in the next listing. Again, the same thing can be achieved using built-in scikit-learn functions, but we find the method shown next to be more illustrative.

Listing 2.9   Shuffling data in unison with a header/list of labels

```
def unison_shuffle_data(data, header):
    p = np.random.permutation(len(header))
    data = data[p]
    header = np.asarray(header)[p]
    return data, header
```

As the very last step of preparing the email dataset for training by our baseline classifiers, we split it into independent training and testing, or validation, sets. This will allow us to evaluate the performance of the classifier on a set of data that was not used for training—an important thing to ensure in machine learning practice. We elect to use 70% of the data for training and 30% for testing/validation afterward. The following code calls the unison shuffling function and then performs the train/test split. The resulting NumPy array variables train_x and train_y will be fed directly to the classifiers in the following sections of this chapter:

```
data, header = unison_shuffle_data(EnronSpamBag.values, header)
idx = int(0.7*data.shape[0])          ◁        Uses 70% of data
train_x = data[:idx]                           for training
train_y = header[:idx]
test_x = data[idx:]         ◁      Uses remaining
test_y = header[idx:]              30% for testing
```

Hopefully, this exercise of building and preprocessing an NLP dataset for machine learning tasks, now complete, has equipped you with useful skills that will carry over to your own projects. We will now proceed to address the preprocessing of the second illustrative example we will use in this and the next chapter, the classification of Internet Movie Database (IMDB) movie reviews. That exercise will be decidedly shorter, given that the IMDB dataset is in a more prepared state than the email dataset we assembled. However, it is an opportunity to highlight a different type of preprocessing required, given that the data is available in separate folders, organized by class.

2.2 *Preprocessing movie sentiment classification example data*

In this section, we preprocess and explore the second example dataset that will be analyzed in this chapter. This second example is concerned with classifying movie reviews from IMDB into positive or negative sentiments expressed. This is a prototypical sentiment analysis example that has been used widely in the literature to study many algorithms. We present the code snippets necessary to preprocess the data, and you are encouraged to run the code as you read for best educational value.

We will use a popular labeled dataset of 25,000 reviews for this,[5] which was assembled by scraping the popular movie review website IMDB and mapping the number of stars corresponding to each review to either 0 or 1, depending on whether it was less than or greater than 5 out of 10 stars, respectively.[6] This dataset has been used widely in prior NLP literature, and this familiarity is part of the reason we chose it as an illustrative example for baselining.

The sequence of steps used to preprocess each IMDB movie review before analysis is very similar to the one presented in figure 2.2 for the email spam classification example. The first major difference is that no email headers are attached to these reviews, so the header extraction step is not applicable. Additionally, because some stop words, including "no" and "not," may change the sentiment of the message, the stop-word removal step may need to be carried out with extra care, first making sure to drop such stop words from the target list. We did experiment with dropping such words from the list and saw little to no effect on the result. This is likely because other non–stop words in the reviews are very predictive features, rendering this step irrelevant. Thus, although we do show you how to do this in our Jupyter notebook, we do not discuss it any further here.

Let's dive right into preparing the IMDB dataset for our purposes, similarly to what was done for the email dataset that we assembled in the previous section. The IMDB dataset can be downloaded and extracted via the following shell commands in our Jupyter notebook:

```
!wget -q "http://ai.stanford.edu/~amaas/data/sentiment/aclImdb_v1.tar.gz"
!tar xzf aclImdb_v1.tar.gz
```

Note that the exclamation sign, !, at the beginning of the command tells the interpreter that these are shell, not Python, commands. Also note that this is a Linux command. If you're running this code locally on Windows, you may need to download and extract the file manually from the provided link. This yields two subfolders—aclImdb/pos/ and aclImdb/neg/—which we load, after tokenizing, removing stop words and punctuations, and shuffling, into a NumPy array using the function and its calling script in the following listing.

---

[5] ai.stanford.edu/~amaas/data/sentiment

[6] A.L. Maas et al., "Learning Word Vectors for Sentiment Analysis," Proc. of NAACL-HLT (2018).

Listing 2.10   Loading IMDB data into a NumPy array

```
def load_data(path):
    data, sentiments = [], []
    for folder, sentiment in (('neg', 0), ('pos', 1)):
        folder = os.path.join(path, folder)
        for name in os.listdir(folder):
            with open(os.path.join(folder, name), 'r') as reader:
                text = reader.read()
            text = tokenize(text)
            text = stop_word_removal(text)
            text = reg_expressions(text)
            data.append(text)
            sentiments.append(sentiment)
    data_np = np.array(data)
    data, sentiments = unison_shuffle_data(data_np, sentiments)

    return data, sentiments

train_path = os.path.join('aclImdb', 'train')
raw_data, raw_header = load_data(train_path)
```

Goes through every file in current folder

Applies tokenization and stop-word analysis routines

Converts to a NumPy array

Tracks corresponding sentiment labels

Calls the function above on the data

Note that on Windows, you may have to specify the parameter encoding=utf-8 to the open function call in listing 2.10. Check dimensions of loaded data to make sure things worked as expected, as shown here:

```
print(raw_data.shape)
print(len(raw_header))
```

This yields the following:

```
(25000,)
25000
```

Take Nsamp*2 random entries of the loaded data for training, as shown next:

```
random_indices = np.random.choice(range(len(raw_header)),size=(Nsamp*2,),
    replace=False)
data_train = raw_data[random_indices]
header = raw_header[random_indices]
```

Before proceeding, we need to check the balance of the resulting data with regard to class. In general, we don't want one of the labels to represent most of the dataset, unless that is the distribution expected in practice. Check the label distribution using the following code:

```
unique_elements, counts_elements = np.unique(header, return_counts=True)
print("Sentiments and their frequencies:")
print(unique_elements)
print(counts_elements)
```

This yields the following:

```
Sentiments and their frequencies:
[0 1]
[1019  981]
```

Having satisfied ourselves that the data is roughly balanced between the two classes, with each class representing roughly half of the dataset, assemble and visualize the bag-of-words representation with the next lines of code:

```
MixedBagOfReviews = assemble_bag(data_train)
print(MixedBagOfReviews)
```

A slice through the resulting DataFrame produced by this snippet looks like this:

	ages	i	series		the	dream	the	movie	film	plays	...	\
0	2	2	0	0	0	0	0	1	0	0	...	
1	0	0	0	0	0	0	0	0	0	1	...	
2	0	0	2	2	2	2	2	0	1	0	...	
3	0	2	0	1	0	0	0	1	1	1	...	
4	0	2	0	0	0	0	1	0	0	0	...	
...	...	..	...	..	...	...	...	...	...	...	...	
1995	0	0	0	0	0	0	0	2	1	0	...	
1996	0	0	0	0	0	0	0	1	0	0	...	
1997	0	0	0	0	0	0	0	0	0	0	...	
1998	0	3	0	0	0	0	1	1	1	0	...	
1999	0	1	0	0	0	0	0	1	0	0	...	

Note that after this, you still need to split this data structure into training and validation sets, similar to what we did for the spam-detection example. We do not repeat that here in the interest of brevity, but this code is included in the companion Kaggle notebook.

With this numerical representation ready, we now proceed to building out our baseline classifiers in the subsequent sections for the two presented example datasets. We start with generalized linear models in the next section.

2.3 Generalized linear models

Traditionally, the development of models in any area of applied mathematics has started with linear models. These models are mappings that preserve addition and multiplication in the input and output spaces. In other words, the net response from a pair of inputs will be the sum of the responses to each individual input. This property enables a significant reduction in associated statistical and mathematical theory.

Here, we use a relaxed definition of linearity from statistics, that of *generalized linear models*. Let Y be a vector of output variables or responses, X be a vector of independent variables and β be a vector of unknown parameters to be estimated by training our classifier. A generalized linear model is defined by the equation in figure 2.3.

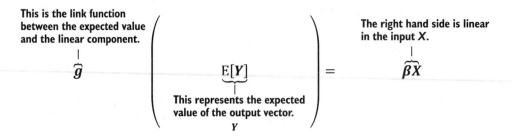

Figure 2.3   Generalized linear model equation

Here, $E[\,]$ stands for the *expected value* of the enclosed quantity, the right-hand side is linear in X, and g is a function that links this linear quantity to the expected value of Y.

In this section, we will apply a pair of the most widely used generalized linear machine learning algorithms to the pair of example problems that were introduced in the previous section—logistic regression and support vector machines (SVMs) with linear kernel. Other popular generalized linear machine learning models that will not be applied include the simple perceptron neural architecture with a linear activation function, latent Dirichlet allocation (LDA), and naive Bayes.

2.3.1   *Logistic regression*

Logistic regression models the relationship between a categorical output variable and a set of input variables by estimating probabilities with the *logistic function*. Assuming the existence of a single input variable x and a single output binary variable y with associated probability $P(y{=}1){=}p$, the logistic equation can be expressed as the equation in figure 2.4.

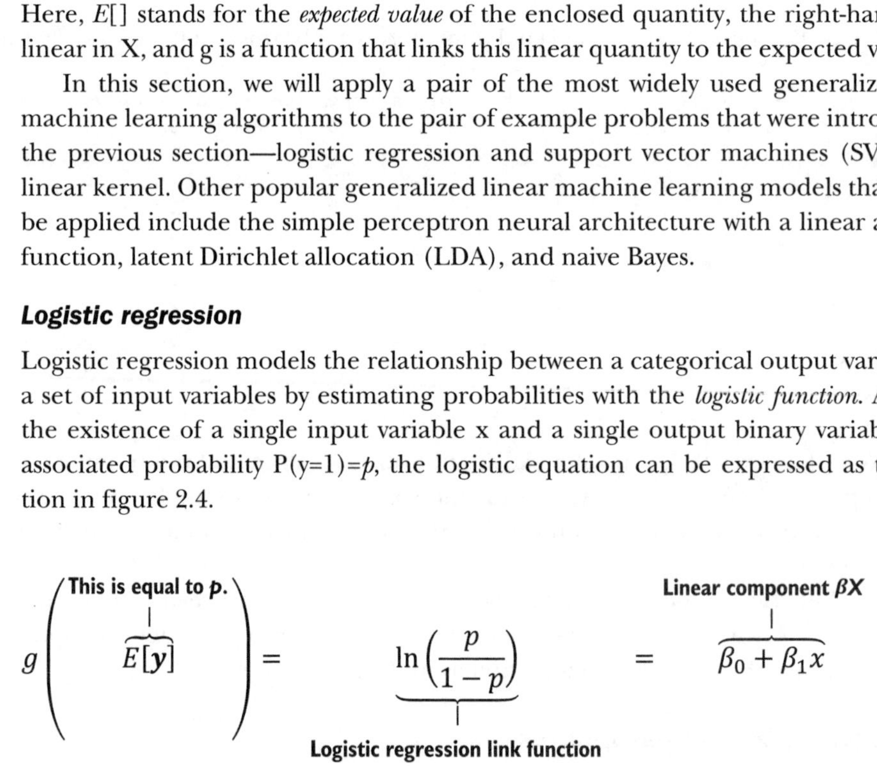

$$
g\left(\underbrace{\overset{\text{This is equal to } p.}{E[y]}}\right) = \underbrace{\ln\left(\frac{p}{1-p}\right)}_{\text{Logistic regression link function}} = \overset{\text{Linear component } \beta X}{\overbrace{\beta_0 + \beta_1 x}}
$$

Figure 2.4   The logistic regression equation

This can be reorganized to yield the prototypical logistic curve equation shown in figure 2.5.

This equation is plotted in figure 2.6. Historically, this curve emerged from the study of bacterial population growth, with initial slow growth, explosion in growth toward the middle, and diminishing growth toward the end, as resources to sustain the population run out.

**This is equal to *E[y]*,
and follows the logistic
curve to the right >>.**

$$\tilde{p} = \frac{1}{1+e^{-(\beta_0+\beta_1 x)}}$$

Linear component βX

Figure 2.5 Reorganized prototypical logistic regression equation

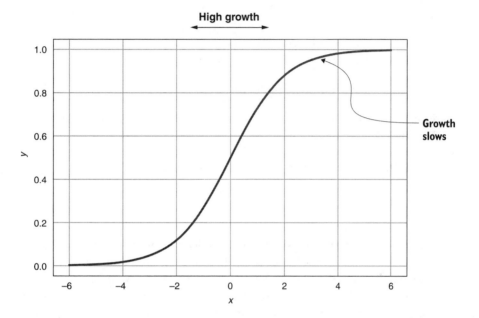

Figure 2.6 Prototypical logistic curve plot

Now let's go ahead and build our classifier using the popular library scikit-learn using the function shown in the next listing.

Listing 2.11 **Building a logistic regression classifier**

```
from sklearn.linear_model import LogisticRegression

def fit(train_x,train_y):
    model = LogisticRegression()          Instantiates
                                          the model
    try:
        model.fit(train_x, train_y)       Fits the model
    except:                               to prepared,
        pass                              labeled data
    return model
```

To fit this model to our data for either the email or IMDB classification example, we need to execute only the following line of code:

```
model = fit(train_x,train_y)
```

This should only take a few seconds on any modern PC. To evaluate performance, we must test on the "hold out" test/validation sets that were put together for each example. This can be performed using the following code:

```
predicted_labels = model.predict(test_x)
from sklearn.metrics import accuracy_score
acc_score = accuracy_score(test_y, predicted_labels)
print("The logistic regression accuracy score is::")
print(acc_score)
```

For the email classification example, this yields:

```
The logistic regression accuracy score is::
0.9766666666666667
```

For the IMDB semantic analysis example, this yields:

```
The logistic regression accuracy score is::
0.715
```

This appears to suggest that the spam classification problem we set up is easier than the IMDB movie review problem. We will address potential ways of improving the performance on the IMDB classifier by the conclusion of the next chapter.

Before proceeding, it is important to address the use of accuracy as the metric for evaluating performance. Accuracy is defined as the ratio of correctly identified samples—the ratio of the number of true positives and negatives to the total number of samples. Other potential metrics that could be used here include precision—the ratio of the number of true positives to all predicted positives—and recall—the ratio of the number of true positives to all actual positives. These two measures could be useful if the costs of false positives and false negatives, respectively, are particularly important. Crucially, the F1-score—the harmonic mean of precision and recall—strikes a balance between the two and is particularly useful for imbalanced datasets. This is the most common situation in practice, making this metric very important. However, remember that the datasets we have constructed so far are roughly balanced. Thus, accuracy is a reasonable enough metric in our case.

2.3.2   *Support vector machines (SVMs)*

SVMs, as was alluded to in chapter 1, have traditionally been the most popular kind of kernel method. These methods attempt to find good decision boundaries by mapping data to a high-dimensional space, using hyperplanes as decision boundaries and the kernel trick to reduce computing cost. When the kernel function is a linear function, SVMs are not only generalized linear models but are indeed linear models.

Let's proceed with building and evaluating an SVM classifier on our two running illustrative example problems using the code shown in the next listing. Note that because this classifier takes a bit longer to train than the logistic regression one, we employ the built-in Python library time to determine the training time.

Listing 2.12 Training and testing an SVM classifier

```
import time
from sklearn.svm import SVC # Support Vector Classification model

clf = SVC(C=1, gamma="auto", kernel='linear',probability=False)

start_time = time.time()
clf.fit(train_x, train_y)
end_time = time.time()
print("Training the SVC Classifier took %3d seconds"%(end_time-start_time))

predicted_labels = clf.predict(test_x)
acc_score = accuracy_score(test_y, predicted_labels)
print("The SVC Classifier testing accuracy score is::")
print(acc_score)
```

Creates a support vector classifier with linear kernel

Fits the classifier using the training data

Tests and evaluates

Training the SVM classifier on the email data took 64 seconds and yielded an accuracy score of 0.670. Training the classifier on the IMDB data took 36 seconds and yielded an accuracy score of 0.697. We see that SVM significantly underperforms logistic regression for the email spam classification problem, while achieving lower but nearly comparable performance for the IMDB problem.

In the next chapter, we will apply some more increasingly sophisticated methods to both classification problems to further baseline them and compare the performance of the various methods. In particular, we will explore decision-tree-based methods, as well as the popular neural-network-based methods ELMo and BERT.

Summary

- It is typical to try a variety of algorithms on any given problem of interest to find the best combination of model complexity and performance for your particular circumstances.
- Baselines usually start with the simplest algorithms, such as logistic regression, and become increasingly complex until the right performance/complexity trade-off is attained.
- A big part of machine learning practice is concerned with assembling and pre-processing data for your problem, and today this is arguably the most important part of the process.
- Important model design choices include metrics for evaluating performance, loss functions to guide the training algorithm, and best validation practices, among many others, and these can vary by model and problem type.

Getting started with baselines: Benchmarking and optimization

This chapter covers

- Analyzing a pair of natural language processing (NLP) problems
- Establishing problem baselines using key traditional methods
- Baselining with representative deep pretrained language models, ELMo and BERT

In this chapter, we continue our direct dive into solving NLP problems we started in the previous chapter. We continue with our goal to establish a set of baselines for a pair of concrete NLP problems, which we will later be able to use to measure progressive improvements gained from leveraging increasingly sophisticated transfer learning approaches. We complete the exercise that we started in chapter 2, where we introduced a pair of practical problems, preprocessed the corresponding data, and initiated baselining by exploring some generalized linear methods. In particular, we introduced the email spam and the Internet Movie Database (IMDB) movie review classification examples and used logistic regression and a support vector machine (SVM) to baseline them.

In this chapter, we explore decision-tree-based and neural-network-based methods. The decision-tree-based methods we look at include random forests and gradient-boosting machines. With regard to the neural-network-based methods, we apply the simplest form of transfer learning to a pair of recently popularized deep pretrained language models, ELMo and BERT. This work involves fine-tuning only a handful of the final layers of each network on a target dataset. This activity will serve as an applied hands-on introduction to the main theme of the book—transfer learning for NLP. Additionally, we explore optimizing the performance of models via hyperparameter tuning.

We begin by exploring decision-tree-based methods in the next section.

3.1 *Decision-tree-based models*

A decision tree is a decision support aid that models decisions and their consequences as *trees*—a graph where any two nodes are connected by exactly one path. An alternative definition of a tree is a flowchart that transforms input values into output categories. More details about this type of model can be found in chapter 1.

In this section, we apply two of the most common decision-tree-based methods— random forests and gradient-boosting machines—to our two running problems.

3.1.1 *Random forests (RFs)*

Random forests (RFs) provide a practical machine learning method for applying decision trees by generating a large number of specialized trees and collecting their outputs. RFs are extremely flexible and widely applicable, making them often the second algorithm practitioners try after logistic regression for baselining. See chapter 1 for more detailed discussions around RFs and their historical context.

Let's build our classifier using the popular library scikit-learn, as shown next.

> **Listing 3.1 Training and testing a random forest classifier**

```
from sklearn.ensemble import RandomForestClassifier        ⟵─┤ Loads scikit's
                                                                 random forest
       ┌─▷ clf = RandomForestClassifier(n_jobs=1, random_state=0)   classifier library
Creates a │
random    │ start_time = time.time()        ⟵─┤ Trains the classifier to learn how
forest    │ clf.fit(train_x, train_y)           the training features relate to the
classifier│ end_time = time.time()              training response variable
          │ print("Training the Random Forest Classifier took %3d seconds"%(end_time-
                 start_time))

          predicted_labels = clf.predict(test_x)

          acc_score = accuracy_score(test_y, predicted_labels)

          print("The RF testing accuracy score is::")
          print(acc_score)
```

Training the RF classifier on the email example data with this code took under a second in our experience and achieved an accuracy score of 0.945. Training it on the IMDB example similarly took under a second and achieved an accuracy score of 0.665. This exercise further confirms the initial hunch from the previous chapter that the IMDB review problem is harder than the email classification problem.

3.1.2   *Gradient-boosting machines (GBMs)*

This variant of decision-tree-based machine learning algorithms iteratively learns new decision-tree-based models that address the weak points of models from the previous iterations. At the time of this writing, they are widely considered to be the best class of methods for addressing nonperceptual machine learning problems. They do present some disadvantages, unfortunately, including a larger model size, a higher risk of overfitting, and less interpretability than some other decision tree models.

The code for training a gradient-boosting machine (GBM) classifier is shown in the next listing. Again, we use the implementation of these models in scikit-learn. Note that the implementation in the Python library XGBoost is widely considered to be more memory-efficient and more readily scalable/parallelizable.

Listing 3.2   Training/testing a gradient-boosting machine classifier

```
from sklearn.ensemble import GradientBoostingClassifier        ◁─┐ GBM
from sklearn import metrics                                        │ algorithm
from sklearn.model_selection import cross_val_score

def modelfit(alg, train_x, train_y, predictors, test_x, performCV=True,
    cv_folds=5):
    alg.fit(train_x, train_y)                       ◁─┐ Fits the algorithm
    predictions = alg.predict(train_x)                │ on the overall data
    predprob = alg.predict_proba(train_x)[:,1]
    if performCV:
        cv_score = cross_val_score(alg, train_x, train_y, cv=cv_folds,
        scoring='roc_auc')
                                                    ┌─ Prints the
    print("\nModel Report")                         │  model report
    print("Accuracy : %.4g" % metrics.accuracy_score(train_y,predictions))
    print("AUC Score (Train): %f" % metrics.roc_auc_score(train_y, predprob))
    if performCV:
        print("CV Score : Mean - %.7g | Std - %.7g | Min - %.7g | Max - %.7g" %
(np.mean(cv_score),np.std(cv_score),np.min(cv_score),np.max(cv_score)))

    return alg.predict(test_x),alg.predict_proba(test_x)    ◁─┐ Predicts the
                                                               │ test data
```

Additional sklearn functions → (imports)

Predicts the training set → `predictions = alg.predict(train_x)`

Performs k-fold cross-validation → `if performCV:`

Note that in listing 3.2, in addition to the usual training accuracy score, we report *k-fold cross-validation* and the *area under the receiver operating characteristic* (ROC) *curve* to evaluate the model. It's necessary to do this here because GBMs are particularly prone to overfitting, and reporting these metrics helps us monitor that risk. Another reason is that the exercise allows you to review these concepts.

More specifically, k-fold cross-validation (with a default value of k=5 folds) randomly splits the training dataset into k partitions, or folds, and trains the model on k–1 of them while evaluating/validating performance on the remaining kth partition, repeating this process k times, with each partition serving as a validation set. It then reports the performance using the statistics of these k evaluation iterations. This process allows us to reduce the risk of the model overfitting on some parts of the dataset and underperforming on others.

> **NOTE** Put simply, overfitting refers to fitting too many parameters to too little data. This scenario hurts the model's ability to generalize to new data and often manifests as improving training metrics with no improvement in validation metrics. It can be alleviated by collecting more data, simplifying the model to reduce the number of training parameters, and other approaches that we will highlight throughout the book.

The following code can be used to call the function and evaluate it on each of the two running examples:

```
gbm0 = GradientBoostingClassifier(random_state=10)
start_time = time.time()
test_predictions, test_probs = modelfit(gbm0, train_x, train_y, predictors,
    test_x)
end_time = time.time()
print("Training the Gradient Boosting Classifier took %3d seconds"%(end_time-
    start_time))

predicted_labels = test_predictions
acc_score = accuracy_score(test_y, predicted_labels)
print("The Gradient Boosting testing accuracy score is::")
print(acc_score)
```

For the email spam classification example, this yields the following result:

```
Model Report
Accuracy : 0.9814
AUC Score (Train): 0.997601
CV Score : Mean - 0.9854882 | Std - 0.006275645 | Min - 0.9770558 | Max -
    0.9922158
Training the Gradient Boosting Classifier took 159 seconds
The Gradient Boosting testing accuracy score is::
0.9483333333333334
```

For the IMDB movie review classification example, this yields the result shown here:

```
Model Report
Accuracy : 0.8943
AUC Score (Train): 0.961556
CV Score : Mean - 0.707521 | Std - 0.03483452 | Min - 0.6635249 | Max -
    0.7681968
Training the Gradient Boosting Classifier took 596 seconds
The Gradient Boosting testing accuracy score is::
0.665
```

At first glance, looking at these results, one may be tempted to conclude that the GBM numerical experiment is more expensive compared to those carried out for the prior methods we looked at—taking almost 10 minutes to complete in the case of the IMDB example on Kaggle. However, we must take into account the fact that when the k-fold cross-validation exercise is carried out, the model is trained repeatedly k=5 times to obtain a more reliable estimate of performance. Each training thus takes approximately two minutes—not as drastic an increase in training time as would be deduced without considering the k-fold cross-validation.

We can see some evidence of overfitting—the testing accuracy is lower than the k-fold training accuracy for the first example. Moreover, in the case of the IMDB example, the k-fold cross-validation scores are noticeably lower than the training score on the overall dataset, underscoring the importance of using the k-fold cross-validation approach for tracking overfitting in this model type. We discuss some approaches to improving the accuracy of the classifier further in the penultimate section of this chapter.

So what exactly is the ROC curve? It is the plot of the false positive rate (FPR) versus the true positive rate (TPR) and an important characteristic used to evaluate and tune classifiers. It shows the trade-off in these important qualities of a classifier as the decision threshold—the probability value beyond which a predicted confidence begins to be classified as a member of a given class—is varied between 0 and 1. The following code can now be used to plot this curve:

```
test_probs_max = []                                    ◁──────────── We first need to find the
for i in range(test_probs.shape[0]):                                maximum probabilities for
    test_probs_max.append(test_probs[i,test_y[i]])                  each example.

fpr, tpr, thresholds = metrics.roc_curve(test_y, np.array(test_probs_max))

import matplotlib.pyplot as plt                         ◁──────── Generates the labeled ROC curve
fig,ax = plt.subplots()                                            plot with the matplotlib library
plt.plot(fpr,tpr,label='ROC curve')
plt.plot([0, 1], [0, 1], color='navy', linestyle='--')
plt.xlabel('False Positive Rate')
plt.ylabel('True Positive Rate')
plt.title('Receiver Operating Characteristic for Email Example')
plt.legend(loc="lower right")
plt.show()
```

Calculates the ROC curve values (annotation pointing to `fpr, tpr, thresholds = metrics.roc_curve(...)`)

The resulting ROC curve for the email classification example is shown in figure 3.1. The straight line with a slope of 1 represents the FPR-versus-TPR trade-off corresponding to random chance. The further to the left the ROC curve is from this line, the better performing the classifier. As a result, the area under the ROC curve can be used as a measure of performance.

One important property of decision-tree-based methods is that they can provide features an importance score, which can be used to detect the most important features in a given dataset. We do this by inserting a couple lines of code right before the return statement of the function in listing 3.2, as shown in listing 3.3.

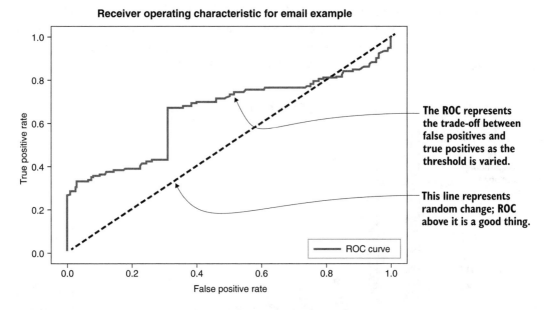

Receiver operating characteristic for email example

The ROC represents the trade-off between false positives and true positives as the threshold is varied.

This line represents random change; ROC above it is a good thing.

Figure 3.1 ROC curve for the email classification example

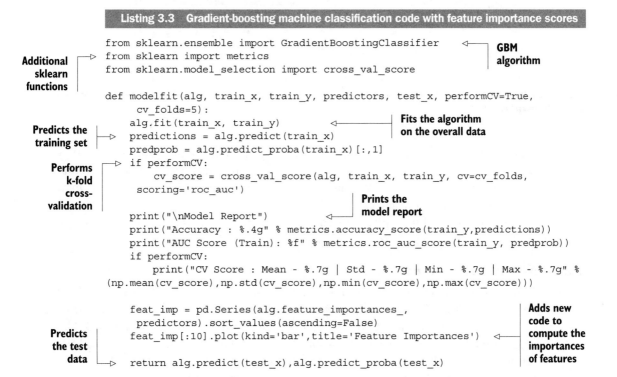

Listing 3.3 Gradient-boosting machine classification code with feature importance scores

```python
from sklearn.ensemble import GradientBoostingClassifier
from sklearn import metrics
from sklearn.model_selection import cross_val_score

def modelfit(alg, train_x, train_y, predictors, test_x, performCV=True,
        cv_folds=5):
    alg.fit(train_x, train_y)
    predictions = alg.predict(train_x)
    predprob = alg.predict_proba(train_x)[:,1]
    if performCV:
        cv_score = cross_val_score(alg, train_x, train_y, cv=cv_folds,
        scoring='roc_auc')

    print("\nModel Report")
    print("Accuracy : %.4g" % metrics.accuracy_score(train_y,predictions))
    print("AUC Score (Train): %f" % metrics.roc_auc_score(train_y, predprob))
    if performCV:
        print("CV Score : Mean - %.7g | Std - %.7g | Min - %.7g | Max - %.7g" %
(np.mean(cv_score),np.std(cv_score),np.min(cv_score),np.max(cv_score)))

    feat_imp = pd.Series(alg.feature_importances_,
        predictors).sort_values(ascending=False)
    feat_imp[:10].plot(kind='bar',title='Feature Importances')

    return alg.predict(test_x),alg.predict_proba(test_x)
```

Additional sklearn functions

GBM algorithm

Predicts the training set

Fits the algorithm on the overall data

Performs k-fold cross-validation

Prints the model report

Adds new code to compute the importances of features

Predicts the test data

For the IMDB example, this yields the plot in figure 3.2. We see that words like "worst" and "awful" are very important to the classification decision, which makes qualitative sense, because one can imagine a negative critic using these words. On the other hand, words like "loved" may be used by a positive reviewer.

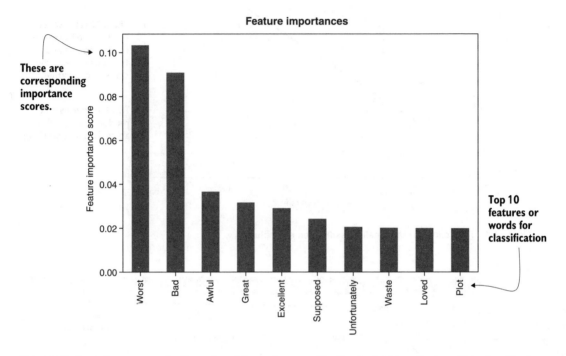

Figure 3.2   Importance scores for the various tokens discovered by the gradient-boosting machine classifier for the IMDB classification example

A point of caution: Importance scores seem to work well for this example, but they should not always be blindly trusted. For instance, it has been widely recognized that these importance scores can be biased toward continuous variables, as well as high cardinality categorical variables.

We now proceed to applying to our two running examples some neural network models, arguably the most important class of models for NLP today.

3.2   Neural network models

As we discussed in chapter 1, neural networks are the most important class of machine learning algorithms for handling perceptual problems such as computer vision and NLP.

In this section, we will train two representative pretrained neural network language models on the two example problems we have been baselining in this and the previous chapter. We consider the Embeddings from Language Models (ELMo) and Bidirectional Encoder Representations from Transformers (BERT).

ELMo includes elements of convolutional and recurrent (specifically *long short-term memory* [LSTM]) elements, whereas the appropriately named BERT is transformer-based. These terms were introduced in chapter 1 and will be addressed in more detail in subsequent chapters. We employ the simplest form of transfer learning fine-tuning, where a single dense classification layer is trained on top of the corresponding pre-trained embedding over our dataset of labels from the previous sections.

3.2.1 Embeddings from Language Models (ELMo)

The Embeddings from Language Models (ELMo) model, named after the popular *Sesame Street* character, was among the first models to demonstrate the effectiveness of transferring pretrained language model knowledge to general NLP tasks. The model was trained to predict the next word in a sequence of words, which can be done in an unsupervised manner on very large corpora, and showed that the weights obtained as a result could generalize to a variety of other NLP tasks. We will not discuss the architecture of this model in detail in this section—we'll get to that in a later chapter. Here we focus on building intuition, but it suffices to mention that the model employs character-level convolutions to build up preliminary embeddings of each word token, followed by bidirectional LSTM layers, which introduce the context of surrounding words into the final embeddings produced by the model.

Having briefly introduced ELMo, let's proceed to train it for each of the two running example datasets. The ELMo model is available through the TensorFlow Hub, which provides an easy platform for sharing TensorFlow models. We will use Keras with a TensorFlow backend to build our model. In order to make the TensorFlow Hub model usable by Keras, we need to define a custom Keras layer that instantiates it in the right format. This is achieved using the function shown in the next listing.

Listing 3.4 Instantiating TensorFlow Hub ELMo as a custom Keras layer

```
import tensorflow as tf                              ◁──┐  Imports the
import tensorflow_hub as hub                            │  required
from keras import backend as K                          │  dependencies
import keras.layers as layers
from keras.models import Model, load_model
from keras.engine import Layer
import numpy as np
                                          ┌──  Initializes the
                                          │    session
sess = tf.Session()          ◁───────────┘
K.set_session(sess)


class ElmoEmbeddingLayer(Layer):          ◁──┐  Creates a custom layer
    def __init__(self, **kwargs):            │  that allows us to
        self.dimensions = 1024               │  update weights
        self.trainable=True
        super(ElmoEmbeddingLayer, self).__init__(**kwargs)
```

Extracts the trainable parameters— four weights in the weighted average of the ELMo model layers; see the earlier TensorFlow Hub link for more details

Downloads the pretrained ELMo model from TensorFlow Hub

```
def build(self, input_shape):
    self.elmo =hub.Module('https://tfhub.dev/google/elmo/2',
   trainable=self.trainable,
                            name="{}_module".format(self.name))

    self.trainable_weights +=
  K.tf.trainable_variables(scope="^{}_module/.*".format(self.name))
    super(ElmoEmbeddingLayer, self).build(input_shape)

def call(self, x, mask=None):
    result = self.elmo(K.squeeze(K.cast(x, tf.string), axis=1),
                  as_dict=True,
                  signature='default',
                  )['default']
    return result

def compute_output_shape(self, input_shape):
    return (input_shape[0], self.dimensions)
```

Specifies the shape of the output

Before using this function to train a model, we will need to adapt our preprocessed data a bit for this model architecture. In particular, recall that we assembled a bag-of-words representation for the traditional models from the variable raw_data, which was produced by listing 2.7 and is a NumPy array containing a list of word tokens per email. In this case, we instead use the function and code in listing 3.5 to combine each such list into a single text string. This is the format in which the ELMo TensorFlow Hub model expects the input, and we are glad to oblige.

> **NOTE** The combined string in this case has stop words removed, a step that is often not required in deep learning practice due to the uncanny ability of artificial neural networks to figure out what is important and what isn't— feature engineering, automatically. In our case, because we are trying to compare the strengths and weaknesses of the different model types for this problem, applying the same kind of preprocessing for all algorithms makes sense and is arguably the right approach. We note, however, that ELMo was pretrained on a corpus containing stop words, as was BERT.

Listing 3.5 Converting data to the form expected by the ELMo TensorFlow Hub model

```
def convert_data(raw_data,header):
    converted_data, labels = [], []
    for i in range(raw_data.shape[0]):
        out = ' '.join(raw_data[i])
        converted_data.append(out)
        labels.append(header[i])
    converted_data = np.array(converted_data, dtype=object)[:, np.newaxis]

    return converted_data, np.array(labels)

raw_data, header = unison_shuffle(raw_data, header)
```

Converts data into the right format

Concatenates the tokens for each email into a single string

Shuffles the raw data first

```
idx = int(0.7*data_train.shape[0])
train_x, train_y = convert_data(raw_data[:idx],header[:idx])
test_x, test_y = convert_data(raw_data[idx:],header[idx:])
```

**Converts 70% of the
data for training**

**Converts the remaining
30% of the data for testing**

Having converted the data into the right format, we use the code in the next listing to build and train the Keras ELMo TensorFlow Hub model.

Listing 3.6 Building ELMo Keras model using custom layer defined in listing 3.4

```
def build_model():
  input_text = layers.Input(shape=(1,), dtype="string")
  embedding = ElmoEmbeddingLayer()(input_text)
  dense = layers.Dense(256, activation='relu')(embedding)
  pred = layers.Dense(1, activation='sigmoid')(dense)

  model = Model(inputs=[input_text], outputs=pred)

  model.compile(loss='binary_crossentropy', optimizer='adam',
                          metrics=['accuracy'])
  model.summary()

  return model

# Build and fit
model = build_model()
model.fit(train_x,
          train_y,
          validation_data=(test_x, test_y),
          epochs=5,
          batch_size=32)
```

**New layer
outputting
256-dimensional
feature vectors**

**Classification
layer**

**Loss, metric,
and optimizer
choices**

**Shows the model
architecture for
inspection**

**Fits the model
for five epochs**

A few things should be noted here, given that this is our first encounter with some detailed aspects of deep learning design. First of all, notice that we have added an additional layer on top the pretrained ELMo embedding, producing 256-dimensional feature vectors. We have also added a classification layer of output dimension 1. The activation function sigmoid transforms its input into the interval between 0 and 1 and is essentially the logistic curve in figure 2.6. We can interpret its output as the probability of the positive class, and when it exceeds some prespecified threshold (usually 0.5), we can classify the corresponding input to the network as the said positive class.

The model is fitted for five "major steps," or epochs, over the whole dataset. The Keras code statement model.summary() in listing 3.6 prints the model details and produces the following output:

```
Layer (type)                     Output Shape            Param #
=================================================================
input_2 (InputLayer)             (None, 1)               0

elmo_embedding_layer_2 (Elmo     (None, 1024)            4
```

```
dense_3 (Dense)              (None, 256)               262400

dense_4 (Dense)              (None, 2)                 514
=================================================================
Total params: 262,918
Trainable params: 262,918
Non-trainable params: 0
```

We note—without delving into too much further detail, because this will be addressed in chapter 4—that most of the trainable parameters in this case (approximately 260 thousand of them) are coming from the layers we added on top of the custom ELMo model. This is our first instance of transfer learning: learning a pair of new layers on top of the pretrained model shared by ELMo's creators. It is important to use a powerful GPU for most neural network experiments, and the value of the batch_size parameter, which specifies how much data is fed to the GPU at each step, can be extremely important to the speed of convergence. It will vary with the GPU being used, or the lack thereof. In practice, one can increase the value of this parameter until the speed of convergence of a typical problem instance does not benefit from the increase, or whenever the GPU memory is no longer large enough for a single data batch to fit on it during an iteration of the algorithm—whichever happens first. Additionally, when dealing with a multi-GPU scenario, some evidence has been experimentally shown[1] that the optimal scaling-up schedule of the batch size is linear in the number of GPUs.

On a free NVIDIA Tesla K80 GPU via a Kaggle Kernel (see our companion GitHub repository[2] for Kaggle notebook links), we achieve the performance on our email dataset for the first five epochs as shown in figure 3.3 for a typical run. We found a batch_size of 32 to work well for us in that context.

Each epoch takes approximately 10 seconds to complete—this information is printed by our code. We see that a validation accuracy of approximately 97.3% is attained at the fourth epoch (meaning the results were reached in under a minute). This performance is comparable to the performance of the logistic regression approach, which is only slightly better at 97.7% (see also table 3.1). We note that the behavior of the algorithm is stochastic—it behaves differently from run to run. Thus, your own convergence will vary somewhat, even on architecture similar to what we used. It is typical in practice to try the algorithm run a few times and pick the best set of parameters among the stochastic and varying results attained. Finally, we note that the divergence of training and validation accuracies is suggestive of the beginning of overfitting, as indicated in the figure. This lends credence to the hypothesis that increasing the amount of signal by increasing the length of tokens, as specified by the hyperparameter maxtokenlen, and the number of tokens per email, as specified by maxtokens, may increase performance further. Naturally, increasing the number of samples per class by cranking up Nsamp should also work to improve performance.

---

[1] P. Goyal et al., "Accurate, Large Minibatch SGD: Training ImageNet in 1 Hour," *arXhiv* (2018).
[2] https://github.com/azunre/transfer-learning-for-nlp

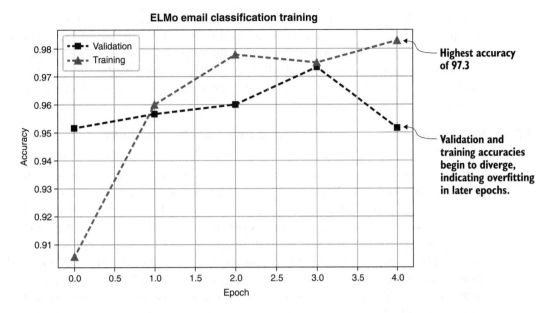

Figure 3.3 Convergence of the validation and training accuracy scores for the first five epochs of training the ELMo model on the email classification example

For the IMDB example, the ELMo model code yields the convergence output shown in figure 3.4.

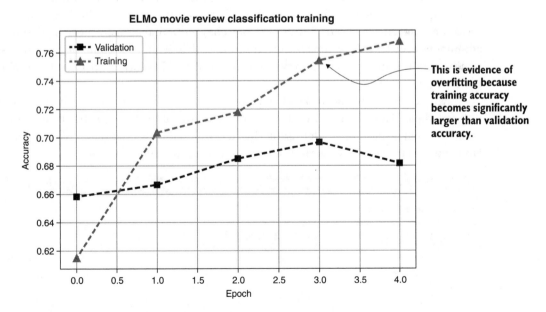

Figure 3.4 Convergence of the validation and training accuracy scores for the first five epochs of training the ELMo model on the IMDB movie review classification example

Each epoch again takes approximately 10 seconds and achieves a validation accuracy of approximately 70% in under a minute at the second epoch. We will see how to improve the performances of these models in the next and final sections of this chapter. Note that some evidence of overfitting can be observed at the third and later epochs, as the training accuracy continues to improve—the fit to the data improves, whereas the validation accuracy remains lower.

3.2.2   *Bidirectional Encoder Representations from Transformers (BERT)*

The Bidirectional Encoder Representations from Transformers (BERT) model was also named after a popular *Sesame Street* character as a nod to the trend started by ELMo. At the time of writing, its variants achieve some of the best performance in transferring pretrained language model knowledge to downstream NLP tasks. The model was similarly trained to predict words in a sequence of words, although the exact *masking* procedure is somewhat different and will be discussed in detail later in the book. It can also be done in an unsupervised manner on very large corpuses, and the resulting weights similarly generalize to a variety of other NLP tasks. Arguably, to familiarize yourself with transfer learning in NLP, it is indispensable to also familiarize yourself with BERT.

Just as we did with ELMo, we will avoid discussing the architecture of this deep learning model in complete detail in this section—we will cover that in a subsequent chapter. It will suffice to mention here that the model employs character-level convolutions to build up preliminary embeddings of word tokens, followed by transformer-based encoders with self-attention layers that provide the model with a context of surrounding words. The transformer functionally replaced the role of the bidirectional LSTMs employed by ELMo. Recalling from chapter 1 that transformers have some advantages over LSTMs with respect to training scalability, we see some of the motivation behind this model. Again, we will use Keras with a TensorFlow backend to build our model.

Having briefly introduced BERT, let's proceed to train it for each of the two running example datasets. The BERT model is also available through the TensorFlow Hub. To make the hub model usable by Keras, we similarly define a custom Keras layer that instantiates it in the right format, as shown in the next listing.

> ### Listing 3.7   Instantiating TensorFlow Hub BERT as a custom Keras layer

```
import tensorflow as tf
import tensorflow_hub as hub
from bert.tokenization import FullTokenizer
from tensorflow.keras import backend as K

# Initialize session
sess = tf.Session()


class BertLayer(tf.keras.layers.Layer):
    def __init__(
```

Choice of regularization type

```
    self,
    n_fine_tune_layers=10,
    pooling="mean",
    bert_path="https://tfhub.dev/google/bert_uncased_L-12_H-768_A-12/1",
    **kwargs,
):
    self.n_fine_tune_layers = n_fine_tune_layers
    self.trainable = True
    self.output_size = 768
    self.pooling = pooling
    self.bert_path = bert_path

    super(BertLayer, self).__init__(**kwargs)

def build(self, input_shape):
    self.bert = hub.Module(
        self.bert_path, trainable=self.trainable,
name=f"{self.name}_module"
    )

    trainable_vars = self.bert.variables
    if self.pooling == "first":
        trainable_vars = [var for var in trainable_vars if not "/cls/" in
var.name]
        trainable_layers = ["pooler/dense"]

    elif self.pooling == "mean":
        trainable_vars = [
            var
            for var in trainable_vars
            if not "/cls/" in var.name and not "/pooler/" in var.name
        ]
        trainable_layers = []
    else:
        raise NameError("Undefined pooling type")

    for i in range(self.n_fine_tune_layers):
        trainable_layers.append(f"encoder/layer_{str(11 - i)}")

    trainable_vars = [
        var
        for var in trainable_vars
        if any([l in var.name for l in trainable_layers])
    ]

    for var in trainable_vars:
        self._trainable_weights.append(var)

    for var in self.bert.variables:
        if var not in self._trainable_weights:
            self._non_trainable_weights.append(var)

    super(BertLayer, self).build(input_shape)

def call(self, inputs):
    inputs = [K.cast(x, dtype="int32") for x in inputs]
```

Default number of top layers to unfreeze for training

Pretrained model to use; this is the large, uncased original version of the model.

BERT embedding dimension, that is, the size of the resulting output semantic vectors

Removes unused layers

Enforces the number of unfrozen layers to fine-tune

Trainable weights

Inputs to
BERT take a
very specific
triplet form;
we will show
how to
generate it
in the next
listing.

```
        input_ids, input_mask, segment_ids = inputs
        bert_inputs = dict(
            input_ids=input_ids, input_mask=input_mask,
    segment_ids=segment_ids
        )
        if self.pooling == "first":
            pooled = self.bert(inputs=bert_inputs, signature="tokens",
    as_dict=True)[
                "pooled_output"
            ]
        elif self.pooling == "mean":
            result = self.bert(inputs=bert_inputs, signature="tokens",
    as_dict=True)[
                "sequence_output"
            ]
```

BERT
"masks"
some words
and then
attempts to
predict them
as learning
target.

```
        mul_mask = lambda x, m: x * tf.expand_dims(m, axis=-1)
        masked_reduce_mean = lambda x, m: tf.reduce_sum(mul_mask(x, m),
    axis=1) / (
                    tf.reduce_sum(m, axis=1, keepdims=True) + 1e-10)
        input_mask = tf.cast(input_mask, tf.float32)
        pooled = masked_reduce_mean(result, input_mask)
        else:
            raise NameError("Undefined pooling type")

        return pooled

    def compute_output_shape(self, input_shape):
        return (input_shape[0], self.output_size)
```

Similar to what we did for ELMo in the previous subsection, we perform a sequence of analogous postprocessing steps on the data from the prior sections to put it into the format required by the BERT model. In addition to what we did in listing 3.5 to concatenate the bag-of-words token representations into a list of strings, we subsequently need to convert each concatenated string into three arrays—*input IDs, input masks,* and *segment IDs*—prior to feeding them to the BERT model. The code for doing this is shown in listing 3.8. Having converted the data into the right format, we use the remaining code in the same listing 3.8 to build and train the Keras BERT TensorFlow Hub model.

Listing 3.8 Converting data to form expected by BERT, building and training model

Function for
building model

```
def build_model(max_seq_length):
    in_id = tf.keras.layers.Input(shape=(max_seq_length,), name="input_ids")
    in_mask = tf.keras.layers.Input(shape=(max_seq_length,),
     name="input_masks")
    in_segment = tf.keras.layers.Input(shape=(max_seq_length,),
     name="segment_ids")
    bert_inputs = [in_id, in_mask, in_segment]
```

We do not retrain any BERT layers but rather use the pretrained model as an embedding and retrain some new layers on top of it.

```
bert_output = BertLayer(n_fine_tune_layers=0)(bert_inputs)
dense = tf.keras.layers.Dense(256, activation="relu")(bert_output)
pred = tf.keras.layers.Dense(1, activation="sigmoid")(dense)

model = tf.keras.models.Model(inputs=bert_inputs, outputs=pred)
model.compile(loss="binary_crossentropy", optimizer="adam",
 metrics=["accuracy"])
model.summary()

return model
```

Vanilla TensorFlow initialization calls

```
def initialize_vars(sess):
    sess.run(tf.local_variables_initializer())
    sess.run(tf.global_variables_initializer())
    sess.run(tf.tables_initializer())
    K.set_session(sess)
```

Converts data to the "InputExample" format using a function in the BERT source repository

Creates a compatible tokenizer using a function in the BERT source repository

```
bert_path = "https://tfhub.dev/google/bert_uncased_L-12_H-768_A-12/1"
tokenizer = create_tokenizer_from_hub_module(bert_path)

train_examples = convert_text_to_examples(train_x, train_y)
test_examples = convert_text_to_examples(test_x, test_y)

# Convert to features
(train_input_ids,train_input_masks,train_segment_ids,train_labels) =
    convert_examples_to_features(tokenizer, train_examples,
    max_seq_length=maxtokens)
(test_input_ids,test_input_masks,test_segment_ids,test_labels) =
    convert_examples_to_features(tokenizer, test_examples,
    max_seq_length=maxtokens)
```

Builds the model

```
model = build_model(maxtokens)
```

Converts the InputExample format into the triplicate final BERT input format, using a function in the BERT source repository

Instantiates the variables

```
initialize_vars(sess)
```

Trains the model

```
history = model.fit([train_input_ids, train_input_masks, train_segment_ids],
train_labels,validation_data=([test_input_ids, test_input_masks,
test_segment_ids],test_labels), epochs=5, batch_size=32)
```

Similar to the ELMo model we built in the previous subsection, we put a pair of layers on top of the pretrained model and train only those, which amounts to about 200 thousand parameters. With hyperparameters set at comparable values with all of the prior methods, we achieved validation accuracies of approximately 98.3% and 71% for the email and movie review classification problems, respectively (within five epochs).

3.3 *Optimizing performance*

In looking at the performance results of the various algorithms from the previous sections of the chapter, as well as those from the previous chapter, we might be tempted to make conclusions right away about which algorithm is best-performing for each problem we looked at. For instance, we may conclude that BERT and logistic regression are the best algorithms for the email classification problem, with an accuracy of around 98%, whereas ELMo is not that far behind, followed by the decision-tree-based methods and SVM in last place. On the other hand, for the IMDB movie review classification problem, BERT appears to be the winner with a performance of approximately 71%, followed by ELMo, and only then logistic regression.

We must remember, however, that we know this to be true for sure only at the *hyperparameter settings* at which we initially evaluated the algorithms—Nsamp = 1000, maxtokens = 50, maxtokenlen = 20—in addition to any algorithm-specific default parameter values. To make general statements with confidence, we need to explore the space of hyperparameters more thoroughly by evaluating the performance of all algorithms at many hyperparameter settings, a process typically referred to as *hyperparameter tuning or optimization.* It may be that the best performance found through this process for each algorithm will change their performance ranking, and in general, this will help us achieve better accuracies for our problems of interest.

3.3.1   Manual hyperparameter tuning

Hyperparameter tuning is often initially performed manually, driven by intuition. We describe such an approach here for the hyperparameters Nsamp, maxtokens and maxtokenlen, which are general across all the algorithms.

Let's first assume that the initial amount of data trained—with Nsamp=1000, for example—is all the data we have. We hypothesize that if we increase the number of tokens in the data for each document—maxtokens—and increase the maximum length of any such token—maxtokenlen—we would be able to increase the amount of signal for making the classification decision and, thereby, the resulting accuracy.

For the email classification problem, we first increase both of these, from values of 50 and 20, respectively, to 100 each. Accuracy results for doing this for logistic regression (LR), support vector machines (SVMs), random forests (RFs), gradient-boosting machines (GBMs), ELMo, and BERT are shown in second row of table 3.1. Furthermore, we increase maxtokens to 200 to yield the results in the third row of table 3.1.

Table 3.1   Comparison of algorithm accuracies at different general hyperparameter settings explored during the manual tuning process for the email classification example

General hyperparameter settings	LR	SVM	RF	GBM	ELMo	BERT
Nsamp = 1000 maxtokens = 50 maxtokenlen = 20	97.7%	70.2%	94.5%	94.2%	97.3%	98.3%
Nsamp = 1000 maxtokens = 100 maxtokenlen = 100	99.2%	72.3%	97.2%	97.3%	98.2%	98.8%
Nsamp = 1000, maxtokens = 200, maxtokenlen = 100	98.7%	90.0%	97.7%	97.2%	99.7%	98.8%

We see based on this that, although SVMs is clearly the worst-performing classifier for this problem, logistic regression, ELMo, and BERT can achieve nearly perfect performance. Note also that ELMo is the clear winner in the presence of more signal—something we would have missed without the optimization step. However, the simplicity and speed of logistic regression would likely result in it being picked as the classifier of choice for this email classification problem in production.

We now repeat a similar sequence of hyperparameter testing steps for the IMDB movie review classification problem. We first increase maxtokens and maxtokenlen to 100 each and then increase maxtokens further to 200. The resulting algorithm performances are listed in table 3.2, along with the performances at the initial hyperparameter settings.

Table 3.2 Comparison of algorithm accuracies at different general hyperparameter settings explored during the manual tuning process for the IMDB movie review classification example

General hyperparameter settings	LR	SVM	RF	GBM	ELMo	BERT
Nsamp = 1000 maxtokens = 50 maxtokenlen = 20	69.1%	66.0%	63.9%	67.0%	69.7%	71.0%
Nsamp = 1000 maxtokens = 100 maxtokenlen = 100	74.3%	72.5%	70.0%	72.0%	75.2%	79.1%
Nsamp = 1000 maxtokens = 200 maxtokenlen = 100	79.0%	78.3%	67.2%	77.5%	77.7%	81.0%

BERT appears to be the best model for this problem across the board, followed by ELMo and logistic regression. Observe that this problem has more headroom for improvement, consistent with our earlier observation that this problem is more difficult than the email classification one. This leads us to hypothesize that pretrained knowledge transfer has more of an effect on harder problems, which makes intuitive sense. This concept is also consistent with general advice that stipulates that neural network models are likely to be preferable to other approaches when significant labeled data is available, assuming the problem to be solved is complex enough for the additional data to be needed in the first place.

3.3.2 *Systematic hyperparameter tuning*

A number of tools exist for more systematic and exhaustive hyperparameter searches on ranges of hyperparameters. These include the Python methods GridSearchCV, which performs an exhaustive search over a specified parameter grid, and HyperOpt, which does a random search over parameter ranges. Here, we present code for using GridSearchCV to tune an algorithm of choice as an illustrative example. Note that we tune only some internal algorithm-specific hyperparameters in this exercise, with the general ones we tuned in the last subsection fixed, for simplicity of illustration.

We pick email classification with RF with the initial general hyperparameter settings as our illustrative example. The reason for this choice is that it takes about a second for each fit of this algorithm on this problem, and because the grid search will perform a lot of fits, this example can be executed quickly for the greatest learning value for the reader.

We first import the required method and check which RF hyperparameters are available for tuning as follows:

```
from sklearn.model_selection import GridSearchCV
print("Available hyper-parameters for systematic tuning available with RF:")
print(clf.get_params())
```

GridSearchCV scikit-learn import statement

clf is the RF classifier from listing 2.13.

This yields the following output:

```
{'bootstrap': True, 'class_weight': None, 'criterion': 'gini', 'max_depth':
None, 'max_features': 'auto', 'max_leaf_nodes': None,
'min_impurity_decrease': 0.0, 'min_impurity_split': None, 'min_samples_leaf':
1, 'min_samples_split': 2, 'min_weight_fraction_leaf': 0.0, 'n_estimators':
10, 'n_jobs': 1, 'oob_score': False, 'random_state': 0, 'verbose': 0,
'warm_start': False}
```

We pick three of these hyperparameters to search over and specify three values for each of them, as shown next:

```
param_grid = {
    'min_samples_leaf': [1, 2, 3],
    'min_samples_split': [2, 6, 10],
    'n_estimators': [10, 100, 1000]
}
```

We then carry out the grid search using the following code, making sure to print out final test accuracy and best hyperparameter values:

```
grid_search = GridSearchCV(estimator = clf, param_grid = param_grid,
                    cv = 3, n_jobs = -1, verbose = 2)

grid_search.fit(train_x, train_y)

print("Best parameters found:")
print(grid_search.best_params_)

print("Estimated accuracy is:")
acc_score = accuracy_score(test_y,
        grid_search.best_estimator_.predict(test_x))
print(acc_score)
```

Defines the grid search object with a specified hyperparameter grid

Fits the grid search to the data

Displays the results

This experiment required training the classifier at 3*3*3=27 points, because each of the three hyperparameter grids has three requested points on it. The overall experiment took less than five minutes to complete and yielded an accuracy of 95.7%. This is an improvement of more than 1% over the original score of 94.5%. The raw output from the code is shown next, specifying best hyperparameter values:

```
Best parameters found:
{'min_samples_leaf': 2, 'min_samples_split': 10, 'n_estimators': 1000}
Estimated accuracy is:
0.9566666666666667
```

Indeed, when we performed the tuning across the board on all classifiers, we found that we could boost the performance of each by 1–2%, without affecting the conclusions on the best classifier for each problem reached in the previous subsection.

Summary

- It is typical to try a variety of algorithms on any given problem of interest to find the best combination of model complexity and performance for your circumstances.

- Baselines usually start with the simplest algorithms, such as logistic regression, and become increasingly complex until the right performance/complexity trade-off is attained.

- Important model design choices include metrics for evaluating performance, loss functions to guide the training algorithm, and best validation practices, among many others, and these can vary by model and problem type.

- Hyperparameter tuning is an important step of the model-development pipeline, because initial hyperparameter settings may severely misrepresent the best attainable performance that can be found by tuning it.

- Simple models tend to work best when the amount of available data isn't very large and/or for easier problems, whereas complex neural network models tend to do better, and as such be worth the extra complexity, when more data is available.

Part 2

Shallow transfer learning and deep transfer learning with recurrent neural networks (RNNs)

Chapters 4, 5, and 6 dive deeper into some important transfer learning NLP approaches based on shallow neural networks, that is, neural networks with relatively few layers. They also begin to explore deep transfer learning via representative techniques that employ recurrent neural networks (RNNs) for key functions, such as ELMo.

Shallow transfer
learning for NLP

This chapter covers

- Using pretrained word embeddings in a semisupervised fashion to transfer pretrained knowledge to a problem
- Using pretrained embeddings of larger sections of text in a semisupervised fashion to transfer pretrained knowledge to a problem
- Using multitask learning to develop better-performing models
- Modifying target domain data to reuse knowledge from a resource-rich source domain

In this chapter, we will cover some prominent shallow transfer learning approaches and concepts. This allows us to explore some major themes in transfer learning, while doing so within the context of relatively simple models in the class of eventual interest—shallow neural networks. Several authors have suggested various classification systems for categorizing transfer learning methods into groups.[1,2,3] Roughly speaking, categorization is based on whether transfer occurs between different languages, tasks, or data domains. Each of these types of categorization is usually correspondingly referred to as *cross-lingual learning*, *multitask learning*, and *domain adaptation*, as visualized in figure 4.1.

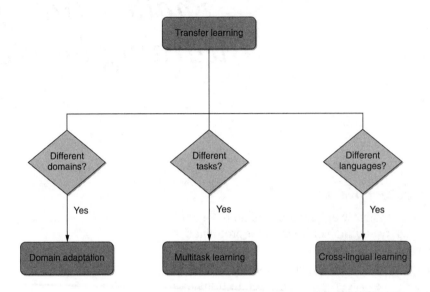

Figure 4.1   Visualizing the categorization of transfer learning into multitask learning, domain adaptation, and cross-lingual learning

The methods we will look at here will involve components that are neural networks in one way or another, but unlike those discussed in chapter 3, these neural networks do not have many layers. This is the reason the label "shallow" is appropriate to describe this collection of methods. Just as in the previous chapter, we present these methods in the context of specific hands-on examples to facilitate the advancement of your practical NLP skills. Cross-lingual learning will be addressed in later chapters of the book, given that modern neural machine translation methods are deep in general. We will explore the other two types of transfer learning briefly in this chapter.

We begin by exploring a common form of semisupervised learning that employs pretrained word embeddings, such as word2vec, in the context of applying it to one of the examples from the previous two chapters of the book. Recall from chapter 1 that

---

[1] S. J. Pan and Q. Yang, "A Survey on Transfer Learning," IEEE Transactions on Knowledge and Data Engineering (2009).

[2] S. Ruder, "Neural Transfer Learning for Natural Language Processing," National University of Ireland, Galway, Ireland (2019).

[3] D. Wang and T. F. Zheng, "Transfer Learning for Speech and Language Processing," Proceedings of 2015 Asia-Pacific Signal and Information Processing Association Annual Summit and Conference (APSIPA).

these methods differ from those in chapter 3 in that they produce a single vector per word, regardless of context.

We revisit the IMDB movie review sentiment classification. Recall that this example is concerned with classifying movie reviews from IMDB into positive or negative based on the sentiments expressed. It is a prototypical sentiment analysis example that has been used widely in the literature to study many algorithms. We combine feature vectors generated by pretrained word embeddings for each review with some traditional machine learning classification methods, namely random forests and logistic regression. We then demonstrate that using higher-level embeddings, which vectorize bigger sections of text—at the sentence, paragraph, and document level—can lead to improved performance. The general idea of vectorizing text and then applying a traditional machine learning classification method to the resulting vectors is visualized in figure 4.2.

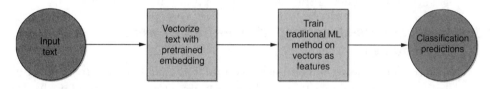

Figure 4.2 **Sequence of typical steps for semisupervised learning with word, sentence, or document embeddings**

Subsequently, we cover multitask learning and learn how to train a single system simultaneously to perform multiple tasks—in our case, represented by both of our running examples from the previous chapter, the email spam classification and the IMDB movie review sentiment analysis. You can gain several potential benefits from multitask learning. By training a single machine learning model for multiple tasks, a shared representation is learned on a larger and more varied collection of data from the combined data pool, which can lead to performance improvements. Moreover, it has been widely observed that this shared representation has a better ability to generalize to tasks beyond those that were trained on, and this improvement can be achieved without any increase in model size. We explore some of these benefits in the context of our running examples. Specifically, we focus on shallow neural multitask learning, where a single additional dense layer, as well as a classification layer, is trained for each specific task in the setup. Different tasks also share a layer between them, a setup typically referred to as *hard-parameter sharing*.

Finally, we introduce a popular dataset as another running example for the remainder of the chapter. This is the Multi-Domain Sentiment Dataset, which describes Amazon.com product reviews for a set of different products. We use this dataset to explore domain adaptation. Assume that we are given one *source* domain, which can be defined as a particular distribution of data for a specific task, and a classifier that has been trained to perform well on data in that domain for that task. The goal of domain adaptation is to modify, or adapt, data in a different *target* domain in such a way that the pretrained knowledge from the source domain can aid learning in the target domain. We apply a simple *autoencoding* approach to "project" samples in the target domain into the source domain feature space.

An autoencoder is a system that learns to reconstruct inputs with very high accuracy, typically by encoding them into an efficient latent representation and learning to decode that representation efficiently. They have traditionally been heavily used in model reduction applications, because the latent representation is often of a smaller dimension than the original space from which the encoding happens, and the said dimension value can also be picked to strike the right balance of computational efficiency and accuracy.[4] In the extreme scenario, improvements can be obtained with no labeled data in the target domain being used for training. This is typically referred to as *zero-shot domain adaptation*, where learning happens with no labeled data in the target domain. We demonstrate an instance of it in our experiments.

4.1   Semisupervised learning with pretrained word embeddings

The concept of word embeddings is central to the field of NLP. It is a name given to a collection of techniques that produce a set of vectors of real numbers for each word that needs to be analyzed. A major consideration in word embedding design is the dimension of the vector generated. Bigger vectors generally can achieve better representation capability of words within a language and thereby better performance on many tasks, while naturally being more expensive computationally. Picking the optimal dimension requires striking a balance between these competing factors and has often been done empirically, although some recent approaches argue for a more thorough theoretical optimization approach.[5]

As was outlined in the first chapter of this book, this important subarea of NLP research has a rich history, originating with the *term-vector model of information retrieval* in the 1960s. This culminated with pretrained, shallow neural-network-based techniques such as fastText, GloVe, and word2vec, which came in several variants in the mid-2010s, including Continuous Bag of Words (CBOW) and Skip-Gram. Both CBOW and Skip-Gram are extracted from shallow neural networks that were trained for various goals. Skip-Gram attempts to predict words neighboring any target word in a sliding window, whereas CBOW attempts to predict the target word given the neighbors. GloVe—which stands for global vectors—attempts to extend word2vec by incorporating global information into the embeddings. It optimizes the embeddings such that the cosine product between words reflects the number of times they cooccur, with the

---

[4] Jing Wang, Haibo Hea Danil, and V.Prokhorov, "A Folded Neural Network Autoencoder for Dimensionality Reduction," Procedia Computer Science 13 (2012): 120–27.

[5] Z. Yin and Y. Shen, "On the Dimensionality of Word Embedding," 32nd Conference on Neural Information Processing Systems (NeurIPS 2018), Montreal, Canada.

goal of making the resulting vectors more interpretable. The technique fastText attempts to enhance word2vec by repeating the Skip-Gram methods on character n-grams (versus word n-grams), thereby being able to handle previously unseen words. Each of these variants of pretrained embeddings has its strengths and weaknesses, and these are summarized in table 4.1.

Table 4.1 Comparison of strengths and weaknesses of various popular word-embedding methods

Word-embedding method	Strengths	Weaknesses
Skip-Gram word2vec	Works well with a small training dataset and rare words	Slower training, plus lower accuracy for frequent words
CBOW word2vec	Several times faster in training and better accuracy for frequent words	Doesn't work as well with little training data and rare words
GloVe	Vectors have more interpretability than other methods	Higher memory requirement during training to store co-occurrences of words
fastText	Can handle out-of-vocabulary words	Higher computing cost; larger and more complex model

To reiterate, fastText is known for its ability to handle out-of-vocabulary words, which comes from it having been designed to embed subword character n-grams, or *subwords* (versus entire words, as is the case with word2vec). This enables it to build up embeddings for previously unseen words by aggregating composing character n-gram embeddings. That comes at the expense of a larger pretrained embedding and a higher computing resource requirement and cost. For these reasons, we will use the fastText software framework in this section to load embeddings in the word2vec input format, without the subword information. This allows us to keep the computing cost lower, making the exercise easier for the reader, while also showcasing how out-of-vocabulary issues would be handled and providing a solid experience platform from which the reader can venture into subword embeddings.

Let's begin the computing experiment! The first thing we need to do is obtain the appropriate pretrained word-embedding file. Because we will be using the fastText framework, we could obtain these pretrained files from the authors' official website,[6] which hosts appropriate embedding files in a number of formats. Note that these files are extremely large, because they attempt to capture vectorization information about all possible words within a language. For instance, the .vec format embedding for the English language, which was trained on Wikipedia 2017 and provides vectorization information without handling subwords and out-of-vocabulary words, is about 6 GB. The corresponding .bin format embedding, which contains the famous fastText subword information and can handle out-of-vocabulary words, is about 25% larger, at approximately 7.5 GB. We also note that Wikipedia embeddings are provided in up to

---

[6] https://fasttext.cc/docs/en/english-vectors.html

294 languages, even including traditionally unaddressed African languages such as Twi, Ewe, and Hausa. It has been shown, however, that for many of the included low-resource languages, the quality of these embeddings is not very good.[7]

Due to the size of these embeddings, it is a lot easier to execute this example using the recommended cloud-based notebooks we have hosted on Kaggle (versus running them locally) because the embedding files have already been openly hosted in the cloud environment by other users.[8] As such, we can simply attach them to a running notebook without having to obtain and run the files locally.

Once the embedding is available, we can load it using the following code snippet, making sure to time the loading function call:

```
import time
from gensim.models import FastText, KeyedVectors

start=time.time()
FastText_embedding =
    KeyedVectors.load_word2vec_format("../input/jigsaw/wiki.en.vec")
end = time.time()
print("Loading the embedding took %d seconds"%(end-start))
```

Loads a pretrained fastText embedding in "word2vec" format (without subword information)

Loading the embedding takes more than 10 minutes the first time on the Kaggle environment we used for execution. In practice, in such a situation, it is not uncommon to load the embedding once into memory and then serve access to it using an approach such as Flask for as long as it is needed. This can also be achieved using the Jupyter notebook that comes along with this chapter of the book.

Having obtained and loaded the pretrained embedding, let's look back at the IMDB movie review classification example, which we will analyze in this section. In particular, we pick up right after listing 2.10 in the preprocessing stage of the pipeline, which generates a NumPy array raw_data that contains word-level tokenized representations of movie reviews, with stop words and punctuation removed. For the reader's convenience, we show listing 2.10 again next.

Listing 2.10   (Duplicated from chapter 2) Loading the IMDB data into a NumPy array

```
def load_data(path):
    data, sentiments = [], []
    for folder, sentiment in (('neg', 0), ('pos', 1)):
        folder = os.path.join(path, folder)
        for name in os.listdir(folder):
            with open(os.path.join(folder, name), 'r') as reader:
                text = reader.read()
            text = tokenize(text)
            text = stop_word_removal(text)
            text = reg_expressions(text)
```

Goes through every file in the current folder

Applies tokenization and stop word analysis routines

---

[7] J. Alabi et al., "Massive vs. Curated Word Embeddings for Low-Resourced Languages. The Case of Yorùbá and Twi," The International Conference on Language Resources and Evaluation (LREC 2020), Marseille, France.

[8] https://www.kaggle.com/yangjia1991/jigsaw

```
                        data.append(text)
                        sentiments.append(sentiment)
  Converts to           data_np = np.array(data)
  a NumPy               data, sentiments = unison_shuffle_data(data_np, sentiments)
  array

                    return data, sentiments

train_path = os.path.join('aclImdb', 'train')
raw_data, raw_header = load_data(train_path)
```

Converts to a NumPy array

Tracks corresponding sentiment labels

Calls the function above on the data

If you have already worked through chapter 2, you may recall that after listing 2.10, we proceeded to generate a simple bag-of-words representation for the output NumPy array, which simply counts occurrence frequencies of possible word tokens in each review. We then used the resulting vectors as numerical features for further machine learning tasks. Here, instead of the bag-of-words representation, we extract corresponding vectors from the pretrained embedding instead.

Because our embedding of choice does not handle out-of-vocabulary words out of the box, the next thing we do is develop a methodology for addressing this situation. The simplest thing to do, quite naturally, is to simply skip any such words. Because the fastText framework errors out when such a word is encountered, we will use a *try and except* block to catch these errors without interrupting execution. Assume that you are given a pretrained input embedding that serves as a dictionary, with words as keys and corresponding vectors as values, and an input list of words in a review. The next listing shows a function that produces a two-dimensional NumPy array with rows representing embedding vectors for each word in the review.

Listing 4.1   Producing a 2-D Numpy array of movie review word embedding vectors

```
def handle_out_of_vocab(embedding,in_txt):
    out = None
    for word in in_txt:
        try:
            tmp = embedding[word]
            tmp = tmp.reshape(1,len(tmp))

            if out is None:
                out = tmp
            else:
                out = np.concatenate((out,tmp),axis=0)
        except:
            pass

    return out
```

Loops through every word

Extracts the corresponding embedding vector, and enforces "row shape"

Handles the edge case of the first vector and an empty-out array

Concatenates the row embedding vector to the output NumPy array

Skips the execution on the current word, and continues the execution from the next word when out-of-vocabulary errors occur

The function in this listing can now be used to analyze the entire dataset as captured by the variable raw_data. However, before doing so we must decide how we will combine or *aggregate* the embedding vectors for individual words in a review into a single vector representing the entire review. It has been found in practice that the heuristic of simply averaging the words works as a strong baseline. Because the embeddings were trained in a way that ensures that similar words are closer to each other in the resulting vector space, it makes intuitive sense that their average would represent the average meaning of the collection. The averaging baseline for summarization/aggregation is often recommended as a first attempt at embedding bigger sections of text from word embeddings. This is also the approach we use in this section, as demonstrated by the code in listing 4.2. Effectively, this code calls the function from listing 4.1 repeatedly on every review in the corpus, averages the output, and concatenates the resulting vectors into a single two-dimensional NumPy array. The rows of this resulting array correspond to aggregated-by-averaging embedding vectors for each review.

Listing 4.2   Loading IMDB data into a NumPy array

```
def assemble_embedding_vectors(data):
    out = None
    for item in data:                               ← Loops through every IMDB review
        tmp = handle_out_of_vocab(FastText_embedding,item)   ← Extracts the embedding vectors for every word in the review, making sure to handle out-of-vocabulary words
        if tmp is not None:
            dim = tmp.shape[1]
            if out is not None:                      ← Averages the word vectors in each review
                vec = np.mean(tmp,axis=0)
                vec = vec.reshape((1,dim))
                out = np.concatenate((out,vec),axis=0)   ← Concatenates the average row vector to output the NumPy array
            else:
                out = np.mean(tmp,axis=0).reshape((1,dim))
        else:
            pass                                     ← Out-of-vocabulary edge case handling

    return out
```

We can now assemble embedding vectors for the whole dataset using the next function call:

```
EmbeddingVectors = assemble_embedding_vectors(data_train)
```

These can now be used as feature vectors for the same logistic regression and random forest codes as were used in listings 2.11 and 3.1, respectively. Using these codes to train and evaluate these models, we found the corresponding accuracy scores to be 77% and 66%, respectively, when the hyperparameters `maxtokens` and `maxtokenlen` are set to 200 and 100, respectively, and the value of `Nsamp`—the number of samples from each class—is equal to 1,000. These are only slightly lower than the corresponding values obtained from the bag-of-words baseline that was initially developed in the previous chapters (corresponding to accuracy scores of 79% and 67%, respectively). We hypothesize that this slight reduction is likely due to the aggregation of individual word vectors by the naive averaging approach that was described. In the next section, we attempt to perform more intelligent aggregation using embedding methods that were designed to embed at a higher text level.

4.2 *Semisupervised learning with higher-level representations*

Several techniques, inspired by word2vec, try to embed larger sections of text into vector spaces in such a way that sentences with similar meanings would be closer to each other in the induced vector space. This enables us to perform arithmetic on sentences to make inferences about analogies, combined meanings, and so on. One prominent approach is paragraph vectors, or *doc2vec*, which exploits the concatenation (versus averaging) of words from pretrained word embeddings in summarizing them. Another is sent2vec, which extends the classic Continuous Bag-of-Words (CBOW) of word2vec—where a shallow network is trained to predict a word in a sliding window from its context—to sentences by optimizing word and word n-gram embeddings for an accurate averaged representation. In this section, we use a pretrained sent2vec model as an illustrative representative method and apply it to the IMDB movie classification example.

You can find a few open source implementations of sent2vec online. We are employing a heavily used implementation that builds on fastText.[9] To install that implementation directly from its hosted URL, execute the following command:

```
pip install git+https://github.com/epfml/sent2vec
```

Quite naturally, just as in the case of the pretrained word embeddings, the next step is to obtain the pretrained sent2vec sentence embedding to be loaded by the particular implementation/framework we have installed. These are hosted by the authors of the framework on their GitHub page and on Kaggle by other users.[10] For simplicity, we choose the smallest 600-dimensional embedding `wiki_unigrams.bin`, approximately 5 GB in size, which captures just the unigram information on Wikipedia. Note that significantly larger models are available pretrained on book corpora and Twitter, and also include bigram information.

Having obtained the pretrained embedding, we load it using the following code snippet, making sure to time the loading process as before:

```
import time
import sent2vec

model = sent2vec.Sent2vecModel()
start=time.time()
model.load_model('../input/sent2vec/wiki_unigrams.bin')    ←── Loads sent2vec embedding
end = time.time()
print("Loading the sent2vec embedding took %d seconds"%(end-start))
```

---

[9] https://github.com/epfml/sent2vec
[10] https://www.kaggle.com/maxjeblick/sent2vec

It's worth mentioning that we found the load time during the first execution to be less than 10 seconds—a notable improvement over the fastText word embedding loading time of over 10 minutes. This increased speed is attributed to the significantly more efficient implementation of the current package versus the gensim implementation that we used in the previous section. It is not uncommon to try different packages to find the most efficient one for your application in practice.

Next, we define a function to generate vectors for a collection of reviews. It is essentially a simpler form of the function presented in listing 4.2 for pretrained word embeddings. It is simpler because we do not need to worry about out-of-vocabulary words. This function is shown in the following listing.

Listing 4.3   Loading IMDB data into a NumPy array

```
def assemble_embedding_vectors(data):        Loops through
    out = None                               every IMDB review
    for item in data:
        vec = model.embed_sentence(" ".join(item))    Extracts the
        if vec is not None:                           embedding vectors
            if out is not None:                       for every review
                out = np.concatenate((out,vec),axis=0)
            else:
                out = vec
        else:
            pass


    return out
```

Edge case handling

We can now use this function to extract sent2vec embedding vectors for each review as follows:

```
EmbeddingVectors = assemble_embedding_vectors(data_train)
```

We can also split this into training and test datasets and train logistic regression and random forest classifiers on top of the embedding vectors as before, using code analogous to what is shown in listings 2.11 and 3.1, respectively. This yields accuracy scores of 82% and 68% for the logistic regression and random forest classifiers, respectively (at the same hyperparameter values as in the previous section). This value for the logistic regression classifier combined with sent2vec is an improvement on the corresponding values of 79% and 67%, respectively, for the bag-of-words baseline, as well as an improvement over the averaged word embedding approach from the previous section.

4.3   *Multitask learning*

Traditionally, machine learning algorithms have been trained to perform a single task at a time, with the data collected and trained on being independent for each separate task. This is somewhat antithetical to the way humans and other animals learn, where training for multiple tasks occurs simultaneously, and information from training on one task may inform and accelerate the learning of other tasks. This additional information may improve performance not just on the current tasks being trained on but also on future tasks, and sometimes even in cases where no labeled data is available on such future tasks. This scenario of transfer learning with no labeled data in the target domain is often referred to as zero-shot transfer learning.

In machine learning, multitask learning has historically appeared in a number of settings, from *multiobjective optimization* to *l2* and other forms of *regularization* (which can itself be framed as a form of multiobjective optimization). Figure 4.3 shows the

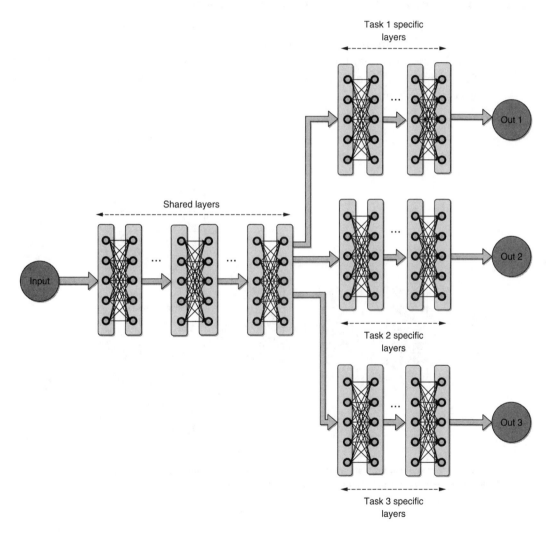

Figure 4.3 The general form of neural multitask learning we will employ—*hard parameter sharing* (in this case, three tasks)

form of neural multitask learning we will employ, where some layers/parameters are shared between all tasks, that is, *hard parameter sharing*.[11]

In the other prominent type of neural multitask learning, *soft parameter sharing*, all tasks have their own layers/parameters that are not shared. Instead, they are encouraged to be similar via various constraints imposed on the task-specific layers across the various tasks. We do not address this type of multitask learning further, but it is good to be aware of its existence for your own future potential literature explorations.

Let's proceed to our illustrative example for this section, by setting it up and baselining it in the next subsection.

4.3.1 *Problem setup and a shallow neural single-task baseline*

Consider figure 4.3 again, but with only two tasks—the first task being IMDB movie review classification from the previous two sections, and the second task being email spam classification from the previous chapter. The resulting setup represents the specific example we will address in this section. This setup is shown in figure 4.4 to facilitate conceptualizing.

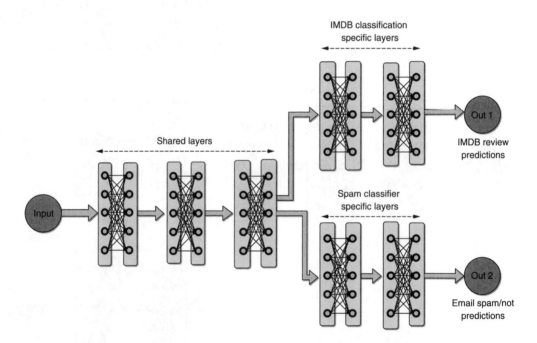

Figure 4.4   The specific form of neural multitask hard parameter sharing we will employ, with two specific tasks shown—IMDB reviews and email spam classification

---

[11] S. Ruder, "Neural Transfer Learning for Natural Language Processing," National University of Ireland, Galway, Ireland (2019).

Before proceeding, we must decide how the inputs to the resulting neural network will be converted into numbers for analysis. One popular choice is to encode the input at the character level using one-hot encoding, where each character is replaced by a sparse vector of a dimension equal to the total number of possible characters. This vector contains 1 in the column corresponding to the character and 0 otherwise. An illustration of this method, which aims to help you concisely visualize the process of one-hot encoding, is shown in figure 4.5.

One-hot encodings allow one to convert categorical variables into numerical data.

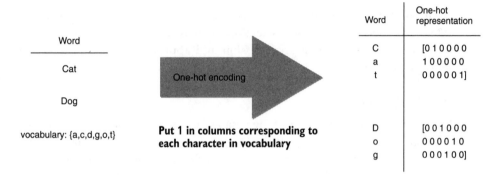

Figure 4.5 A visualization of the process of one-hot encoding characters into row-vector representations. The process replaces every character in the vocabulary with a sparse vector with a dimension equal to the size of the vocabulary. 1 is placed in the column corresponding to the vocabulary character index.

This method can be expensive from a memory perspective, given the significant inherent increase in dimension, and as such, it is common to perform the one-hot encoding "on the fly" via specialized neural network layers. Here, we take an even more straightforward approach: we pass each review through the sent2vec embedding function and use the embedding vectors as input features to the setup shown in figure 4.4.

Before proceeding to the exact two-task setup shown in figure 4.4, we perform another baseline. We use the IMDB movie classification task as the only one present, to see how the task-specific shallow neural classifier compares with the model from the previous section. The code corresponding to this shallow neural baseline is shown in the next listing.

Listing 4.4 Shallow single-task Keras neural network

```
from keras.models import Model
from keras.layers import Input, Dense, Dropout

input_shape = (len(train_x[0]),)
sent2vec_vectors = Input(shape=input_shape)
```

The input must match the dimension of the sent2vec vectors.

```
dense = Dense(512, activation='relu')(sent2vec_vectors)   ◀─┐  A dense neural
dense = Dropout(0.3)(dense)                                 │  layer trained on
output = Dense(1, activation='sigmoid')(dense)              │  top of the sent2vec
model = Model(inputs=sent2vec_vectors, outputs=output)      │  vectors
model.compile(loss='binary_crossentropy', optimizer='adam',
    metrics=['accuracy'])
history = model.fit(train_x, train_y, validation_data=(test_x, test_y),
    batch_size=32, nb_epoch=10, shuffle=True)
```

The output indicates a single binary classifier—is review "positive" or "negative"?

Applies dropout to reduce overfitting

We found that the performance of this classifier was about 82% at the hyperparameter values specified in the previous section. This is higher than the baseline of bag-of-words combined with logistic regression and approximately equal to sent2vec combined with logistic regression from the previous section.

4.3.2   Dual-task experiment

We now introduce another task: the email spam classification problem from the previous chapter. We will not repeat the preprocessing steps and associated code here for this auxiliary task; see chapter 2 for these details. Assuming the availability of the sent2vec vectors `train_x2` corresponding to the emails in the data sample, listing 4.5 shows how one can create a multiple-output shallow neural model to train it simultaneously for email spam classification and the classification of IMDB movie reviews via hard-parameter sharing.

Listing 4.5   Shallow dual-task hard parameter sharing Keras neural network

```
from keras.models import Model
from keras.layers import Input, Dense, Dropout
from keras.layers.merge import concatenate

input1_shape = (len(train_x[0]),)
input2_shape = (len(train_x2[0]),)
sent2vec_vectors1 = Input(shape=input1_shape)
sent2vec_vectors2 = Input(shape=input2_shape)
combined = concatenate([sent2vec_vectors1,sent2vec_vectors2])
dense1 = Dense(512, activation='relu')(combined)
dense1 = Dropout(0.3)(dense1)
output1 = Dense(1, activation='sigmoid',name='classification1')(dense1)
output2 = Dense(1, activation='sigmoid',name='classification2')(dense1)
model = Model(inputs=[sent2vec_vectors1,sent2vec_vectors2],
    outputs=[output1,output2])
```

Concatenates the sent2vec vectors for the different tasks

Shared dense neural layer

Two task-specific outputs, each being a binary classifier

Having defined the hard-parameter sharing setup for the two-task multitask scenario involving IMDB movie reviews and email spam classification, we can compile and train the resulting model via the following:

```
model.compile(loss={'classification1': 'binary_crossentropy',
                    'classification2': 'binary_crossentropy'},
              optimizer='adam', metrics=['accuracy'])
history = model.fit([train_x,train_x2],[train_y,train_y2],
                    validation_data=([test_x,test_x2],[test_y,test_y2]),
              batch_size=8,nb_epoch=10, shuffle=True)
```

Specifies two loss functions (both binary_crossentropy in our case)

Specifies the training and validation data for each input

For this experiment, we set the hyperparameters `maxtokens` and `maxtokenlen` both to 100 and the value of `Nsamp`—the number of samples from each class—to 1,000 (as in the previous section).

We found, upon training the multitask system, that the IMDB classification performance dropped slightly, from approximately 82% in the single-task shallow setup in listing 4.4 to about 80%. The email classification accuracy similarly dropped from 98.7% to 98.2%. Given the drop in performance, one may rightfully ask: What was the point of all this?

First of all, observe that the trained model can be deployed independently for each task, by simply replacing the omitted task input with zeros to respect the expected overall input dimension and ignoring the corresponding output. Moreover, we expect the shared pretrained layer `dense1` of the multitask setup to be more readily generalizable to arbitrary new tasks than that from listing 4.4. This is because it has been trained to be predictive on a more varied and general set of data and tasks.

To make this more concrete, consider replacing either or both task-specific layers with new ones, initializing the shared layer `dense1` to pretrained weights from the previous experiment, and fine-tuning the resulting model on the new task dataset. Having seen a broader range of task data, potentially similar to the newly added tasks, these shared weights are more likely to contain useful information for the downstream tasks being considered.

We will return to the idea of multitask learning later in the book, which will give us the opportunity to investigate and think about these phenomena further. The experiment in this section has hopefully armed you with the required foundation for further exploration.

4.4 Domain adaptation

In this section, we briefly explore the idea of *domain adaptation*, one of the oldest and most prominent ideas in transfer learning. An implicit assumption made often by machine learning practitioners is that the data during the inference phase will come from the same distribution as the data that was used for training. This is, of course, rarely true in practice.

Enter domain adaptation to attempt to address this issue. Let's define domain as a particular distribution of data for a specific task. Assume that we are given a *source* domain and an algorithm that has been trained to perform well on data in that domain. The goal of domain adaptation is to modify, or adapt, data in a different *target* domain in such a way that the pretrained knowledge from the source domain can be applicable to faster learning and/or direct inference in the target domain. A variety of approaches have been explored, ranging from multitask learning (as introduced in the previous section)—where learning on different data distributions occurs simultaneously—to coordinate transformations—which enable more effective learning on a single combined feature space[12]—to methods that exploit measures of similarity between the source and target domains to help us select which data should be used for training.[13]

We apply a simple *autoencoding* approach to "project" samples in the target domain into the source domain feature space. An autoencoder is a system that can learn to reconstruct inputs with high accuracy, typically by encoding them into an efficient latent representation and learning to decode the said representation. A technical way of describing the process of reconstructing input is "learning the identity function." Autoencoders have traditionally been heavily used in model dimensionality-reduction applications, because the latent representation is often of a smaller dimension than the original space from which the encoding happens, and the said dimension value can also be picked to strike the right balance between computational efficiency and accuracy.[14] In the extreme favorable scenario, you can obtain improvements with no labeled data in the target domain, which is typically referred to as *zero-shot domain adaptation.*

The idea of zero-shot transfer learning arises in many contexts. You can think of it as a sort of "holy grail" of transfer learning, because obtaining labeled data in the target domain can be an expensive exercise. Here, we explore whether a classifier trained to predict the polarity of IMDB movie reviews can be used to predict the polarity of reviews in some other domain. For example, can a classifier trained on IMDB review data predict the polarity of book reviews or DVD reviews obtained from a completely different data source?

A natural alternative source of reviews, given its ubiquity in the contemporary world, is Amazon.com. Few sources of data today contain as much variety with regard to categories of products and sheer volume of data as this e-commerce website, which many Americans have come to rely on for basic daily-need purchases, at the expense of business for more traditional brick-and-mortar stores. A rich repository of reviews is available. Indeed, one of the most prominently and heavily explored datasets in the space of NLP domain adaptation happens to be a collection of reviews for different product categories on Amazon—the Multi-Domain Sentiment Dataset.[15] This dataset

---

[12] Hal Daumé III, "Frustratingly Easy Domain Adaptation," Proceedings of the 45th Annual Meeting of the Association of Computational Linguistics (2007), Prague, Czech Republic.

[13] S. Ruder and B. Plank, "Learning to Select Data for Transfer Learning with Bayesian Optimization," Proceedings of the 2017 Conference on Empirical Methods in Natural Language Processing (2017), Copenhagen, Denmark.

[14] Jing Wang, Haibo Hea Danil, and V.Prokhorov, "A Folded Neural Network Autoencoder for Dimensionality Reduction," Procedia Computer Science 13 (2012): 120–127.

[15] https://www.cs.jhu.edu/~mdredze/datasets/sentiment/

represents 25 categories, from which we picked the product category of book reviews, feeling that it was sufficiently different from IMDB reviews to present a challenging test case.

The data in this dataset is contained in a markup language format, where tags are used to define various elements, and is organized by category and polarity into separate files. It suffices to note for our purposes that reviews are contained within appropriately named `<review_text>...</review_text>` tags. Given this information, the code in the next listing can be used to load positive and negative book reviews and prepare them for analysis.

Listing 4.6 Loading reviews from the Multi-Domain Sentiment Dataset

```
def parse_MDSD(data):
    out_lst = []
    for i in range(len(data)):          Locates the first line of review,
        txt = ""                        and combines all subsequent
        if(data[i]=="<review_text>\n"): characters until the end tag
            j=i                         into the review text
            while(data[j]!="</review_text>\n"):
                txt = txt+data[j]
                j = j+1
            text = tokenize(txt)
            text = stop_word_removal(text)
            text = remove_reg_expressions(text)
            out_lst.append(text)

    return out_lst


input_file_path = \
"../input/multi-domain-sentiment-dataset-books-and-
    dvds/books.negative.review"
with open (input_file_path, "r", encoding="latin1") as myfile:
    data=myfile.readlines()
neg_books = parse_MDSD(data)         Reads lines from the source text file,
                                     both positive and negative reviews,
                                     by leveraging defined function

input_file_path = \
"../input/multi-domain-sentiment-dataset-books-and-
    dvds/books.positive.review"
with open (input_file_path, "r", encoding="latin1") as myfile:
    data=myfile.readlines()
pos_books = parse_MDSD(data)
                                     Creates labels for the positive
                                     and negative classes
header = [0]*len(neg_books)
header.extend([1]*len(pos_books))    Appends, shuffles, and
neg_books.extend(pos_books)          extracts the corresponding
MDSD_data = np.array(neg_books)      sent2vec vectors
data, sentiments = unison_shuffle_data(np.array(MDSD_data), header)
EmbeddingVectors = assemble_embedding_vectors(data)
```

Having loaded the book review text and prepared it for further processing, we now test the trained IMDB classifier from the previous section directly on the target data to see how accurate it is without any processing, using the following code:

```
print(model.evaluate(x=EmbeddingVectors,y=sentiments))
```

This yields an accuracy of about 74%. Although this is a decrease from the performance of the same classifier of 82% on the IMDB data, it is still sufficiently high to demonstrate an instance of zero-shot knowledge transfer from the movie review task to the book review task. Let's attempt to improve this number via zero-shot domain adaptation with an autoencoder.

> **NOTE** Zero-shot domain transfer is more likely to be successful the more "similar" the source and target domains. Similarity can be measured by techniques such as cosine similarity applied to the sent2vec vectors from the two domains. A suggested take-home exercise is to explore the MDSD cosine similarities across some domains, along with the efficacy of the zero-shot transfer experiment described here between them. The library scikit-learn has a simple method for computing cosine similarity.

We train an autoencoder to reconstruct the IMDB data. The autoencoder takes the form of a shallow neural network that is similar to the multitask layers we used in the previous section. The Keras Python code is shown in listing 4.7. A major difference from the previous neural networks is that because this is a regression problem, there is no activation in the output layer. The encoding dimension `encoding_dim` was empirically tuned for the right balance of accuracy and computing cost.

Listing 4.7   Keras shallow neural autoencoder

```
encoding_dim = 30                                      The input size must be the
                                                       same as the dimension of
input_shape = (len(train_x[0]),)                       the sent2vec vectors.
sent2vec_vectors = Input(shape=input_shape)
encoder = Dense(encoding_dim, activation='relu')(sent2vec_vectors)
dropout = Dropout(0.1)(encoder)
decoder = Dense(encoding_dim, activation='relu')(dropout)          Encodes into
dropout = Dropout(0.1)(decoder)                                    the space of the
output = Dense(len(train_x[0]))(dropout)                           specified latent
autoencoder = Model(inputs=sent2vec_vectors, outputs=output)      dimension,
                                                                  encoding_dim
```

Decodes from the space of the
specified latent dimension back
into the sent2vec space

We train the autoencoder for 50 epochs, which takes only a few seconds, by setting both the input and output to the IMDB sent2vec vectors from the previous chapter, as shown via the following compilation and training code:

```
autoencoder.compile(optimizer='adam',loss='mse',metrics=["mse","mae"])
autoencoder.fit(train_x,train_x,validation_data=(test_x, test_x),
batch_size=32,nb_epoch=50, shuffle=True)
```

We use mean squared error (mse) as a loss function for this regression problem and mean absolute error (mae) as an additional metric. A minimum validation mae value of approximately 0.06 was achieved.

We next project the book reviews into the IMDB feature space using the autoencoder trained to reconstruct the features just described. This just means we preprocess the book review feature vectors using the autoencoder. We then repeat the accuracy evaluation experiment of the IMDB classifier on these preprocessed vectors as input as follows:

```
EmbeddingVectorsScaledProjected = autoencoder.predict(EmbeddingVectors)
print(model.evaluate(x=EmbeddingVectorsScaledProjected,y=sentiments))
```

An accuracy of approximately 75% is now observed, demonstrating an improvement of about 1% and an instance of zero-shot domain adaptation. Repeating this several times, we find the improvement to consistently stay around 0.5–1%, giving us confidence that the autoencoding domain adaptation did indeed lead to some positive transfer.

Summary

- Pretrained word embeddings, as well as embeddings at higher levels of text— such as sentences—are ubiquitous in NLP and can be used to convert text into numbers/vectors. This simplifies further processing to extract meaning from them.
- Such an extraction represents a form of semisupervised shallow transfer learning, which has been widely used in practice with immense success.
- Techniques like hard-parameter sharing and soft-parameter sharing allow us to create multitask learning systems, which have potential benefits, including simplified engineering design, improved generalization, and reduced overfitting.
- Sometimes it may be possible to achieve zero-shot transfer learning with no labeled data in the target domain, which is an ideal scenario because labeled data can be expensive to collect.
- It is sometimes possible to modify or adapt data in a target domain to be more similar to the data in the source domain, for instance, via projection methods such as autoencoders, and this can improve performance.

Preprocessing data for recurrent neural network deep transfer learning experiments

This chapter covers

- An overview of modeling architectures for transfer learning in NLP that rely on recurrent neural networks (RNNs)
- Preprocessing and modeling tabular text data
- Analyzing a new pair of representative NLP problems

In the previous chapter, we looked in some detail at some important shallow neural network architectures important in transfer learning for NLP, including word2vec and sent2vec. Recall also that the vectors produced by these methods are static and noncontextual, in the sense that they produce the same vector for the word or sentence in question, regardless of the surrounding context. This means these methods are unable to disambiguate, or distinguish, between different possible meanings of a word or sentence.

In this and the next chapter, we will cover some representative deep transfer learning modeling architectures for NLP that rely on recurrent neural networks (RNNs) for key functions. Specifically, we will be looking at the modeling frameworks

SIMOn,[1] ELMo,[2] and ULMFiT.[3] The deeper nature of the neural networks employed by these methods will allow the resulting embedding to be contextual, that is, to produce word embeddings that are functions of context and allow disambiguation. Recall that we first encountered ELMo in chapter 3. In the next chapter, we will take a closer look at its architecture.

Semantic Inference for the Modeling of Ontologies (SIMOn) was developed during DARPA's Data-Driven Discovery of Models (D3M) program, which was an attempt to automate some typical tasks faced by data scientists,[4] including the automatic construction of processing pipelines for data cleaning, feature extraction, feature importance ranking, and model selection for any given data science problem. These tasks fall under what is often referred to as *automatic machine learning,* or *AutoML.* Specifically, the model looks to classify every column in a tabular dataset into a fundamental type, such as integer, string, float, or address. The idea is that an AutoML system can decide what to do with input tabular data—an important kind of data encountered in practice—based on this information. One can download pre-packaged Docker images of various tools developed during the program, including SIMOn, from the aforementioned D3M program webpage.

SIMOn's development was motivated by analogies to transfer learning in computer vision, which were discussed at the conclusion of chapter 1. Its training procedure demonstrates how transfer learning can be used to augment a small set of manually labeled data with simulated data. The process of expanding the set of handled classes beyond those that were initially trained for is another task where transfer learning is illustratively employed within this framework. This model has been heavily used within D3M, and we use it in this chapter as a comparatively simple practical example of leveraging transfer learning to solve real, practical challenges. SIMOn has also been applied to detecting potentially harmful communication on social media.[5] Column-type classification is used as an illustrative example for this modeling framework.

We begin the chapter with a section that introduces the column data type classification example. The related simulated data generation and preprocessing procedures are also briefly touched on in that section. We follow this up with a section describing equivalent steps for a "fake news" detection example, to be used as a running example for ELMo later in the next chapter.

A visualization of the SIMOn architecture is shown, in the context of the tabular column-type classification example, in figure 5.1. Roughly speaking, it employs convolutional neural networks (CNNs) to build preliminary embeddings for sentences and

---

[1] P. Azunre et al., "Semantic Classification of Tabular Datasets via Character-Level Convolutional Neural Networks," *arXiv* (2019).

[2] M. E. Peters et al., "Deep Contextualized Word Representations," Proc. of NAACL-HLT (2018).

[3] J. Howard et al., "Universal Language Model Fine-Tuning for Text Classification," Proc. of the 56th Annual Meeting of the Association for Computational Linguistics (2018).

[4] https://docs.datadrivendiscovery.org/

[5] N. Dhamani et al., "Using Deep Networks and Transfer Learning to Address Disinformation," AI for Social Good ICML Workshop (2019).

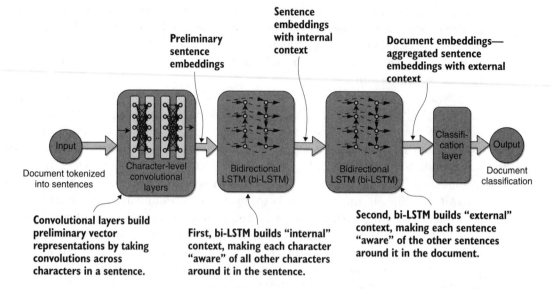

Figure 5.1   Visualizing SIMOn architecture in the context of the tabular column-type classification example

a pair of RNNs to first build internal context for characters in a sentence and then to build external context for sentences in a document.

We see from the figure that the architecture is composed of elements of character-level convolutional neural networks (CNNs) and bidirectional long short-term memory (bi-LSTM) networks, a type of recurrent neural network (RNN). It is also worth highlighting at this stage that the input text is tokenized into sentences, not words, in this framework. Additionally, viewing each sentence as a cell of a column that corresponds to a given document allows for the conversion of unstructured text into the tabular dataset context considered by the framework.

Embeddings from Language Models (ELMo) is arguably the most popular early pretrained language model associated with the ongoing NLP transfer learning revolution. It shares a lot of architectural similarities with SIMOn, also being composed of character-level CNNs followed by bi-LSTMs. This similarity makes a deeper dive into the architecture of ELMo a natural next step after the introduction of SIMOn. We will apply ELMo to an illustrative example problem, namely, "fake news" detection, to provide a practical context.

Figure 5.2 shows a visualization of the ELMo architecture in the context of tabular column-type classification. Some similarities and differences between the two frameworks are immediately evident. We can see that both frameworks employ character-level CNNs and bi-LSTMs. However, whereas SIMOn has two context-building stages with RNNs—one for characters in a sentence and another for sentences in a document—ELMo has a single stage, focusing on building context for words in the input document.

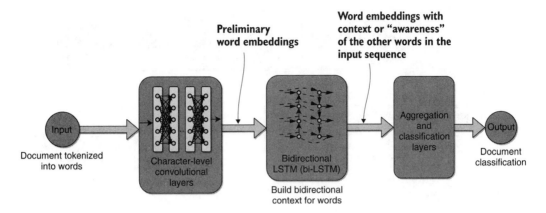

Figure 5.2 Visualizing ELMo architecture in the context of the tabular column-type classification example

Finally, we will take a look at the Universal Language Model Fine-Tuning (ULMFiT) framework, which introduces and demonstrates some key techniques and concepts enabling more effective adaptation of a pretrained language model for new settings, such as discriminative fine-tuning and gradual unfreezing. Discriminative fine-tuning stipulates that because the different layers of a language model contain different type of information, they should be tuned at different rates. Gradual unfreezing describes a procedure for fine-tuning progressively more parameters in a gradual manner that aims to reduce the risks of overfitting. The ULMFiT framework also includes innovations in varying the learning rate in a unique way during the adaptation process. We will introduce the model after ELMo in the next chapter, along with several of these concepts.

5.1 *Preprocessing tabular column-type classification data*

In this section, we introduce the first example dataset that will be explored in this and the subsequent chapter. Here, we are interested in developing an algorithm that can ingest a tabular dataset and determine for the user which fundamental type is in each column, that is, which columns are integer, string, float, address, and so on. The key motivation for doing this is that an automatic machine learning system can decide what to do with the input tabular data—an important kind of data encountered in practice—based on this information. Detected latitude and longitude coordinate values could be plotted on a map and displayed to the user, for instance. Detected float columns could be potential candidate inputs or outputs of a regression problem, and categorical columns are candidates for classification problem dependent variables. We visualize the essence of this problem with a simple example in figure 5.3.

We stress that this is a multilabel, multiclass problem, because there are multiple possible classes for each input example, and each input sample can be assigned multiple such classes. For instance, in figure 5.3, the first column, Customer ID, has multiple output labels, namely `categorical` and `int`. This also helps to handle the cases

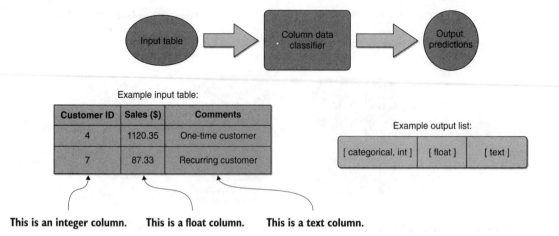

Figure 5.3   **Visualizing the tabular column data-type classification problem with a simple example**

where the input columns are not "clean," in the sense that they contain multiple types. Such columns can be labeled with all types present and passed to a relevant parser for further cleaning.

Now that we have gained a better sense of the problem, let's go ahead and obtain some tabular data for the experiments in this section.

5.1.1   *Obtaining and visualizing tabular data*

We will use two simple datasets to illustrate the tabular column-type classification example in the next chapter. The first of these datasets is the baseball player statistics dataset made available by OpenML.[6] This dataset describes the baseball statistics for a set of players, as well as whether or not they ended up in the Hall of Fame.

On a Linux system, we can obtain the dataset as follows:

```
!wget https://www.openml.org/data/get_csv/3622/dataset_189_baseball.arff
```

Recall from the previous chapters that the exclamation sign (!) is required only when executing in a Jupyter environment, such as the Kaggle environment we recommend for these exercises. When executing via a terminal, it should be dropped. Also observe that the .arff format is functionally equivalent to .csv for our purposes.

Having obtained the dataset of interest, let us peek at it as usual, using Pandas:

```
import pandas as pd
raw_baseball_data = pd.read_csv('dataset_189_baseball.arff', dtype=str)   ◁
print(raw_baseball_data.head())
```
The .arff format is functionally equivalent to .csv for our purposes.

---

[6] https://www.openml.org/d/185

This displays the top five lines of the DataFrame, as shown next:

```
        Player Number_seasons Games_played At_bats  Runs  Hits Doubles  \
0   HANK_AARON             23         3298   12364  2174  3771     624
1  JERRY_ADAIR             13         1165    4019   378  1022     163
2 SPARKY_ADAMS             13         1424    5557   844  1588     249
3 BOBBY_ADAMS             14         1281    4019   591  1082     188
4  JOE_ADCOCK             17         1959    6606   823  1832     295

   Triples Home_runs  RBIs Walks Strikeouts Batting_average On_base_pct  \
0       98       755  2297  1402       1383           0.305       0.377
1       19        57   366   208        499           0.254       0.294
2       48         9   394   453        223           0.286       0.343
3       49        37   303   414        447           0.269        0.34
4       35       336  1122   594       1059           0.277       0.339

   Slugging_pct Fielding_ave    Position Hall_of_Fame
0         0.555         0.98    Outfield            1
1         0.347        0.985 Second_base            0
2         0.353        0.974 Second_base            0
3         0.368        0.955  Third_base            0
4         0.485        0.994  First_base            0
```

We see that this is a dataset of baseball statistics for some players, as advertised.

Let's proceed to obtaining another tabular dataset. Without getting into too many details, this dataset will be used to expand our SIMOn classifier beyond the set of classes the pretrained model we will use was designed to detect. This exercise will provide an interesting use case for transfer learning that can stimulate ideas for your own applications.

The second dataset we will look at is the multiyear British Columbia public library statistics dataset, which we obtained from the BC Data Catalogue[7] but have also attached to our companion Kaggle notebook for your convenience. To load the dataset using Pandas, we execute the following command, where the location of the file in our Kaggle environment should be replaced by your local path if you chose to work locally:

```
raw_data = pd.read_csv('../input/20022018-bc-public-libraries-open-data-
    v182/2002-2018-bc-public-libraries-open-data-csv-v18.2.csv', dtype=str)
```

We can peek at the dataset using the following command

```
print(raw_data.head())
```

---

[7] https://catalogue.data.gov.bc.ca/dataset/bc-public-libraries-statistics-2002-present

which yields

```
      YEAR                        LOCATION                         LIB_NAME  \
0     2018    Alert Bay Public Library & Museum      Alert Bay Public Library
1     2018            Beaver Valley Public Library  Beaver Valley Public Library
2     2018             Bowen Island Public Library    Bowen Island Public Library
3     2018                 Burnaby Public Library        Burnaby Public Library
4     2018              Burns Lake Public Library      Burns Lake Public Library

                        LIB_TYPE SYMBOL        Federation           lib_ils  \
0    Public Library Association    BABM     Island Link LF      Evergreen Sitka
1    Public Library Association    BFBV        Kootenay LF      Evergreen Sitka
2            Municipal Library    BBI        InterLINK LF      Evergreen Sitka
3            Municipal Library     BB        InterLINK LF  SirsiDynix Horizon
4    Public Library Association   BBUL   North Central LF      Evergreen Sitka


      POP_SERVED srv_pln STRAT_YR_START  ... OTH_EXP    TOT_EXP EXP_PER_CAPITA  \
0            954     Yes          2,013  ...    2488      24439        25.6174
1          4,807     Yes          2,014  ...   15232  231314.13       48.12027
2          3,680     Yes          2,018  ...   20709  315311.17       85.68238
3        232,755     Yes          2,019  ...  237939   13794902       59.26791
4          5,763     Yes          2,018  ...     NaN     292315       50.72271

      TRANSFERS_TO_RESERVE AMORTIZATION EXP_ELEC_EBOOK EXP_ELEC_DB  \
0                        0            0              0         718
1                    11026            0        1409.23      826.82
2                    11176        40932           2111       54.17
3                        0      2614627         132050           0
4                      NaN          NaN              0           0

      EXP_ELEC_ELEARN EXP_ELEC_STREAM EXP_ELEC_OTHER
0                   0               0            752
1             1176.11               0        1310.97
2                3241               0              0
3                   0               0         180376
4                   0               0           7040

[5 rows x 235 columns]
```

We are only interested in a pair of columns, of type percent and integer, which we extract and display as follows:

```
COLUMNS = ["PCT_ELEC_IN_TOT_VOLS","TOT_AV_VOLS"]
raw_library_data = raw_data[COLUMNS]
print(raw_library_data)
```

There are lots of columns in this dataset; let's just focus on these two.

This yields the following output, showcasing the two remaining columns we will use:

```
      PCT_ELEC_IN_TOT_VOLS TOT_AV_VOLS
0                   90.42%          57
1                   74.83%       2,778
2                   85.55%       1,590
```

```
3                    9.22%         83,906
4                   66.63%          4,261
...                    ...            ...
1202                 0.00%         35,215
1203                 0.00%        109,499
1204                 0.00%            209
1205                 0.00%         18,748
1206                 0.00%           2403
```

```
[1207 rows x 2 columns]
```

5.1.2 Preprocessing tabular data

Now let's preprocess the obtained tabular data into a form that the SIMOn framework can accept. Because we will be using a pretrained model, which comes prepackaged with an encoder that we will apply for this purpose, we will need to install SIMOn as a first step using the following command:

```
!pip install git+https://github.com/algorine/simon
```

Having done this, we need to also make a few required imports, shown here:

```
from Simon import Simon
from Simon.Encoder import Encoder
```

Imports the SIMOn model class

Imports the SIMOn data encoder class for converting input text into numbers

These imports respectively represent the SIMOn model class, the data encoder class, a utility for standardizing all input data to a fixed length, and a class for generating simulated data.

Next we obtain a pretrained SIMOn model, which comes with its own encoder for transforming text to numbers. The model is composed of two files: one containing the encoder and other configurations, and the second one containing the model weights. We obtain these files using the following commands:

A pretrained SIMOn model configuration, encoder, and so on

```
!wget https://raw.githubusercontent.com/algorine/simon/master/Simon/scripts/
    pretrained_models/Base.pkl
!wget https://raw.githubusercontent.com/algorine/simon/master/Simon/scripts/
    pretrained_models/text-class.17-0.04.hdf5
```

Corresponding model weights

Before we can load the model weights themselves, we first need to load their configurations, which include the encoder, via the following sequence of commands:

The model weights are at the current level.

```
checkpoint_dir = ""
execution_config = "Base.pkl"
```

The name of our pretrained model configuration that was downloaded

```
Classifier = Simon(encoder={})
config = Classifier.load_config(execution_config, checkpoint_dir)
encoder = config['encoder']
checkpoint = config['checkpoint']
```

**Loads
the model
configuration**

**Extracts the
encoder**

**Creates a text classifier instance
for loading the encoder from
model configurations**

**Extract the
checkpoint name**

To make sure that we downloaded the right set of weights, double-check the weights file the model expects via

```
print(checkpoint)
```

which should confirm that we obtained the right file by printing the following:

```
text-class.17-0.04.hdf5
```

Finally, we need to specify two key parameters for modeling the tabular data. The parameter max_cells specifies the maximum numbers of cells in every column of the table. The parameter max_len specifies the maximum length of each cell. These are visualized in figure 5.4.

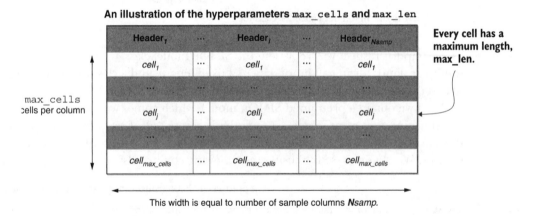

An illustration of the hyperparameters `max_cells` and `max_len`

**Every cell has a
maximum length,
max_len.**

max_cells
cells per column

This width is equal to number of sample columns *Nsamp.*

Figure 5.4   Visualizing the tabular data-modeling parameters. The parameter `max_cells` specifies the maximum number of cells or rows per column in the table. The parameter `max_len` specifies the maximum length of each cell or row.

The maximum number of cells per column must match the value of 500 used in training and can be extracted from the encoder as follows:

```
max_cells = encoder.cur_max_cells
```

Additionally, we set max_len to 20 for consistency with the pretrained model settings and extract the categories supported by the pretrained model as follows:

```
max_len = 20 # maximum length of each tabular cell
Categories = encoder.categories
category_count = len(Categories)          ◄───┤  The number of categories
print(encoder.categories)                      the pretrained model
                                               supports
```

We find that the handled categories are as follows:

```
['address', 'boolean', 'datetime', 'email', 'float', 'int', 'phone', 'text',
    'uri']
```

5.1.3   Encoding preprocessed data as numbers

We will now use the encoder to convert the tabular data into a set of numbers that the SIMOn model can use to make predictions. This involves converting each character in every input string into a unique integer representing that character in the model's encoding scheme.

Because convolutional neural networks (CNNs) require all inputs to be of a fixed, prespecified length, the encoder will also standardize the length of each input column. This step replicates random cells in columns shorter than max_cells and discards some random cells in columns that are longer. This ensures that all columns are of length max_cells exactly. Additionally, all cells are standardized to length max_len, with added padding if needed. We will not worry about these details too much, because the SIMOn API will handle it for us behind the scenes.

We encode the baseball dataset and display its shape using the following code:

```
                                          Encodes the data (standardization,
                                     transposition, conversion to NumPy array)

X_baseball = encoder.encodeDataFrame(raw_baseball_data)    ◄───┘
print(X_baseball.shape)        ◄───┐
print(X_baseball[0])   ◄───┐        Displays the shape of
                            │       the encoded data
          Displays the encoded
              first column
```

Executing this yields the following output, where the output shape tuple is displayed first, followed by the encoded first column:

```
(18, 500, 20)
[[-1 -1 -1 ... 50 37 44]
 [-1 -1 -1 ... 54 41 46]
 [-1 -1 -1 ... 37 52 55]
 ...
 [-1 -1 -1 ... 49 45 46]
 [-1 -1 -1 ... 51 54 43]
 [-1 -1 -1 ... 38 37 43]]
```

We see that each encoded column is a max_cells=500 by max_len=20 array as expected. We also note that the −1 entries of the encoded column represent the padding of cells shorter than max_len by the empty character.

We also encode the library data for later use as follows:

```
X_library = encoder.encodeDataFrame(raw_library_data)
```

At this stage, we have converted the example input datasets into NumPy arrays of an appropriate shape. This encodes the text into numbers compatible for ingestion and analysis by the first stage of the SIMOn neural net—the CNNs producing the preliminary input sentence embeddings.

5.2   *Preprocessing fact-checking example data*

In this section, we introduce the second example dataset that will be examined in this and the subsequent chapter. Here, we are interested in developing an algorithm to distinguish between factual news and potentially false information or misinformation. This application area is increasingly important and is frequently referred to as "automated fake news detection."

Conveniently, for us, an applicable dataset is available on Kaggle[8] for this purpose. This dataset contains more than 40,000 articles divided into two categories: "fake" and "true." The true articles were collected from reuters.com, a reputable news website. The fake articles, on the other hand, were collected from a variety of sources flagged by PolitiFact—a fact-checking organization—as unreliable. Most of the articles center on politics and world news.

5.2.1   *Special problem considerations*

The subject of what can be called fake is undoubtedly a hot-button topic that deserves a brief discussion. It is certainly true that the biases ingrained in whoever prepared the labels for the training data will likely transfer to the classification system. In this sensitive context, the validity of the labels deserves particular attention and consideration in how they are created.

Moreover, although our purpose in this section is to develop a content-based classification system for true versus potentially fake articles, it is important to stress that the realistic scenario is significantly more complex. In other words, detection of potentially false information spread is only one aspect of the problem of detecting *influence operations*. To understand the difference between the two, consider that even true information can be used to influence opinion to harm a brand if it is taken out of context or unnaturally amplified.

Detecting influence operations can be naturally framed as an anomaly-detection problem,[9] but such a system can be effective only as part of a bigger strategy for mitigation. It must be cross-platform to be effective, with as many potential information channels as possible monitored and analyzed for anomalies. Moreover, most practical

---

[8] https://www.kaggle.com/clmentbisaillon/fake-and-real-news-dataset
[9] P. Azunre et al., "Disinformation: Detect to Disrupt," Conference for Truth and Trust Online 1, no. 1 (2019).

systems today have humans embedded, in the sense that the detection systems only flag aggregated suspicious activity and leave the final call of action to a human analyst.

5.2.2 Loading and visualizing fact-checking data

Now we jump directly into loading the fact-checking data and preparing it for classification using the ELMo modeling framework. Recall from section 3.2.1, where we applied ELMo to spam detection and movie review sentiment analysis, that the model expects each input document as a single string. This makes things easier—no tokenization is required. Also note that the dataset has already been attached to the companion Jupyter notebook for the book on Kaggle.

We load the true and fake data from the dataset using the code in listing 5.1. Note that we are choosing to load 1,000 samples of each here, to be consistent with section 3.2.1.

Listing 5.1   Loading 1,000 samples each of true and fake articles

```
import numpy as np                                              Reads the true news data
import pandas as pd                                             into a Pandas DataFrame

DataTrue = pd.read_csv("/kaggle/input/fake-and-real-news-dataset/True.csv")   ◁
DataFake = pd.read_csv("/kaggle/input/fake-and-real-news-dataset/Fake.csv")   ◁

Nsamp =1000                         ◁       Number of samples      Reads the fake news data
DataTrue = DataTrue.sample(Nsamp)           to generate in each    into a Pandas DataFrame
DataFake = DataFake.sample(Nsamp)           class—true, fake
raw_data = pd.concat([DataTrue,DataFake], axis=0).values

raw_data = [sample[0].lower() + sample[1].lower() + sample[3].lower() for
      sample in raw_data]        ◁
                                          Combines the title, body
                                          text, and topics into one
Categories = ['True','False']     ◁       string per document
header = (([1]*Nsamp)
header.extend(([0]*Nsamp))                Corresponding labels
```

Concatenated true and fake samples points to the `raw_data = pd.concat(...)` line.

70% of data for training points to the `train_x = raw_data[:idx]` block.

Secondly, we shuffle the data and split it into 70% training/30% validation using the following code, replicated here from section 3.2.1 for your convenience:

```
def unison_shuffle(a, b):                  ◁       A function for shuffling data in
    p = np.random.permutation(len(b))              unison with the label header, to
    data = np.asarray(a)[p]                         remove any potential order bias
    header = np.asarray(b)[p]
    return data, header

                                                            Shuffles data by
raw_data, header = unison_shuffle(raw_data, header)   ◁     calling a previously
                                                            defined function

idx = int(0.7*raw_data.shape[0])    ◁             Splits into independent
                                                 70% training and 30%
train_x = raw_data[:idx]            The remaining  testing sets
train_y = header[:idx]              30% for
test_x = raw_data[idx:]     ◁       validation
test_y = header[idx:]
```

Having introduced and preprocessed the example problem data, we proceed to apply the three RNN-based neural network models—which were overviewed at the beginning of the chapter—to the example problem data in the next chapter.

Summary

- Character-level models, as opposed to word-level models, can handle misspellings and other social media features, such as emoticons and niche vernacular.
- Bidirectional language modeling is key for building word embeddings that are aware of their local context.
- SIMOn and ELMo both employ character-level CNNs and bi-LSTMs, with the latter helping to achieve bidirectional context-building.

Deep transfer learning for NLP with recurrent neural networks

6

This chapter covers

- Three representative modeling architectures for transfer learning in NLP relying on RNNs
- Applying these methods to the two problems introduced in the previous chapter
- Transferring knowledge obtained from training on simulated data to real labeled data
- An introduction to some more sophisticated model adaptation strategies via ULMFiT

In the previous chapter, we introduced two example problems for the experiment we will conduct in this chapter—column-type classification and fake news detection. Recall that the goal of the experiment is to study the deep transfer learning methods for NLP that rely on recurrent neural networks (RNNs) for key functions. In particular, we will focus on three such methods—SIMOn, ELMo, and ULMFiT— which were briefly introduced in the previous chapter. In this chapter, we will apply them to the example problems, starting with SIMOn in the next section.

6.1 Semantic Inference for the Modeling of Ontologies (SIMOn)

As we discussed briefly in the previous chapter, SIMOn was designed as a component of an automatic machine learning (AutoML) pipeline for the Data-Driven Discovery of Models (D3M) DARPA program. It was developed as a classification tool for the column type in a tabular dataset but can also be viewed as a more general text classification framework. We will present the model in the context of arbitrary text input first and then specialize it to the tabular case.

By design, SIMOn is a character-level model, as opposed to a word-level model, in order to handle misspellings and other social media features, such as emoticons and niche vernacular. Because it encodes input text at the character level, the input needs to be expressed with only allowable characters to be useful for classification. This allows the model to easily adapt to the dynamic nature of social media language. The character-level nature of the model is contrasted with word-level models in figure 6.1. On the left of the figure, we show the word-level encoder, for which input has to be a valid word. Obviously, an out-of-vocabulary word due to misspelling or vernacular is an invalid input. For character-level encoders, shown on the right and resembling those of ELMo and SIMOn, input only has to be a valid character, which helps in handling misspellings.

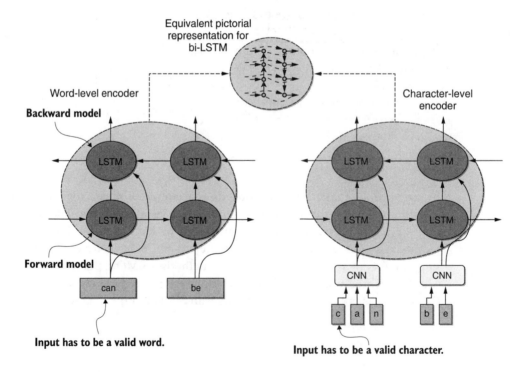

Figure 6.1 Contrasting word-level to character-level models for text classification

6.1.1 General neural architecture overview

The network, which can be split into two major coupled components, takes a document tokenized into sentences as an input. The first component is a network that encodes each individual sentence, whereas the second takes the encoded sentences and creates an encoding for the entire document.

The sentence encoder first one-hot encodes the input sentence at the character level using a dictionary of 71 characters. This includes all possible English alphabets, as well as numbers and punctuation marks. The input sentence is also standardized to a length of `max_len`. It is then passed through a sequence of convolutional, max-pooling, dropout, and bidirectional LSTM layers. Please refer to the first two stages of figure 5.1, duplicated here for your convenience, for a summary visualization. The convolutions essentially form the concept of "words" in each sentence, whereas the bidirectional LSTM "looks" in both directions around a word to determine its local context. The output from this stage is an embedding vector of a default dimension 512 for each sentence. Also compare the equivalent pictorial representation of the bi-LSTMs in figure 5.1 and figure 6.1 to make things concrete.

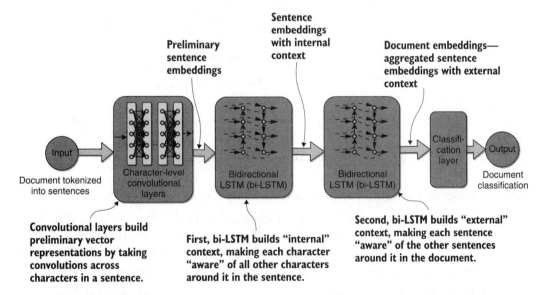

Figure 5.1 (Duplicated from the previous chapter for your convenience.) Visualizing SIMOn architecture in the context of the tabular column-type classification example

The document encoder takes the sentence-embedding vectors as input and similarly passes them through a sequence of dropout and bidirectional LSTM layers. The length of each document is standardized to `max_cells` such embedding vectors. This can be thought of as a process of forming higher-level "concepts" or "topics" from sentences, within their context with respect to other concepts present in the document. This produces an embedding vector for each document, which is then passed through a classification layer that outputs probabilities for each different type or class.

6.1.2   Modeling tabular data

Modeling tabular data is surprisingly straightforward; it just requires viewing every cell of a column within a tabular dataset as a sentence. Naturally, each such column is viewed as a document to be classified.

This means that to apply the SIMOn framework to unstructured text, one just needs to transform the text into a table with one document per column and one sentence per cell. An illustration of this process is shown in figure 6.2. Note that in this simple example, we have chosen `max_cells` to be equal to 3 for the sake of illustration.

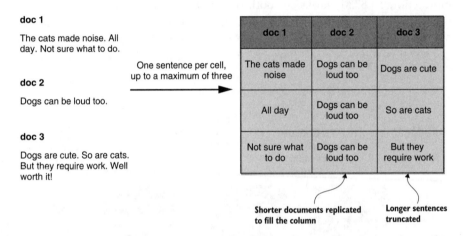

Figure 6.2   The process of converting unstructured text for consumption by SIMOn

6.1.3   Application of SIMOn to tabular column-type classification data

In its original form, SIMOn was initially trained on simulated data for a set of base classes. It was then transferred to a smaller set of hand-labeled data. Knowing how to generate simulated data can be useful, and so we briefly illustrate the process using the following set of commands, which use the library Faker under the hood:

Number of columns to generate, chosen arbitrarily for the sake of simple illustration

Simulated/fake data– generation utility (using the library Faker)

```
from Simon.DataGenerator import DataGenerator

data_cols = 5
data_count = 10

try_reuse_data = False
simulated_data, header = DataGenerator.gen_test_data((data_count, data_cols),
    try_reuse_data)
```

Number of cells/rows per column, chosen arbitrarily for the sake of simple illustration

Don't reuse data, but rather generate fresh data for more variability in the dataset.

```
print("SIMULATED DATA")                    ⟵┐  Prints
print(simulated_data)                        │  results
print("SIMULATED DATA HEADER:")
print(header)
```

Executing this code yields the following output, which shows generated samples of various data types and their corresponding labels:

```
SIMULATED DATA:
[['byoung@hotmail.com' 'Jesse' 'True' 'PPC' 'Lauraview']
 ['cindygilbert@gmail.com' 'Jason' 'True' 'Intel' 'West Brandonburgh']
 ['wilsonalexis@yahoo.com' 'Matthew' 'True' 'U; Intel'
  'South Christopherside']
 ['cbrown@yahoo.com' 'Andrew' 'False' 'U; PPC' 'Loganside']
 ['christopher90@gmail.com' 'Devon' 'True' 'PPC' 'East Charlesview']
 ['deanna75@gmail.com' 'Eric' 'False' 'U; PPC' 'West Janethaven']
 ['james80@hotmail.com' 'Ryan' 'True' 'U; Intel' 'Loriborough']
 ['cookjennifer@yahoo.com' 'Richard' 'True' 'U; Intel' 'Robertsonchester']
 ['jonestyler@gmail.com' 'John' 'True' 'PPC' 'New Kevinfort']
 ['johnsonmichael@gmail.com' 'Justin' 'True' 'U; Intel' 'Victormouth']]
SIMULATED DATA HEADER:
[list(['email', 'text']) list(['text']) list(['boolean', 'text'])
 list(['text']) list(['text'])]
```

The top level of the SIMOn repository contains the file types.json, which specifies mappings from the Faker library classes to the classes displayed previously. For instance, the second column of names in the previous example is labeled "text" because we did not require identifying names for our purposes. You could quickly change this mapping and generate simulated data for your own projects and sets of classes.

We do not train on simulated data here, because that process can take a few hours, and we already have access to the pretrained model capturing that knowledge. We do, however, perform an illustrative transfer learning experiment that involves expanding the set of classes supported beyond those available in the pretrained model.

Recall that we loaded the SIMOn Classifier class in section 5.1.2, along with model configurations, including the encoder. We can then generate a Keras SIMOn model, load our downloaded weights into it, and compile it using the following sequence of commands:

Generates the model

```
model = Classifier.generate_model(max_len, max_cells, category_count)  ⟵┘
Classifier.load_weights(checkpoint, None, model, checkpoint_dir)   ⟵┐  Loads the
model.compile(loss='binary_crossentropy',optimizer='adam',            │  weights
    metrics=['accuracy'])    ⟵┐ Compiles the model, using
                              │ binary_crossentropy loss for
                              │ multilabel classification
```

It is a good idea to take a look at the model architecture before proceeding, which we can do using this command:

```
model.summary()
```

This displays the following output and allows you to get a better sense for what is going on under the hood:

Layer (type)	Output Shape	Param #	Connected to
input_1 (InputLayer)	(None, 500, 20)	0	
time_distributed_1 (TimeDistrib	(None, 500, 512)	3202416	input_1[0][0]
lstm_3 (LSTM)	(None, 128)	328192	time_distributed_1[0][0]
lstm_4 (LSTM)	(None, 128)	328192	time_distributed_1[0][0]
concatenate_2 (Concatenate)	(None, 256)	0	lstm_3[0][0] lstm_4[0][0]
dropout_5 (Dropout)	(None, 256)	0	concatenate_2[0][0]
dense_1 (Dense)	(None, 128)	32896	dropout_5[0][0]
dropout_6 (Dropout)	(None, 128)	0	dense_1[0][0]
dense_2 (Dense)	(None, 9)	1161	dropout_6[0][0]

The `time_distributed_1` layer is the sentence encoder applied to every input sentence. We see that is followed by forward and backward LSTMs that are concatenated, some regularization via dropout, and output probabilities from the `dense_2` layer. Recall that the number of classes handled by the pretrained model is exactly 9, which matches the dimension of the output `dense_2` layer. Also note that, coincidentally, the model has 9 layers total.

Having gained a sense for the compiled model's architecture, let's go ahead and see what it thinks the types of the baseball dataset columns are. We do this by executing the following sequence of commands:

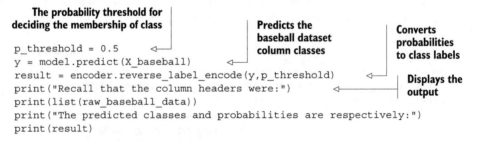

```
p_threshold = 0.5
y = model.predict(X_baseball)
result = encoder.reverse_label_encode(y,p_threshold)
print("Recall that the column headers were:")
print(list(raw_baseball_data))
print("The predicted classes and probabilities are respectively:")
print(result)
```

The probability threshold for deciding the membership of class

Predicts the baseball dataset column classes

Converts probabilities to class labels

Displays the output

The corresponding code output looks as follows:

```
Recall that the column headers were:
['Player', 'Number_seasons', 'Games_played', 'At_bats', 'Runs', 'Hits',
     'Doubles', 'Triples', 'Home_runs', 'RBIs', 'Walks', 'Strikeouts',
```

```
        'Batting_average', 'On_base_pct', 'Slugging_pct', 'Fielding_ave',
        'Position', 'Hall_of_Fame']
The predicted classes and probabilities are respectively:
([('text',), ('int',), ('int',), ('int',), ('int',), ('int',), ('int',),
    ('int',), ('int',), ('int',), ('int',), ('int',), ('float',),
    ('float',), ('float',), ('float',), ('text',), ('int',)],
 [[0.9970826506614685], [0.9877430200576782], [0.9899477362632751],
  [0.9903284907341003], [0.9894667267799377], [0.9854978322982788],
  [0.9892633557319641], [0.9895514845848083], [0.989467203617096],
  [0.9895854592323303], [0.9896339178085327], [0.9897230863571167],
  [0.9998295307159424], [0.9998230338096619], [0.9998272061347961],
  [0.9998039603233337], [0.9975670576095581], [0.9894945025444031]]])
```

Looking back to section 5.1.1 for a displayed slice of this data, which we are replicating here, we see that the model gets every column exactly right with high confidence:

	Player	Number_seasons	Games_played	At_bats	Runs	Hits	Doubles	\
0	HANK_AARON	23	3298	12364	2174	3771	624	
1	JERRY_ADAIR	13	1165	4019	378	1022	163	
2	SPARKY_ADAMS	13	1424	5557	844	1588	249	
3	BOBBY_ADAMS	14	1281	4019	591	1082	188	
4	JOE_ADCOCK	17	1959	6606	823	1832	295	

	Triples	Home_runs	RBIs	Walks	Strikeouts	Batting_average	On_base_pct	\
0	98	755	2297	1402	1383	0.305	0.377	
1	19	57	366	208	499	0.254	0.294	
2	48	9	394	453	223	0.286	0.343	
3	49	37	303	414	447	0.269	0.34	
4	35	336	1122	594	1059	0.277	0.339	

	Slugging_pct	Fielding_ave	Position	Hall_of_Fame
0	0.555	0.98	Outfield	1
1	0.347	0.985	Second_base	0
2	0.353	0.974	Second_base	0
3	0.368	0.955	Third_base	0
4	0.485	0.994	First_base	0

Now, suppose we were interested in detecting columns with percentage values in them for a project. How could we use the pretrained model to achieve this quickly? We can investigate this scenario using the second tabular dataset we prepared in the previous chapter—the multiyear British Columbia public library statistics dataset. Naturally, the first step is to predict that data using the pretrained model directly. The following sequence of commands achieves this:

```
X = encoder.encodeDataFrame(raw_library_data)          ⟵ | Encodes the data using
y = model.predict(X)                                        | the original frame
result = encoder.reverse_label_encode(y,p_threshold)   ⟵
print("Recall that the column headers were:")               | Converts
print(list(raw_library_data))                               | probabilities
print("The predicted class/probability:")                   | to class labels
print(result)
```

Predicts the classes ⟶ (bracket to y = model.predict(X))

This produces the following output:

```
Recall that the column headers were:
['PCT_ELEC_IN_TOT_VOLS', 'TOT_AV_VOLS']
The predicted class/probability:
([('text',), ('int',)], [[0.7253058552742004], [0.7712462544441223]])
```

Looking back to section 5.1.1 for a displayed slice of this data, we see that the integer column is correctly identified, whereas the percent column is identified as text:

```
      PCT_ELEC_IN_TOT_VOLS TOT_AV_VOLS
0                   90.42%          57
1                   74.83%       2,778
2                   85.55%       1,590
3                    9.22%      83,906
4                   66.63%       4,261
...                    ...         ...
1202                 0.00%      35,215
1203                 0.00%     109,499
1204                 0.00%         209
1205                 0.00%      18,748
1206                 0.00%        2403

[1207 rows x 2 columns]
```

That is not incorrect, but it is not exactly what we are looking for, either, because it is not specific enough.

We will quickly transfer the pretrained model to a very small set of training data that includes percentage samples. Let's first inform ourselves of the size of the raw library DataFrame using the following command:

```
print(raw_library_data.shape)
```

We find the size to be (1207,2), which appears to be a sufficient number of rows to build a small dataset!

In listing 6.1, we show the script that can be used to split this dataset into many smaller columns of 20 cells each. The number 20 was chosen arbitrarily, driven by the desire to create sufficient unique columns—approximately 50—in the resulting dataset. This process yields a new DataFrame, new_raw_data, of size 20 rows by 120 columns— the first 60 corresponding to percentage values and the next 60 corresponding to integer values. It also produces a corresponding list of header labels.

Listing 6.1   Transforming long library data into many shorter sample columns

| Turns the data into two lists

```
percent_value_list = raw_library_data['PCT_ELEC_IN_TOT_VOLS'].values.tolist()
int_value_list = raw_library_data['TOT_AV_VOLS'].values.tolist()
```

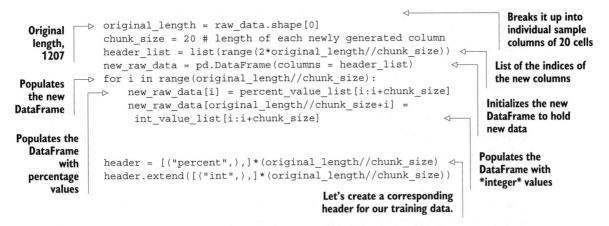

Original length, 1207 →
Populates the new DataFrame →
Populates the DataFrame with percentage values

```
original_length = raw_data.shape[0]
chunk_size = 20 # length of each newly generated column
header_list = list(range(2*original_length//chunk_size))
new_raw_data = pd.DataFrame(columns = header_list)
for i in range(original_length//chunk_size):
    new_raw_data[i] = percent_value_list[i:i+chunk_size]
    new_raw_data[original_length//chunk_size+i] =
        int_value_list[i:i+chunk_size]


header = [("percent",),]*(original_length//chunk_size)
header.extend([("int",),]*(original_length//chunk_size))
```

Breaks it up into individual sample columns of 20 cells

List of the indices of the new columns

Initializes the new DataFrame to hold new data

Populates the DataFrame with *integer* values

Let's create a corresponding header for our training data.

Recall that the final layer of the pretrained model has an output dimension of 9, matching the number of handled classes. To add another class, we need to increase the output dimension to a size of 10. We should also initialize this new dimension's weights to those of the text class because that is the most similar class handled by the pretrained model. This was determined when we predicted the percentage data as text with the pretrained model earlier. This is accomplished by the script shown in the next listing. In the script, we add percent to the list of supported categories, increase the output dimension by 1 to accommodate this addition, and then initialize the corresponding dimension weights to those of the closest category text values.

Listing 6.2   Creating new weights for the final output layer, including the percent class

Sorts the new list alphabetically →
Finds the index of the new category →

Grabs the last layer weights for initialization

Finds the old weight index for the closest category—text

```
import numpy as np

old_weights = model.layers[8].get_weights()
old_category_index = encoder.categories.index('text')
encoder.categories.append("percent")
encoder.categories.sort()
new_category_index = encoder.categories.index('percent')

new_weights = np.copy(old_weights)
new_weights[0] = np.insert(new_weights[0], new_category_index,
    old_weights[0][:,old_category_index], axis=1)
new_weights[1] = np.insert(new_weights[1], new_category_index, 0)
```

Updates the encoder with the new category list

Initializes the new weights to old weights

Inserts the text weights at the percent weight location

Inserts the text biases at the percent biases location

After executing the code in listing 6.2, you should double-check the shapes of the arrays old_weights and new_weights. You should find that the former is (128,9), whereas the latter is (128,10), if things worked as expected.

Now that we have prepared the weights with which to initialize the new model before pretraining, let's actually build and compile this new model. SIMOn API includes the following function that makes it very easy to build the model:

```
model = Classifier.generate_transfer_model(max_len, max_cells,
    category_count, category_count+1, checkpoint, checkpoint_dir)
```

The transfer model returned by this function is exactly analogous to the one we built before, with the exception that the final layer now has a new dimension, as specified by the input `category_count+1`. Additionally, because we did not give it any initialization information for the newly created output layer, this layer is presently initialized to weights of all zeros.

Before we can train this new transfer model, let's make sure that only the final output layer is trainable. We do this, along with compiling the model, via the following code snippet:

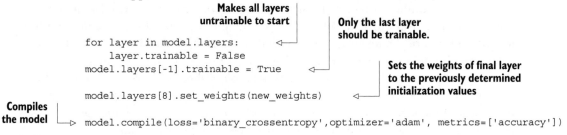

```
for layer in model.layers:            ⟵  Makes all layers
    layer.trainable = False               untrainable to start
model.layers[-1].trainable = True     ⟵  Only the last layer
                                          should be trainable.
model.layers[8].set_weights(new_weights)  ⟵  Sets the weights of final layer
                                              to the previously determined
                                              initialization values
```

Compiles the model ⟶ `model.compile(loss='binary_crossentropy',optimizer='adam', metrics=['accuracy'])`

We can now train the built, initialized, and compiled transfer model on the new data using the code in the following listing.

Listing 6.3   Training the initialized and compiled new transfer model

```
import time

X = encoder.encodeDataFrame(new_raw_data)    ⟵  Encodes the new data
                                                 (standardization, transposition,
                                                 conversion to NumPy array)
y = encoder.label_encode(header)             ⟵  Encodes the labels
data = Classifier.setup_test_sets(X, y)      ⟵  Prepares the data in the
                                                 expected format -> 60/30/10
                                                 train/validation/test data split
batch_size = 4
nb_epoch = 10
start = time.time()
history = Classifier.train_model(batch_size, checkpoint_dir, model, nb_epoch, data)
end = time.time()
print("Time for training is %f sec"%(end-start))
```

Trains the data ⟶

We visualize the convergence information produced by this code in figure 6.3. We see that a validation accuracy of 100% is achieved at the seventh epoch, and the time for training was 150 seconds. It appears that our experiment worked, and we have successfully fine-tuned the pretrained model to handle a new class of data! We note that for this new model to handle all 10 classes accurately, we need to include a few samples of each class in the training data during the transfer step. The fine-tuned model at this stage is suitable only for predicting classes included in the transfer step—integer and percent. Because our goal here was merely illustrative, we leave this as a caution for the reader and do not concern ourselves further with it here.

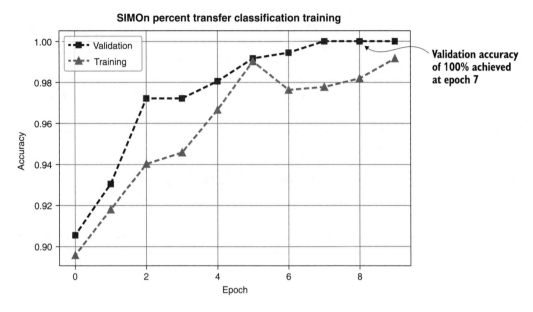

Figure 6.3   Visualization of the convergence of the percent class transfer tabular data experiment

As a final step of our transfer experiment, let's dig even deeper into its performance by comparing predicted labels for the test set with true labels. This can be done via the following code snippet:

```
y = model.predict(data.X_test)                                    Predicts classes
result = encoder.reverse_label_encode(y,p_threshold)
```
Converts probabilities to class labels

```
print("The predicted classes and probabilities are respectively:")
print(result)
print("True labels/probabilities, for comparision:")
    print(encoder.reverse_label_encode(data.y_test,p_threshold))
```
Inspects

The produced output follows:

```
The predicted classes and probabilities are respectively:
([[('percent',), ('percent',), ('int',), ('int',), ('percent',), ('int',),
    ('percent',), ('int',), ('int',), ('percent',), ('percent',), ('int',)],
    [[0.7889140248298645], [0.7893422842025757], [0.7004106640815735],
    [0.7190601229667664], [0.7961368560791016], [0.9885498881340027],
    [0.8160757422447205], [0.8141483068466187], [0.5697212815284729],
    [0.8359809517860413], [0.8188782930374146], [0.5185337066650391]]])
```

```
True labels/probabilities, for comparision:
([('percent',), ('percent',), ('int',), ('int',), ('percent',), ('int',),
    ('percent',), ('int',), ('int',), ('percent',), ('percent',), ('int',)],
    [[1], [1], [1], [1], [1], [1], [1], [1], [1], [1], [1], [1]])
```

We see that the fine-tuned model has predicted every single example correctly, further validating our transfer learning experiment.

In closing, remember that the SIMOn framework can be applied to arbitrary input text, not just tabular data, via the adaptation procedure described in section 6.1.2. Several application examples have yielded promising results.[1] Hopefully, the exercise in this section has sufficiently prepared you to deploy it in your own classification applications, as well as to adapt the resulting classifiers to new situations via transfer learning.

We will now proceed to exploring the application of ELMo to the fake news classification example.

6.2 *Embeddings from Language Models (ELMo)*

As was mentioned briefly in the previous chapter, Embeddings from Language Models (ELMo) is arguably one of the most popular early pretrained language models associated with the ongoing NLP transfer learning revolution. It shares some similarities with SIMOn, in that it is also composed of character-level CNNs and bidirectional LSTMs. Please refer to figure 5.2, duplicated here, for a bird's-eye view of these modeling components.

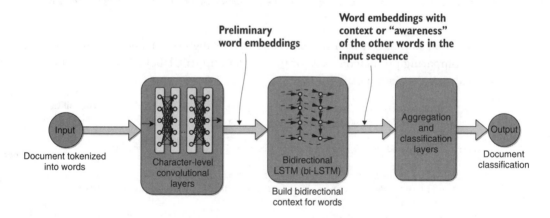

Figure 5.2 (Duplicated) Visualizing ELMo architecture in the context of the tabular column-type classification example

---

[1] N. Dhamani et al., "Using Deep Networks and Transfer Learning to Address Disinformation," AI for Social Good ICML Workshop (2019).

Also review figure 6.1, particularly the more detailed (than what is shown in figure 5.2) equivalent pictorial representation of bi-LSTMs, which are composed of a forward model and a backward model. If you have been following this book chronologically, then you have also applied ELMo to the problems of spam detection and IMDB movie review sentiment classification in section 3.2.1. As you have probably picked up by now, ELMo produces word representations that are a function of the entire input sentence. In other words, the model is a word embedding that is context-aware.

This section takes a deeper dive into the modeling architecture of ELMo. What exactly does ELMo do to the input text to build context and disambiguate? To answer this, bidirectional language modeling with ELMo is first expounded, followed by applying the model to the fake news detection problem to make things concrete.

6.2.1 *ELMo bidirectional language modeling*

Recall that language modeling attempts to model the probability of a token, usually a word, appearing in a given sequence. Consider a scenario where we have a sequence of N tokens, for instance, words in a sentence or paragraph. A word-level forward language model computes the joint probability of the sequence by taking a product of the probabilities of every token in the sequence conditioned on its left-to-right history, as visualized in figure 6.4. Consider the short sentence, "*You can be.*" According to the formula in figure 6.4, the forward language model computes the probability of the sentence as the probability of the first word in a sentence being "*You,*" times the probability of the second word being "*can,*" given that the first word is "*You,*" times the probability of the third word being "*be,*" given that the first two are "*You can.*"

Token sequence

$$p(t_1, t_2,..., t_N) = \prod_{k=1}^{N} p\,(t_k | t_1, t_2,..., t_{k-1})$$

Sequence probability   **Conditional probabilities**

Figure 6.4 Forward language model equation

A word-level backward language model does the same thing, but in reverse, as expressed by the equation in figure 6.5. It models the joint probability of the sequence by taking a product of the probabilities of every token conditioned on the right-to-left token history.

Token sequence

$$p(t_1, t_2,..., t_N) = \prod_{k=1}^{N} p\,(t_k | t_{k+1}, t_{k+2},..., t_N)$$

Sequence probability   **Conditional probabilities**

Figure 6.5 Backward language model equation.

Again, consider the short sentence, "*You can be.*" According to the formula in figure 6.5, the backward language model computes the probability of the sentence as the probability of the last word in a sentence being "*be,*" times the probability of the second word being "*can,*" given that the last word is "*be,*" times the probability of the first word being "*You,*" given that the other two are "*can be.*"

A bidirectional language model combines the forward and backward models. The ELMo model specifically looks to maximize the joint log likelihood of the two directions—the quantity shown in figure 6.6. Note that although separate parameters are maintained for the forward and backward language models, the token vectors and the final layer parameters are shared between the two. This is an example of the soft-parameter sharing multitask learning scenario discussed in chapter 4.

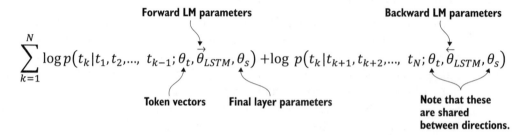

Figure 6.6   The joint bidirectional language modeling (LM) objective equation that ELMo uses to build bidirectional context for any given token in a sequence

The ELMo representation for each token is derived from the internal states of the bidirectional LSTM language model. For any given task, it is a linear combination of the internal states of all LSTM layers (in both directions) corresponding to the target token.

Combining all internal states, versus using just the top layer, as, for instance, in SIMOn, offers significant advantages. Although the lower layers of the LSTM enable good performance on syntax-based tasks, such as part-of-speech tagging, the higher layers enable context-dependent disambiguation in meaning. Learning a linear combination for each task across both types of representations allows the final model to select the kind of signal it needs for the task at hand.

6.2.2   Application to fake news detection

Now let's proceed to build an ELMo model for the fake news classification dataset we assembled in section 5.2. For readers who have already worked through chapters 3 and 4, this is our second application of the ELMo modeling framework to a practical example.

Because we have already built the ELMo model, we will be able to reuse some of the functions that we already defined in chapter 3. Refer to listing 3.4, which employs the TensorFlow Hub platform to load the weights made available by ELMo's authors and builds a Keras-ready model using them via the class `ElmoEmbeddingLayer`. Having defined this class, we can train our required ELMo model for fake news detection via the following code (slightly modified from listing 3.6):

```
def build_model():
  input_text = layers.Input(shape=(1,), dtype="string")
  embedding = ElmoEmbeddingLayer()(input_text)
  dense = layers.Dense(256, activation='relu')(embedding)       ◁─── A new layer outputting 256-dimensional feature vectors
  pred = layers.Dense(1, activation='sigmoid')(dense)       ◁─── The classification layer

  model = Model(inputs=[input_text], outputs=pred)

  model.compile(loss='binary_crossentropy', optimizer='adam',
                                metrics=['accuracy'])       ◁─── Loss, metric, and optimizer choices
  model.summary()       ◁─── Shows the model architecture for inspection

  return model

# Build and fit
model = build_model()
model.fit(train_x,       ◁─── Fits the model for 10 epochs
          train_y,
          validation_data=(test_x, test_y),
          epochs=10,
          batch_size=4)
```

Let's look at the model structure closer, which is output by the `model.summary()` statement in the previous code snippet:

Layer (type)	Output Shape	Param #
input_1 (InputLayer)	(None, 1)	0
elmo_embedding_layer_1 (Elmo	(None, 1024)	4
dense_1 (Dense)	(None, 256)	262400
dense_2 (Dense)	(None, 1)	257

Total params: 262,661
Trainable params: 262,661
Non-trainable params: 0

The layers `dense_1` and `dense_2` are the new fully connected layers added on top of the pretrained embedding produced by listing 3.4. The pretrained embedding is the `elmo_embedding_layer_1`. Note that it has four trainable parameters, as shown by the printed model summary. The four parameters are the weights in the linear combination of internal bi-LSTM states described in the previous subsection. If you use the

TensorFlow Hub approach to using the pretrained ELMo model as we have done here, the rest of the ELMo model is not trainable. It is possible, however, to build a fully trainable TensorFlow-based ELMo model using another version of the model repository.[2]

The convergence result achieved when we executed the previous code on the fake news dataset is shown in figure 6.7. We see that an accuracy over 98% is achieved.

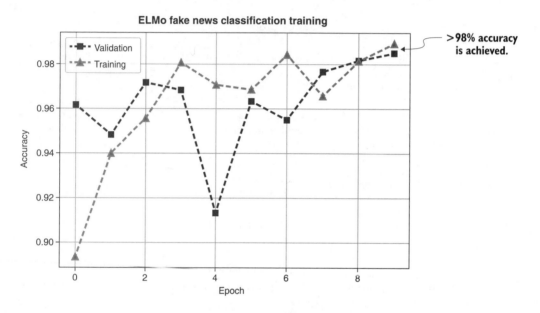

Figure 6.7   **Convergence results for the ELMo model trained on the fake news dataset**

6.3   *Universal Language Model Fine-Tuning (ULMFiT)*

Around the time techniques like ELMo were emerging, it was recognized that NLP language models were different from computer vision models in various ways. Applying the same techniques from computer vision to the fine-tuning of NLP language models came with drawbacks. For instance, the process often suffered from catastrophic forgetting of pretrained knowledge, as well as overfitting on the new data. The impact of this was the loss of any existing pretrained knowledge during training, as well as poor generalizability of the resulting model on any data outside the training set. The method known as Universal Language Model Fine-Tuning (ULMFiT) developed a set of techniques for fine-tuning NLP language models to alleviate some of these drawbacks.

---

[2] https://github.com/allenai/bilm-tf

More specifically, the method stipulates some variable learning-rate schedules for the various layers of the general pretrained language model during fine-tuning. It also specifies a set of techniques for fine-tuning the task-specific layers of the language model for more efficient transfer. Although these techniques were demonstrated by the authors in the context of classification and LSTM-based language models, the techniques are meant to be more general.

We touch on the various techniques introduced by this method in this section. However, we do not actually implement it in the code in this section. We delay the numerical investigation of ULMFiT until chapter 9, where we explore various pretrained model adaptation techniques for new scenarios. We will do that using the fast.ai library,[3] which was written by the ULMFiT authors.

For the procedures discussed next, it is assumed that we have a language model pretrained on a large, general text corpus, such as Wikipedia.

6.3.1 *Target task language model fine-tuning*

No matter how general the initial pretrained model is, the final deployment stage will likely involve data from a different distribution. This motivates us to fine-tune the general pretrained model on a new, smaller dataset from the new distribution to adapt to the new scenario. The authors of ULMFiT found that the techniques of *discriminative fine-tuning* and *slanted learning rates* alleviate the twin problems of overfitting and catastrophic forgetting experienced by researchers when doing this.

Discriminative fine-tuning stipulates that because different layers of the language model capture different information, they should be fine-tuned at different rates. Particularly, the authors found empirically that it was beneficial to first fine-tune the very last layer and note its optimal learning rate. Once they obtain that base rate, they divide this optimal rate by the number 2.6, which yields the suggested rate for the layer right below it. Successively dividing by the same factor yields progressively lower rates for each of the lower layers.

When adapting the language model, we want the model to converge quickly in the beginning, followed by a slower refinement stage. The authors found that the best way to achieve this is to use a slanted triangular learning rate, which linearly increases the learning rate and then linearly decays it. In particular, they increase the rate linearly for the initial 10% of the iterations, up to a maximum value of 0.01. Their suggested rate schedule is illustrated in figure 6.8 for the case of 10,000 total iterations.

---

[3] http://nlp.fast.ai/ulmfit

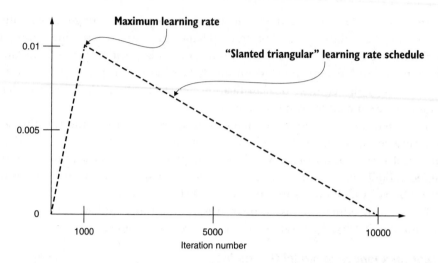

Figure 6.8   Suggested ULMFiT rate schedule for the case of 10,000 total iterations. The rate increases linearly for 10% of the total number of iterations (i.e., 1,000), up to a maximum of 0.01, and then decreases linearly afterward to 0.

6.3.2   *Target task classifier fine-tuning*

In addition to techniques for fine-tuning the language model on a small dataset representing the data distribution for the new scenario, ULMFiT provides two techniques for refining the task-specific layers: *concat pooling* and *gradual unfreezing*.

At the time ULMFiT was developed, it was standard practice to pass the hidden state of the final unit of an LSTM-based language model to the task-specific layer. The authors instead recommend concatenating these final hidden states with the max-pooled and mean-pooled hidden states of all time steps (as many of them as can fit in memory). In the bidirectional context, they do this separately for forward and backward language models and average predictions. This process, which they call *concat pooling*, performs a similar function to the bidirectional language modeling approach described for ELMo.

In order to reduce the risks of catastrophic forgetting when fine-tuning, the authors suggest unfreezing and tuning gradually. This process starts with the last layer, which contains the least general knowledge and is the only one unfrozen and refined at the first epoch. At the second epoch, an additional layer is unfrozen, and the process is repeated. The process continues until all task-specific layers are unfrozen and fine-tuned at the last iteration of this gradual unfreezing process.

As a reminder, these techniques will be explored in the code in chapter 9, which will cover various adaptation strategies.

Summary

- Character-level models, as opposed to word-level models, can handle misspellings and other social media features, such as emoticons and niche vernacular.
- Bidirectional language modeling is key for building word embeddings that are aware of their local context.
- SIMOn and ELMo both employ character-level CNNs and bi-LSTMs, with the latter helping to achieve bidirectional context-building.
- Adapting a pretrained language model to a new scenario may benefit from fine-tuning the different layers of the model at different rates, which should initially increase and then decrease according to a slanted triangular schedule.
- Adapting a task-specific layer to a new scenario may benefit from unfreezing and fine-tuning the different layers gradually, starting from the last layer and unfreezing increasingly more until all layers are refined.
- ULMFiT employs discriminative fine-tuning, slanted triangular learning rates, and gradual unfreezing to alleviate overfitting and catastrophic forgetting when fine-tuning language models.

Part 3

Deep transfer learning with transformers and adaptation strategies

Chapters 7 and 8 cover arguably the most important subfield in this space, namely deep transfer learning techniques relying on transformer neural networks for key functions, such as BERT and GPT. This model architecture class is proving to have the most impact on recent applications, partly due to better scalability on parallel computing architecture than prior methods. Chapters 9 and 10 dig deeper into various adaptation strategies for making the transfer learning process more efficient. Chapter 11 concludes the book by reviewing important topics and briefly discussing emerging research topics and directions.

7
Deep transfer learning for NLP with the transformer and GPT

This chapter covers:

- Understanding the basics of the transformer neural network architecture
- Using the Generative Pretrained Transformer (GPT) to generate text

In this chapter and the following chapter, we cover some representative deep transfer learning modeling architectures for NLP that rely on a recently popularized neural architecture—*the transformer*[1]—for key functions. This is arguably the most important architecture for natural language processing (NLP) today. Specifically, we will be looking at modeling frameworks such as GPT,[2] Bidirectional Encoder Representations from Transformers (BERT),[3] and multilingual BERT (mBERT).[4] These methods employ neural networks with even more parameters than the deep convolutional and recurrent neural network models that we looked at in

---

[1] A. Vaswani et al., "Attention Is All You Need," NeurIPS (2017).

[2] A. Radford et al., "Improving Language Understanding by Generative Pre-Training," *arXiv* (2018).

[3] M. E. Peters et al., "BERT: Pre-Training of Deep Bidirectional Transformers for Language Understanding," Proc. of NAACL-HLT (2019).

[4] https://github.com/google-research/bert/blob/master/multilingual.md

the previous two chapters. Despite the larger size, these frameworks have exploded in popularity because they scale comparatively more effectively on parallel computing architecture. This enables even larger and more sophisticated models to be developed in practice. To make the content more digestible, we have split the coverage of these models into two chapters/parts: we cover the transformer and GPT neural network architectures in this chapter, whereas in the next chapter, we focus on BERT and mBERT.

Until the arrival of the transformer, the dominant NLP models relied on recurrent and convolutional components, as we saw in the previous two chapters. Additionally, the best *sequence modeling* and *transduction* problems, such as machine translation, relied on an encoder-decoder architecture with an *attention mechanism* to detect which parts of the input influence each part of the output. The transformer aims to replace the recurrent and convolutional components entirely with attention.

The goal of this and the following chapters is to provide you with a working understanding of this important class of models and to help you develop a good sense about where some of its beneficial properties come from. We introduce an important library—aptly named *transformers*—that makes the analysis, training, and application of these types of models in NLP particularly user-friendly. Additionally, we use the *tensor2tensor* TensorFlow package to help visualize attention functionality. The presentation of each transformer-based model architecture—GPT, BERT, and mBERT—is followed by representative code applying it to a relevant task.

GPT, which was developed by OpenAI,[5] is a transformer-based model that is trained with a *causal modeling objective*: to predict the next word in a sequence. It is also particularly suited for text generation. We show how to employ pretrained GPT weights for this purpose with the transformers library.

BERT is a transformer-based model that we encountered briefly in chapter 3. It was trained with the *masked modeling objective*: to fill in the blanks. Additionally, it was trained with the *next sentence prediction* task: to determine whether a given sentence is a plausible subsequent sentence after a target sentence. Although not suited for text generation, this model performs well on other general language tasks such as classification and question answering. We have already explored classification in some detail, so we will use the question-answering task to explore this model architecture in more detail than we did in chapter 3.

mBERT, which stands for Multilingual BERT, is effectively BERT pretrained on over 100 languages simultaneously. Naturally, this model is particularly well-suited for cross-lingual transfer learning. We will show how the multilingual pretrained checkpoint can facilitate creating BERT embeddings for languages that were not even originally included in the multilingual training corpus. Both BERT and mBERT were created at Google.

---

[5] A. Radfordet al., "Improving Language Understanding by Generative Pre-Training," *arXiv* (2018).

We begin the chapter with a review of fundamental architectural components and visualize them in some detail with the tensor2tensor package. We follow that up with a section overviewing the GPT architecture, with text generation as a representative application of pretrained weights. The first section of chapter 8 then covers BERT, which we apply to the very important question-answering application as a representative example in a stand-alone section. Chapter 8 concludes with an experiment showing the transfer of pretrained knowledge from mBERT pretrained weights to a BERT embedding for a new language. This new language was not initially included in the multilingual corpus used to generate the pretrained mBERT weights. We use the Ghanaian language Twi as the illustrative language in this case. This example also provides an opportunity to further explore fine-tuning pretrained BERT weights on a new corpus. Note that Twi is an example of a *low-resource language*—one for which high-quality training data is scarce, if available at all.

7.1 *The transformer*

In this section, we look closer at the fundamental transformer architecture behind the neural model family covered by this chapter. This architecture was developed at Google[6] and was motivated by the observation that the best-performing translation models up to that point employed convolutional and recurrent components in conjunction with a mechanism called *attention*.

More specifically, such models employ an encoder-decoder architecture, where the encoder converts the input text into some intermediate numerical vector representation, typically called the *context vector*, and a decoder that converts this vector into output text. Attention allows for better performance in these models by modeling dependencies between parts of the output and the input. Typically, attention had been coupled with recurrent components. Because such components are inherently sequential—the internal hidden state at any given position t depends on the hidden state at the previous position t-1—parallelization of the processing of a long input sequence is not an option. Parallelization across such input sequences, on the other hand, quickly runs into GPU memory limitations.

The transformer discards recurrence and replaces all functionality with attention. More specifically, it uses a flavor of attention called *self-attention*. Self-attention is essentially attention as previously described but applied to the same sequence as both input and output. This allows it to learn the dependencies between every part of the sequence and every other part of the same sequence. Figure 7.3 will revisit and illustrate this idea in more detail, so don't worry if you can't visualize it fully yet. These models have better parallelizability versus the aforementioned recurrent models. Looking ahead, we address exactly the reason for this in section 7.1.2, where we use the example sentence, "He didn't want to talk about cells on the cell phone because he considered it boring," to study how various aspects of the infrastructure work.

---

[6] A. Vaswani et al., "Attention Is All You Need," NeurIPS (2017).

Now that we understand the basics of the motivation behind this architecture, let's take a look at a simplified bird's-eye-view representation of the various building blocks, shown in figure 7.1.

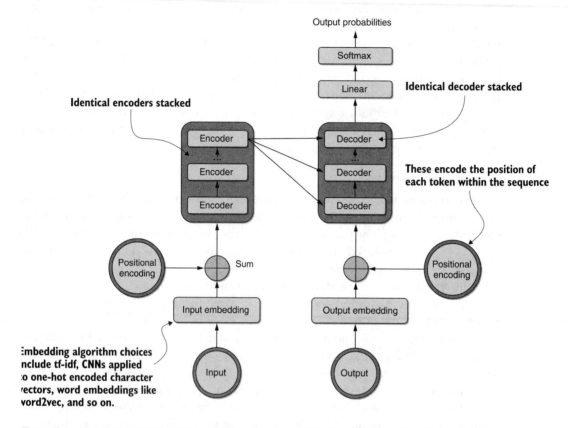

Figure 7.1 A high-level representation of the transformer architecture, showing stacked encoders, decoders, input/output embeddings, and positional encodings

We see from the figure that identical encoders are stacked on the encoding, or left, side of the architecture. The number of stacked encoders is a tunable hyperparameter, with the original paper working with six. Similarly, on the decoding, or right, side of the architecture, six identical decoders are stacked. We also see that both the input and output are converted into vectors using an embedding algorithm of choice. This could be a word embedding algorithm such as word2vec, or even a CNN applied to one-hot encoded character vectors very similar to those we encountered in the previous chapter. Additionally, we encode the sequential nature of the inputs and outputs using *positional encodings*. These allow us to discard recurrent components while maintaining sequential awareness.

Each encoder can be roughly decomposed into a self-attention layer followed by a feedforward neural network, as illustrated in figure 7.2.

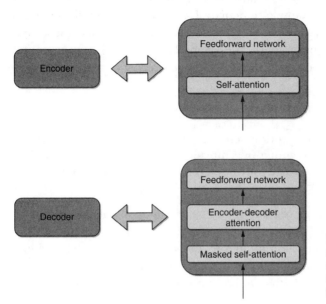

Figure 7.2 A simplified decomposition of the encoder and decoder into self-attention, encoder-decoder attention, and feedforward neural networks

As can be seen in the figure, each decoder can be similarly decomposed with the addition of an encoder-decoder attention layer between the self-attention layer and the feedforward neural network. Note that in the self-attention of the decoder, future tokens are "masked" when computing attention for that token—we will return to this at a more appropriate time. Whereas the self-attention learns the dependencies of every part of its input sequence and every other part of the same sequence, encoder-decoder attention learns similar dependencies between the inputs to the encoder and decoder. This process is similar to the way attention was initially used in the sequence-to-sequence recurrent translation models.

The self-attention layer in figure 7.2 can further be refined into *multihead attention*—a multidimensional analog of self-attention that leads to improved performance. We analyze self-attention in further detail in the following subsections and build on the insights gained to cover multihead attention. The *bertviz* package[7] is used for visualization purposes to provide further insights. We later close the chapter by loading a representative transformer translation model with the transformers library and using it to quickly translate a couple of English sentences into the low-resource Ghanaian language, Twi.

---

[7] https://github.com/jessevig/bertviz

7.1.1   *An introduction to the transformers library and attention visualization*

Before we discuss in detail how various components of multihead attention works, let's visualize it for the example sentence, "He didn't want to talk about cells on the cell phone because he considered it boring." This exercise also allows us to introduce the transformers Python library from Hugging Face. The first step to doing this is to obtain the required dependencies using the following commands:

```
!pip install tensor2tensor
!git clone https://github.com/jessevig/bertviz.git
```

> **NOTE** Recall from the previous chapters that the exclamation sign (!) is required only when executing in a Jupyter environment, such as the Kaggle environment we recommend for these exercises. When executing via a terminal, it should be dropped.

The tensor2tensor package contains the original authors' implementation of the transformers architecture, together with some visualization utilities. The bertviz library is an extension of these visualization utilities to a large set of the models within the transformers library. Note that it requires JavaScript to be activated to render its visualization (we show you how to do that in the companion Kaggle notebook).

The transformers library can be installed with the following:

```
!pip install transformers
```

Note that it is already installed on new notebooks on Kaggle.

For our visualization purposes, we look at the self-attention of a BERT encoder. It is arguably the most popular flavor of the transformers-based architecture and similar to the encoder in the encoder-decoder architecture of the original architecture in figure 7.1. We will visualize BERT architecture explicitly in figure 8.1 of section 8.1. For now, all you need to note is that the BERT encoder is identical to that of the transformer.

For any pretrained model that you want to load in the transformers library, you need to load a tokenizer as well as the model using the following commands:

```
from transformers import BertTokenizer, BertModel          ◁──┤  The transformers BERT
model = BertModel.from_pretrained('bert-base-uncased',            tokenizer and model
    output_attentions=True)
                                                             ◁──┐  Loads the
tokenizer = BertTokenizer.from_pretrained('bert-base-uncased',       uncased BERT
    do_lower_case=True)   ◁──┐  Loads the                              model, making
                             uncased BERT                              sure to output
                             tokenizer                                 attention
```

Note that the uncased BERT checkpoint we are using here is the same as what we used in chapter 3 (listing 3.7) when we first encountered the BERT model through Tensor-Flow Hub.

You can tokenize our running example sentence, encode each token as its index in the vocabulary, and display the outcome using the following code:

```
sentence = "He didnt want to talk about cells on the cell phone because he
    considered it boring"
inputs = tokenizer.encode(sentence, return_tensors='tf',
    add_special_tokens=True)    ◁──┐ Changing return_tensors to "pt"
print(inputs)                        will return PyTorch tensors.
```

This yields the following output:

```
tf.Tensor(
[[  101  2002  2134  2102  2215  2000  2831  2055  4442  2006  1996  3526
    3042  2138  2002  2641  2009 11771   102]], shape=(1, 19), dtype=int32)
```

We could have easily returned a PyTorch tensor simply by setting return_tensors='pt'. To see which tokens these indices correspond to, we can execute the following code on the inputs variable:

```
tokens = tokenizer.convert_ids_to_tokens(list(inputs[0]))    ◁──┐ Extracts a sample of
print(tokens)                                                     batch index 0 from the
                                                                  inputs list of lists
```

This produces the following output:

```
['[CLS]', 'he', 'didn', '##t', 'want', 'to', 'talk', 'about', 'cells', 'on',
'the', 'cell', 'phone', 'because', 'he', 'considered', 'it', 'boring', '[SEP]']
```

We notice immediately that the "special tokens" we requested via the add_special _tokens argument when encoding the inputs variable refers to the '[CLS]' and '[SEP]' tokens in this case. The former indicates the beginning of a sentence/ sequence, whereas the latter indicates the separation point between multiple sequences or the end of a sequence (as in this case). Note that these are BERT-dependent, and you should check the documentation of each new architecture you try to see which special tokens it uses. The other thing we notice from this tokenization exercise is that the tokenization is *subword*—notice how didnt was split into didn and ##t, even without the apostrophe (') , which we deliberately omitted.

Let's proceed to visualizing the self-attention layer of the BERT model we have loaded by defining the following function:

```
from bertviz.bertviz import head_view    ◁──┐ The bertviz attention head
                                               visualization method
```

```
def show_head_view(model, tokenizer, sentence):    ◁──── Function for
    input_ids = tokenizer.encode(sentence, return_tensors='pt',    displaying the
        add_special_tokens=True)                                   multiheaded
    attention = model(input_ids)[-1]                               attention
    tokens = tokenizer.convert_ids_to_tokens(list(input_ids[0]))
    head_view(attention, tokens)    ◁──┐ Calls the internal bertviz
                                         method to display self-attention
```

Be sure to use PyTorch with bertviz. (points to input_ids line)

Gets the attention layer (points to attention line)

```
show_head_view(model, tokenizer, sentence)    ◁──── Calls our function to render visualization
```

Figure 7.3 shows the resulting self-attention visualization of the final BERT layer of our example sentence. You should play with the visualization and scroll through the visualizations of the various words for the various layers. Note that not all the attention visualizations may be as easy to interpret as this example, and it may take some practice to build intuition for it.

That was it! Now that we have a sense for what self-attention does, having visualized it in figure 7.3, let's get into the mathematical details of how it works. We first start with self-attention in the next subsection and then extend our knowledge to the full multiheaded context afterward.

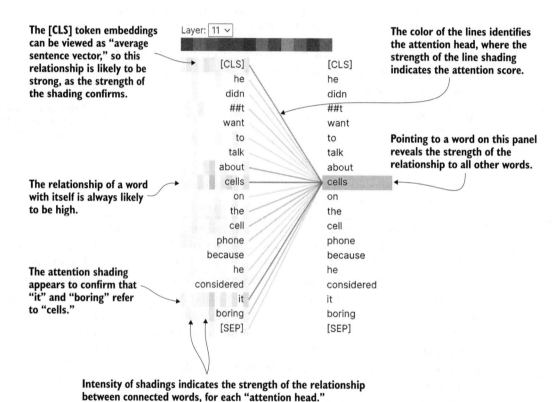

The [CLS] token embeddings can be viewed as "average sentence vector," so this relationship is likely to be strong, as the strength of the shading confirms.

The color of the lines identifies the attention head, where the strength of the line shading indicates the attention score.

The relationship of a word with itself is always likely to be high.

Pointing to a word on this panel reveals the strength of the relationship to all other words.

The attention shading appears to confirm that "it" and "boring" refer to "cells."

Intensity of shadings indicates the strength of the relationship between connected words, for each "attention head."

Figure 7.3 Self-attention visualization in the final encoding layer of the pretrained uncased BERT model for our example sentence. It reveals that "cells" is associated with "it" and "boring." Note that this is a multihead view, with the shadings in each single column representing each head. Multiheaded attention is addressed in detail in section 7.1.2.

7.1.2 Self-attention

Consider again the example sentence, "He didn't want to talk about cells on the cell phone because he considered it boring." Suppose we wanted to figure out which noun the adjective "boring" was describing. Being able to answer a question like this is an important ability a machine needs to have to understand context. We know it refers to "it," which refers to "cells," naturally. This was confirmed by our visualization in figure 7.3. A machine needs to be taught this sense of context. Self-attention is the method that accomplishes this in the transformer. As every token in the input is processed, self-attention looks at all other tokens to detect possible dependencies. Recall that we achieved this same function with bidirectional LSTMs in the previous chapter.

So how does self-attention actually work to accomplish this? We visualize the essential ideas of this in figure 7.4. In the figure, we are computing the self-attention weight for the word "boring." Before delving into further detail, please note that once the

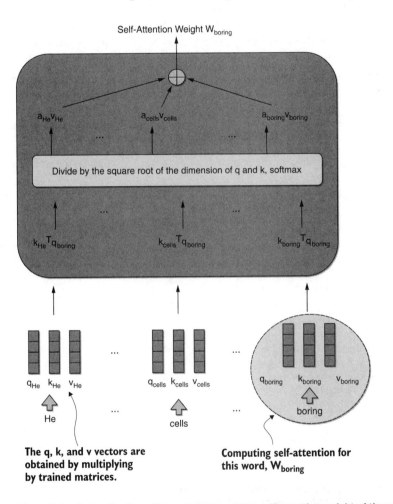

Figure 7.4   A visualization of the calculation of the self-attention weight of the word boring in our example sentence. Observe that the computations of these weights for different words can be carried out independently once key, value, and query vectors have been created. This is the root of the increased parallelizability of transformers over recurrent models. The attention coefficients are what is visualized as intensity of shading in any given column of the multihead attention in figure 7.3.

various query, key, and value vectors for the various words are obtained, they can be processed independently.

Each word is associated with a *query* vector (q), a *key* vector (k), and a *value* vector (v). These are obtained by multiplying the input embedding vectors by three matrices that are learned during training. These matrices are fixed across all input tokens. As shown in the figure, the query vector for the current word boring is used in a dot product with each word's key vector. The results are scaled by a fixed constant—the square root of the dimension of the key and value vectors—and fed to a softmax. The output vector yields the attention coefficients that indicate the strength of the relationship between the current token "boring" and every other token in the sequence. Observe that the entries of this vector indicate the strength of the shadings in any given single column of the multihead attention we visualized in figure 7.3. We duplicate figure 7.3 next for your convenience, so you can inspect the variability in shadings between the various lines.

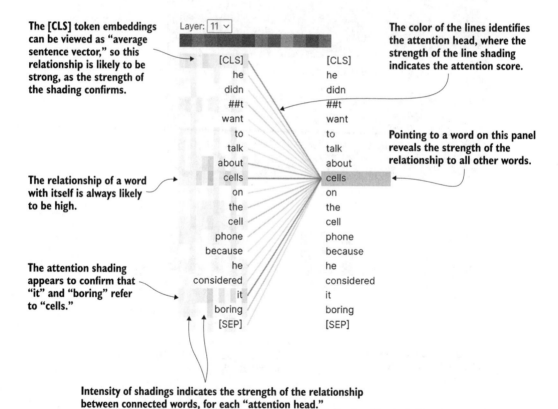

Figure 7.3   (Duplicated) Self-attention visualization in the final encoding layer of the pretrained uncased BERT model for our example sentence. It reveals that "cells" is associated with "it" and "boring." Note that this is a multihead view, with the shadings in each single column representing each head.

We are now in a good position to understand why transformers are more paralleliz-able than recurrent models. Recall from our presentation that the computations of self-attention weights for different words can be carried out independently, once the key, value, and query vectors have been created. This means that for long input sequences, one can parallelize these computations. Recall that recurrent models are inherently sequential—the internal hidden state at any given position t depends on the hidden state at the previous position t-1. This means that parallelization of the processing of a long input sequence is not possible in recurrent models because the steps have to be executed one after the other. Parallelization across such input sequences, on the other hand, quickly runs into GPU memory limitations. An addi-tional advantage of transformers over recurrent model is the increased interpretabil-ity afforded by attention visualizations, such as the one in figure 7.3.

Note that the computation of the weight for every token in the sequence can be carried out independently, although some dependence between computations exists through the key and value vectors. This means that we can vectorize the overall com-putation using matrices as shown in figure 7.5. The matrices Q, K, and V in that equa-tion are simply the matrices made up of query, key and value vectors stacked together as matrices.

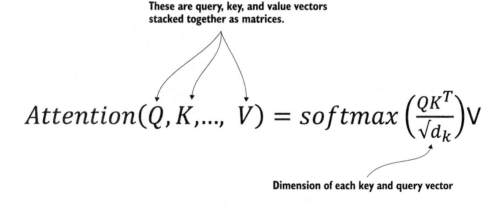

These are query, key, and value vectors stacked together as matrices.

$$Attention(Q, K, ..., V) = softmax\left(\frac{QK^T}{\sqrt{d_k}}\right)V$$

Dimension of each key and query vector

Figure 7.5 Vectorized self-attention calculation for the whole input sequence using matrices

What exactly is the deal with multihead attention? Now that we have presented self-attention, we are at a good point to address this. We have implicitly been presenting multihead attention as a generalization of self-attention from a single column, in the sense of the shadings in figure 7.3, to multiple columns. Let's think about what we were doing when we very looking for the noun which "boring" refers to. Technically, we were looking for a noun-adjective relationship. Assume we had one self-attention mechanism that tracked that kind of relationship. What if we also needed to track subject-verb relationships? What about all other possible kinds of relationships?

Multihead attention essentially addresses that by providing multiple representation dimensions, not just one.

7.1.3 Residual connections, encoder-decoder attention, and positional encoding

The transformer is a complex architecture with many features that we will not cover in as much detail as self-attention. Mastery of these details is not critical for you to begin applying transformers to your own problems. Therefore, we only briefly summarize them here and encourage you to delve into the original source material to deepen your knowledge over time as you gain more experience and intuition.

As a first such feature, we note that the simplified encoder representation in figure 7.2 does not show an additional residual connection between each self-attention layer in the encoder and a normalization layer that follows it. This is illustrated in figure 7.6.

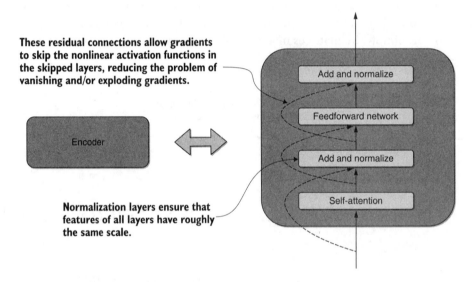

Figure 7.6   A more detailed and accurate breakdown of each transformer encoder, now incorporating residual connections and normalization layers

As shown in the figure, each feedforward layer has a residual connection and a normalization layer after it. Analogous statements are true for the decoder. These residual connections allow gradients to skip the nonlinear activation functions within the layers, alleviating the problem of vanishing and/or exploding gradients. Put simply, normalization ensures that the scale of input features to all layers are roughly the same.

On the decoder side, recall from figure 7.2 the existence of the encoder-decoder attention layer, which we have not yet addressed. We duplicate figure 7.2 next and highlight this layer for your convenience.

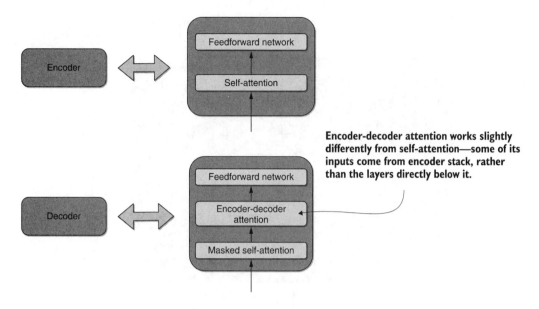

Figure 7.2 (Duplicated, encoder-decoder attention highlighted) Simplified decomposition of the encoder and decoder into self-attention, encoder-decoder attention, and feedforward neural networks

It works analogously to the self-attention layer as described. The important distinction is that the input vectors to each decoder that represent keys and values come from the top of the encoder stack, whereas the query vectors come from the layer immediately below it. If you go through figure 7.4 again with this updated information in mind, you should find it obvious that the effect of this change is to compute attention between every output token and every input token, rather than between all tokens in the input sequence as was the case with the self-attention layer. We duplicate figure 7.4 next—adjusting it slightly for the encoder-decoder attention case—so you can convince yourself.

On both the encoder and decoder sides, recall from figure 7.1 the existence of the positional encoding, which we now address. Because we are dealing with sequences, it is important to model and retain the relative positions of each token in each sequence. Our description of the transformer operation so far has not touched on "positional encoding" and has been agnostic to the order in which the tokens are consumed by each self-attention layer. The positional embeddings address this, by adding to each token input embedding a vector of equal size that is a special function of the token's position in the sequence. The authors used sine and cosine functions of frequencies that are position-dependent to generate these positional embeddings.

This brings us to the end of the transformers architecture exposition. To make things concrete, we conclude this section by translating a couple of English sentences to a low-resource language using a pretrained encoder-decoder model.

Encoder-decoder attention weight $W_{boring,n}$ between output *n* and word "boring"

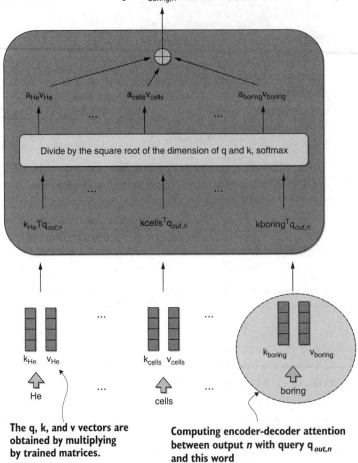

The q, k, and v vectors are obtained by multiplying by trained matrices.

Computing encoder-decoder attention between output *n* with query $q_{out,n}$ and this word

Figure 7.4   (Duplicated, slightly adjusted for encoder-decoder attention calculation) A visualization of the calculation of the encoder-decoder attention weight between the word boring in our example sentence and the output at position *n*. Observe that the computations of these weights for different words can be carried out independently once key, value, and query vectors have been created. This is the root of the increased parallelizability of transformers over recurrent models.

7.1.4   *Application of pretrained encoder-decoder to translation*

The goal of this subsection is to expose you to a large set of translation models available at your fingertips within the transformers library. The Language Technology Research Group at the University of Helsinki[8] has made more than 1,000 pretrained models available. At the time of writing, these are the only available open source

---

[8] https://huggingface.co/Helsinki-NLP

models for many low-resource languages. We use the popular Ghanaian language Twi as an example here. It was trained on the JW300 corpus,[9] which contains the only existing parallel translated datasets for many low-resource languages.

Unfortunately, JW300 is extremely biased data, being religious text translated by the Jehovah's Witnesses organization. However, our investigation revealed that the models are of decent quality as an initial baseline for further transfer learning and refinement. We do not explicitly refine the baseline model on better data here, due to data-collection challenges and the lack of existing appropriate datasets. However, we hope that taken together with the penultimate section of the next chapter—where we fine-tune a multilingual BERT model on monolingual Twi data—you will gain a powerful set of tools for further cross-lingual transfer learning research.

Without further ado, let's load the pretrained English-to-Twi translation model and tokenizer using the following code:

```
from transformers import MarianMTModel, MarianTokenizer

model = MarianMTModel.from_pretrained("Helsinki-NLP/opus-mt-en-tw")
tokenizer = MarianTokenizer.from_pretrained("Helsinki-NLP/opus-mt-en-tw")
```

The MarianMTModel class is a port of encoder-decoder transformer architecture from the C++ library MarianNMT.[10] Note that you can change the source and target languages by simply changing the language codes en and tw to representative codes, if made available by the research group. For instance, loading a French-to-English model would change the input configuration string to Helsinki-NLP/opus-mt-fr-en.

If we were chatting with a friend in Ghana online and wanted to know how to write "My name is Paul" by way of introduction, we could use the following code to compute and display the translation:

```
text = "My name is Paul"                            ← Inputs the English sentence to be translated        Encodes to the input token Ids
inputs = tokenizer.encode(text, return_tensors="pt") ←                                                     Generates the output token Ids
outputs = model.generate(inputs)                     ←
decoded_output = [tokenizer.convert_ids_to_tokens(int(outputs[0][i])) for i
    in range(len(outputs[0]))]                       ←                 Decodes the output token IDs to actual output tokens
print("Translation:")                                ←   Displays the
print(decoded_output)                                    translation
```

The resulting output from running the code is shown next:

```
Translation:
['<pad>', '_Me', '_din', '_de', '_Paul']
```

The first thing we immediately notice is the presence of a special token <pad> in the output that we have not seen before, as well as underscores before each word. This is

---

[9] http://opus.nlpl.eu/JW300.php
[10] https://marian-nmt.github.io/

different from the output the BERT tokenizer produced in section 7.1.1. The technical reason is that BERT uses a tokenizer called WordPiece, whereas our encoder-decoder model here uses SentencePiece. Although we do not get into the detailed differences between these tokenizer types here, we do use this opportunity to warn you once again to review documentation about any new tokenizer you try.

The translation "Me din de Paul" happens to be exactly right. Great! That wasn't too hard, was it? However, repeating the exercise for the input sentence "How are things?" yields the translation "Ɔkwan bɛn so na nneɛma te saa?" which back-translates literally into "In which way are things like this?" We can see that while the semantics of this translation appear close, the translation is wrong. The semantic similarity, however, is a sign that this model is a good baseline that could be improved further via transfer learning, if good parallel English-Twi data were available. Moreover, rephrasing the input sentence to "How are you?" yields the correct translation "Wo ho te dɛn?" from this model. Overall, this result is very encouraging, and we hope that some readers are inspired to work to extend these baseline models to some excellent open source transformer models for some previously unaddressed low-resource languages of choice.

We look at the Generative Pretrained Transformer (GPT) next, a transformer-based model preferred for text generation that has become quite famous in the NLP community.

7.2   *The Generative Pretrained Transformer*

The Generative Pretrained Transformer[11] (GPT) was developed by OpenAI and was among the earliest models to apply the transformer architecture to the semisupervised learning scenario discussed in this book. By this, we mean, of course, the unsupervised (or self-supervised) pretraining of a language-understanding model on a large corpus of text data, followed by supervised fine-tuning on the final target data of interest. The authors found the performance on four types of language-understanding tasks to be significantly improved. These tasks included natural language inference, question answering, semantic similarity, and text classification. Notably, performance on the General Language-Understanding Evaluation (GLUE) benchmark, which includes these along with other difficult and diverse tasks, was improved by more than 5 percentage points.

The GPT model has undergone several iterations—GPT, GPT-2, and, very recently, GPT-3. Indeed, at the time of writing, GPT-3 happens to be one of the largest known pretrained language models, with 175 billion parameters. Its predecessor, the GPT-2, stands at 1.5 billion parameters and was also considered the largest at the time it was released, just a year prior. Before the release of GPT-3 in June 2020, the largest model was Microsoft's Turing-NLG, which stands at 17 billion parameters and was released in February 2020. The sheer speed of progress on some of these metrics has been mind-blowing, and these records are likely to be made obsolete very soon. In fact, when GPT-2 was initially disclosed, the authors felt that not fully open sourcing the technology was the right thing to do, given the potential for abuse by malicious actors.

---

[11] A. Radford et al., "Improving Language Understanding by Generative Pre-Training," *arXiv* (2018).

Although at the time of its initial release, GPT became the state of the art for most of the aforementioned tasks, it has generally come to be preferred as a text-generation model. Unlike BERT and its derivatives, which have come to dominate most other tasks, GPT was trained with the causal modeling objective (CLM) where the next token is predicted, as opposed to BERT's masked language modeling (MLM) fill-in-the-blanks-type prediction objective, which we will cover in more detail in the next chapter.

In the next subsection, we briefly describe the key aspects of the GPT architecture. We follow that with an introduction to the *pipelines* API concept in the transformers library that is used to minimally execute pretrained models for the most common tasks. We do this in the context of applying GPT to the task it has come to excel at—text generation. Like the previous section on the encoder-decoder transformer and translation, we do not explicitly refine the pretrained GPT model on more-specific target data here. However, taken together with the final section of the next chapter—where we fine-tune a multilingual BERT model on monolingual Twi data—you will gain a powerful set of tools for further text-generation transfer learning research.

7.2.1 Architecture overview

You may recall from section 7.1.1, where we visualized BERT self-attention, that BERT is essentially a stacked set of encoders of the original encoder-decoder transformer architecture. GPT is essentially the converse of that, in the sense that it stacks the decoders instead. Recall from figure 7.2 that besides the encoder-decoder attention,

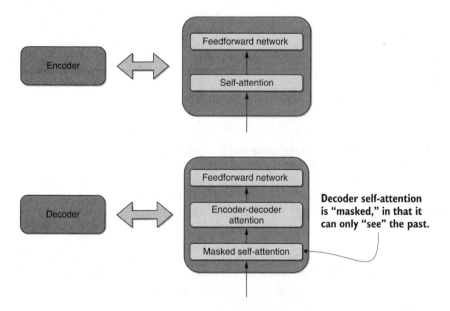

Figure 7.2 (Duplicated, masked layer highlighted) The simplified decomposition of the encoder and decoder into self-attention, encoder-decoder attention, and feedforward neural networks

the other distinguishing feature of the transformer decoder is that its self-attention layer is "masked," that is, future tokens are "masked" when computing attention for any given token. We duplicate figure 7.2 for your convenience, highlighting this masked layer.

In the attention calculation that we went through in figure 7.3, this just means including only the tokens in "he didnt want to talk about cells" in the calculation and ignoring the rest. We duplicate figure 7.3 next, slightly modified so you can clearly see the future tokens being masked.

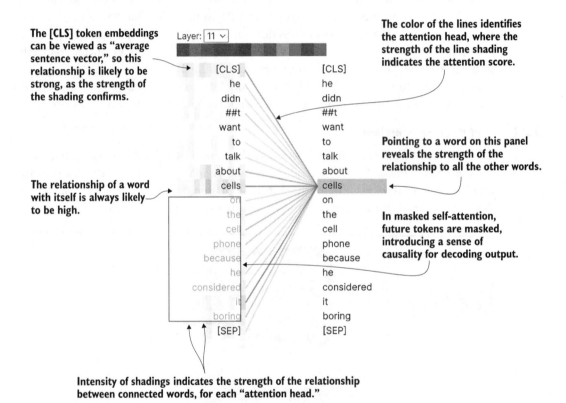

Figure 7.3   (Duplicated again, modified for masked self-attention) A masked self-attention visualization for our example sentence, showing future tokens being masked for causality.

This introduces a sense of causality into the system and suitability for text generation, or predicting the next token. Because there is no encoder, the encoder-decoder attention is also dropped. Taking these factors into account, we show the GPT architecture in figure 7.7.

Note in figure 7.7 that the same output can be used for both text prediction/ generation and classification for some other task. Indeed, the authors devised an input

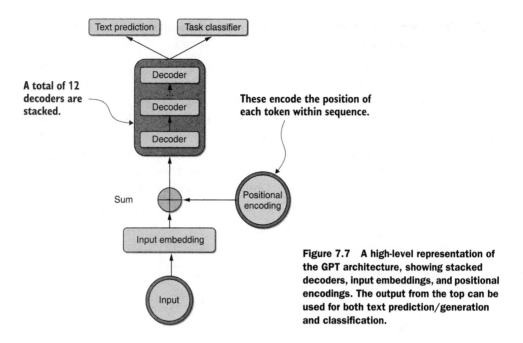

Figure 7.7 **A high-level representation of the GPT architecture, showing stacked decoders, input embeddings, and positional encodings. The output from the top can be used for both text prediction/generation and classification.**

transformation scheme where multiple tasks could be handled by the same architecture without any architectural changes. For instance, consider the task of *textual entailment,* which roughly corresponds to determining if one *premise* statement implies another *hypothesis* statement. The input transformation concatenates the premise and hypothesis statements, separated by a special delimiter token, and feeds the resulting single contiguous string to the same unmodified architecture to classify whether or not entailment exists. On the other hand, consider the important question-answering application. Here, given some context document, a question, and a set of possible answers, the task is to determine which answer is the best potential answer to the question. Here, the input transformation is to concatenate the context, question, and each possible answer before passing each resulting contiguous string through the same model and performing a softmax over the corresponding outputs to determine the best answer. A similar input transformation was devised for the sentence similarity task as well.

Having briefly introduced the architecture of GPT, let's use a pretrained version of it for some fun coding experiments. We first use it to generate some open-ended text given a prompt. We then also use a modification of GPT built at Microsoft— DialoGPT[12]—to perform multiturn conversations with a chatbot in the next subsection.

---

[12] Y. Zhang et al., "DialoGPT: Large-Scale Generative Pretraining for Conversational Response Generation," *arXiv* (2019).

7.2.2 *Transformers pipelines introduction and application to text generation*

The first thing we will do in this subsection is generate some open-ended text using GPT. We will also use this opportunity to introduce pipelines—an API exposing the pretrained models in the transformers library for inference that is even simpler than what we did for translation in section 7.1.4. The stated goal of the transformers authors is for this API to abstract away complex code for some frequently used tasks, including named entity recognition, masked language modeling, sentiment analysis, and question answering. Suitably for our purposes in this subsection, text generation is also an option.

Let's start by initializing the transformers pipeline to the GPT-2 model via the following two lines of code:

```
from transformers import pipeline
gpt = pipeline('text-generation',model='gpt2')
```

By way of reminder, GPT in its original form is well suited for open-ended text generation, such as creative writing of sections of text to complement previous text. Let us see what the model generates when primed by "Somewhere over the rainbow…," up to a maximum of 100 tokens, via the following command:

```
gpt("Somewhere over the rainbow", max_length=100)
```

This generates the following text:

```
[{'generated_text': "Somewhere over the rainbow people live! I wonder how
they get to know each other… They just have a wonderful community out there -
but when they see each other as two of the best in school they never even
realize them, just love, family, friends, and friends. I'm really proud of
their talent and dedication to life. I've seen a lot of people that were
raised by their mother and grandma in the Midwest and didn't understand there
was such an opportunity and I truly cannot"}]
```

This seems very semantically correct, even if the message is a bit incoherent. You could imagine a creative writer using this to generate ideas to get around writer's block! Now, let's see if we can prime the model with something less "creative," something more technical, to see how it will do. Let's prime the model with the text "Transfer learning is a field of study" via the following code:

```
gpt("Transfer learning is a field of study", max_length=100)
```

This produces the following output:

```
[{'generated_text': "Transfer learning is a field of study that has been
around for centuries, and one that requires a thorough grounding in
mathematics in order to understand the complexities of these systems. If you
go to the library for your high school physics course, you know you're on the
right track. The only problem with this position is that people don't ask
questions. The only thing they really do ask is: how do we figure out how to
apply these processes to the rest of physics and other sciences?\n\nIn"}]
```

Again, we can see this text is pretty good in terms of semantic coherence, grammatic structure, spelling, punctuation, and so on—indeed, eerily good. However, as it continues, it becomes arguably factually incorrect. We can all agree that transfer learning requires a thorough grounding in mathematics for true understanding and even argue that it has been around for centuries—via us, the humans! However, it is not a field of physics, even if it might be somewhat similar in terms of the kinds of skills required to master it. We can see that the model's output becomes less plausible the longer it is allowed to speak.

Please be sure to experiment some more to get a sense of the model's strengths and weaknesses. For instance, you could try prompting the model with our example sentence, "He didn't want to talk about cells on the cell phone because he considered it boring." We found this a plausible application in the creative writing space and perhaps in technical writing space with `max_length` set to a smaller number. It is already a plausible aid for many authors out there. One can only imagine what GPT-3, which has not yet been fully released to the public at the time of writing, will be able to do. The future is indeed very exciting.

Having played around with text generation, let us see if we can use it somehow to create a chatbot.

7.2.3 *Application to chatbots*

It seems intuitively that one should be able to adopt GPT without major modification to this application. Luckily for us, the folks at Microsoft already did this via the model DialoGPT, which was also recently included in the transformers library. Its architecture is the same as GPT's, with the addition of special tokens to indicate the end of a participant's turn in a conversation. After seeing such a token, we can add the new contribution of the participant to the priming context text and iteratively repeat the process via direct application of GPT to generate a response from our chatbot. Naturally, the pretrained GPT model was fine-tuned on conversational text to make sure the response would be appropriate. The authors used Reddit threads for the fine-tuning.

Let's go ahead and build a chatbot! We will not use pipelines in this case, because this model isn't yet exposed through that API at the time of writing. This allows us to juxtapose the different methods of calling these models for inference, which is a useful exercise for you to go through.

The first thing to do is load the pretrained model and tokenizer via the following commands:

```
from transformers import GPT2LMHeadModel, GPT2Tokenizer
import torch
```

Note that the DialoGPT model uses the GPT-2 class.

```
tokenizer = GPT2Tokenizer.from_pretrained("microsoft/DialoGPT-medium")
model = GPT2LMHeadModel.from_pretrained("microsoft/DialoGPT-medium")
```

We use Torch here, rather than TensorFlow, because that is the default platform choice in transformers documentation.

A few things are worth highlighting at this stage. First, note that we are using the GPT-2 model classes, which is consistent with our earlier discussion that described DialoGPT as a direct application of that architecture. Additionally, note that we could have used the classes `AutoModelWithLMHead` and `AutoTokenizer` interchangeably with these GPT-specific model classes. These utility classes detect the best classes to load the model that is specified by their input strings—in this case, they would detect that the best classes to use were `GPT2LMHeadModel` and `GPT2Tokenizer`. You are likely to run across these utility classes as you peruse the transformers library documentation, and it is good to be aware of their existence because they can make your code more general. Finally, note that the "LMHead" version of the GPT is used here. This means that the output from the vanilla GPT is passed through one linear layer and one normalization layer, followed by a transformation into a vector of probabilities of a dimension equal to the size of the vocabulary. The maximum value corresponds to the next most likely token if the model is correctly trained.

The code for conversing with our loaded, pretrained DialoGPT model is shown in listing 7.1. We first specify a maximum number of responses of five. We then encode the conversational contribution of the user at each turn, append the contribution to the chat history, and feed that to the loaded pretrained DialoGPT model for generating the next response.

> **Listing 7.1   Conversing with the pretrained DialoGPT model for up to five chatbot responses**

Chats for five lines ▷
Adds new input to the chat history ▷
Displays the response ▷

Encodes new user input, adds an end-of-sentence token, and returns Tensor ◁

Generates a response of up to max_length tokens with chat history as context

```
conversation_length = 5
for step in range(conversation_length):
    new_user_inputs_ids = tokenizer.encode(input("User: ") +
    tokenizer.eos_token, return_tensors='pt')
    bot_input_ids = torch.cat([chat_history_ids, new_user_inputs_ids], dim=1)
        if step > 0 else new_user_inputs_ids
    chat_history_ids = model.generate(bot_input_ids, max_length=1000,
        pad_token_id=tokenizer.eos_token_id)
    print("DialoGPT: {}".format(tokenizer.decode(chat_history_ids[:,
    bot_input_ids.shape[-1]:][0], skip_special_tokens=True)))
```

One could easily play with this bot all day! We had a lot of fun asking it various questions and prompting it in various ways. We include one such exchange here for your amusement:

```
User: Hi there.
DialogGPT: Hi there.
User: How are you today?
DialogGPT: I'm good, how are you?
User: Good! How much money do you have?
DialogGPT: I have about 100k.
User: What will you spend it on?
DialogGPT: I'm not sure, I'm not sure what I want to spend it on.
User: Make a decision, life is short.
DialogGPT: I'm going to go with a lot of things.
```

It's quite plausible that the entity at the other end of this short conversation is a human, isn't it? Does that mean it passes the Turing test? Not quite, as the following exchange illustrates:

```
User: Hi robot.
DialogGPT: Hello, human.
User: Huh?
DialogGPT: I'm a bot.
User: OK, what is your name?
DialogGPT: Robot. I'm a robot.
User: All right then.
DialogGPT: Robot. I'm a robot.
User: Say something else.
DialogGPT: Robot. I'm a robot.
```

As you increase the number of allowable conversational turns, you will find the bot getting stuck in repeated responses that are off-topic. This is analogous to the GPT open-ended text generation becoming more nonsensical as the length of generated text increases. One simple way to improve this is to keep a fixed local context size, where the model is prompted with conversation history only within that context. Of course, this means the conversation will not always take the context of the entire conversation into account—a trade-off that has to be explored experimentally for any given application.

It is exciting to ponder how well GPT-3 will do on some of these problems, isn't it? In the final chapter of this book, we will briefly discuss GPT-3 in more detail and introduce a recent smaller but worthy open source alternative to it: GPT-Neo from EleutherAI. It is already available in the transformers library and can be used directly by setting the `model` string to one of the model names provided by EleutherAI.[13] We also include a companion notebook showing it in action for the exercise we performed in this chapter. Upon inspection, you should find its performance better but naturally at a significantly higher cost (the weights of the largest model are more than 10 GB in size!).

We take a look at arguably the most important member of the transformer family—BERT—in the next chapter.

Summary

- The transformer architecture uses self-attention to build bidirectional context for understanding text. This has enabled it to become a dominant language model in NLP recently.
- The transformer allows tokens in a sequence to be processed independently of each other. This achieves greater parallelizability than bi-LSTMs, which process tokens in order.

---

[13] https://huggingface.co/EleutherAI

- The transformer is a good choice for translation applications.
- The Generative Pretrained Transformer uses the causal modeling objective during training. This makes it the model of choice for text generation, such as chatbot applications.

Deep transfer learning for NLP with BERT and multilingual BERT

This chapter covers

- Using pretrained Bidirectional Encoder Representations from Transformers (BERT) architecture to perform some interesting tasks
- Using the BERT architecture for cross-lingual transfer learning

In this chapter and the previous chapter, our goal is to cover some representative deep transfer learning modeling architectures for natural language processing (NLP) that rely on a recently popularized neural architecture—*the transformer*[1]—for key functions. This is arguably the most important architecture for NLP today. Specifically, our goal has to look at modeling frameworks such as the generative pretrained transformer (GPT),[2] Bidirectional Encoder Representations from Transformers (BERT),[3] and multilingual BERT (mBERT).[4] These methods employ neural networks

[1] A. Vaswani et al., "Attention Is All You Need," NeurIPS (2017).

[2] A. Radford et al., "Improving Language Understanding by Generative Pre-Training," *arXiv* (2018).

[3] M. E. Peters et al., "BERT: Pre-Training of Deep Bidirectional Transformers for Language Understanding," Proc. of NAACL-HLT (2019): 4171–86.

[4] https://github.com/google-research/bert/blob/master/multilingual.md

with even more parameters than the deep convolutional and recurrent neural network models that we looked at previously. Despite their larger size, they have exploded in popularity because they scale comparatively more effectively on parallel computing architecture. This enables even larger and more sophisticated models to be developed in practice. To make the content more digestible, we split the coverage of these models into two chapters/parts: we covered the transformer and GPT neural network architectures in the previous chapter, and in this next chapter, we focus on BERT and mBERT.

As a reminder, BERT is a transformer-based model that we encountered briefly in chapters 3 and 7. It was trained with the *masked modeling objective* to fill in the blanks. Additionally, it was trained with the *next sentence prediction* task, to determine whether a given sentence is a plausible following sentence after a target sentence. mBERT, which stands for "multilingual BERT," is effectively BERT pretrained on over 100 languages simultaneously. Naturally, this model is particularly well-suited for cross-lingual transfer learning. We will show how the multilingual pretrained weights checkpoint can facilitate creating BERT embeddings for languages that were not even originally included in the multilingual training corpus. Both BERT and mBERT were created at Google.

The first section of this chapter dives deeper into BERT, and we apply it to the important question-answering application as a representative example in a standalone section. The chapter concludes with an experiment showing the transfer of pretrained knowledge from mBERT pretrained weights to a BERT embedding for a new language. This new language was not initially included in the multilingual corpus used to generate the pretrained mBERT weights. We use the Ghanaian language Twi as the illustrative language in this case.

Let's proceed to analyzing BERT further in the next section.

8.1   *Bidirectional Encoder Representations from Transformers (BERT)*

In this section we present arguably the most popular and influential transformer-based neural network architecture for NLP transfer learning—the Bidirectional Encoder Representations from Transformers (BERT) model—which, as we previously mentioned, was also named after a popular *Sesame Street* character as a nod to the trend started by ELMo. Recall that ELMo does essentially what the transformer does but with recurrent neural networks. We encountered both of these models first in chapter 1 during our overview of NLP transfer learning history. We also used them for a pair of classification problems, using TensorFlow Hub and Keras, in chapter 3. If you do not recall these exercises, it may be beneficial to review them before you continue with this section. Coupled with the previous chapter, these previews of the model have brought you to a good place to understand in more detail how the model functions, which is our goal in this section.

BERT is an early pretrained language model that was developed after ELMo and GPT but which outperformed both on most tasks in the General Language-Understanding

Evaluation (GLUE) dataset because it is *bidirectionally trained*. We discussed in chapter 6 how ELMo combined left-to-right and right-to-left LSTMs to achieve bidirectional context. In the previous chapter, we also discussed how the masked self-attention of the GPT model, by virtue of its stacking of the transformer decoders, makes it better suited for causal text generation. Unlike these models, BERT achieves bidirectional context for every input token *at the same time* by stacking transformer encoders rather than decoders. Recall from our discussion of self-attention in every BERT layer in section 7.2 that the computation for every token considers every other token in both directions. Whereas ELMo does achieve bidirectionality by putting together the two directions, GPT is a causal unidirectional model. Simultaneous bidirectionality in every layer of BERT appears to give it a deeper sense of language context.

BERT was trained with the masked language modeling (MLM) fill-in-the-blanks type of prediction objective. Tokens in the training text are randomly masked, and the model is tasked with predicting the masked tokens. For illustration, consider again a slightly modified version of our example sentence, "He didn't want to talk about cells on the cell phone, a subject he considered very boring." To use MLM, we may transform it into "He didn't want to talk about cells on the cell phone, a [MASK] he considered very boring." Here [MASK] is a special token indicating which words have been dropped. We then ask the model to predict the dropped word based on all the text it has observed during training up to that point. A trained model might predict that the masked word is "conversation" 40% of the time, "subject" 35% percent of the time, and "topic" the remaining 25% of the time. Repeating this for billions of English examples during training builds up the model's knowledge of the English language.

Additionally, a next-sentence prediction (NSP) objective was used to train BERT. Here, some sentences in the training text are replaced with random sentences, and the model is asked to predict whether a sentence B following a sentence A is a plausible follow-up. For illustration, let's split our example sentence into two sentences: "He didn't want to talk about cells on the cell phone. He considered the subject very boring." We then might drop the second sentence and replace it with the somewhat random sentence, "Soccer is a fun sport." A properly trained model would need to be able to detect the former as a potential plausible completion and the latter as implausible. We address both MLM and NSP objectives in this section via concrete coding exercise examples to aid your understanding of these concepts.

In the next subsection, we briefly describe the key aspects of the BERT architecture. We follow that with an application of the pipelines API concept in the transformers library to the task of question answering with a pretrained BERT model. We follow that up by example executions of the fill-in-the-blanks MLM task and the NSP task. For the NSP task, we use the transformers API directly to build your familiarity with it. Like in the previous chapter, we do not explicitly refine the pretrained BERT model on more-specific target data here. However, we do so in the last section of the chapter, where we will fine-tune a multilingual BERT model on monolingual Twi data.

8.1.1   Model architecture

You may recall from section 7.1.1, where we visualized BERT self-attention, that BERT is essentially a stacked set of encoders of the original encoder-decoder transformer architecture in figure 7.1. The BERT model architecture is shown in figure 8.1.

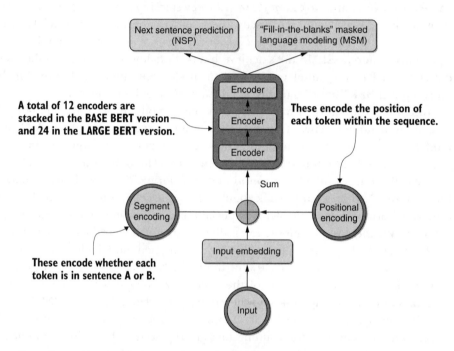

Figure 8.1   A high-level representation of the BERT architecture, showing stacked encoders, input embeddings, and positional encodings. The output from the top is used for both next-sentence prediction and fill-in-blanks masked language modeling objectives during training.

As we discussed in the introduction, and as shown in the figure, during training we use the next-sentence prediction (NSP) and masked language modeling (MSM) objectives. BERT was originally presented in two flavors, BASE and LARGE. As shown in figure 8.1, BASE stacks 12 encoders whereas LARGE stacks 24 encoders. As before—in both the GPT and the original transformer—the input is converted into vectors via an input embedding, and a positional encoding is added to them to give a sense of the position of every token in the input sequence. To account for the next-sentence-prediction task, for which the input is a pair of sentences A and B, an extra segment encoding step is added. The segment embeddings indicate which sentence a given token belongs to and are added to the input and positional encodings to yield the output that is fed to the encoder stack. This entire input transformation is visualized in figure 8.2 for our example sentence pair: "He didn't want to talk about cells on the cell phone. He considered the subject very boring."

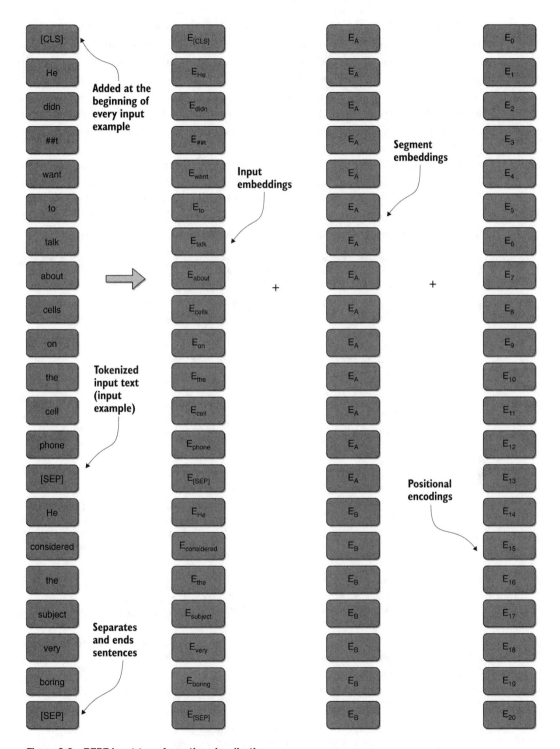

Figure 8.2   BERT input transformation visualization

A brief note about the [CLS] and [SEP] special tokens is worth bringing up at this point. Recall that the [SEP] token separates sentences and ends them, as discussed in previous sections. The [CLS] special token, on the other hand, is added to the beginning of every *input example*. Input example is the terminology used within the BERT framework to refer to the tokenized input text, as illustrated in figure 8.2. The final hidden state of the [CLS] token is used as the aggregate sequence representation for classification tasks, such as entailment or sentiment analysis. [CLS] stands for "classification."

Before proceeding to the concrete examples using some of these concepts in the following subsections, recall that when we first encountered the BERT model in chapter 3, we converted input first into input examples and then into a special triplet form. These were *input IDs*, *input masks*, and *segment IDs*. We replicate listing 3.8 here to help you remember, because at the time, these terms had not been yet introduced.

> **Listing 3.8** **(Duplicated from ch. 3) Converting data to form expected by BERT, training**

```
def build_model(max_seq_length):                    ← Function for building the model
    in_id = tf.keras.layers.Input(shape=(max_seq_length,), name="input_ids")
    in_mask = tf.keras.layers.Input(shape=(max_seq_length,),
     name="input_masks")
    in_segment = tf.keras.layers.Input(shape=(max_seq_length,),
     name="segment_ids")
    bert_inputs = [in_id, in_mask, in_segment]

    bert_output = BertLayer(n_fine_tune_layers=0)(bert_inputs)    ←
    dense = tf.keras.layers.Dense(256, activation="relu")(bert_output)
    pred = tf.keras.layers.Dense(1, activation="sigmoid")(dense)

    model = tf.keras.models.Model(inputs=bert_inputs, outputs=pred)
    model.compile(loss="binary_crossentropy", optimizer="adam",
     metrics=["accuracy"])
    model.summary()                       We do not retrain any BERT layers but
                                          rather use the pretrained model as an
                                          embedding and retrain some new
    return model                          layers on top of it.


def initialize_vars(sess):                      ←  Vanilla
    sess.run(tf.local_variables_initializer())     TensorFlow
    sess.run(tf.global_variables_initializer())    initialization calls
    sess.run(tf.tables_initializer())
    K.set_session(sess)
                                          Creates a compatible tokenizer
Converts data to InputExample format using    using the function in the BERT
the function in the BERT source repository     source repository

    bert_path = "https://tfhub.dev/google/bert_uncased_L-12_H-768_A-12/1"
    tokenizer = create_tokenizer_from_hub_module(bert_path)    ←

    train_examples = convert_text_to_examples(train_x, train_y)
    test_examples = convert_text_to_examples(test_x, test_y)
```

```
# Convert to features
(train_input_ids,train_input_masks,train_segment_ids,train_labels) =
    convert_examples_to_features(tokenizer, train_examples,
    max_seq_length=maxtokens)
(test_input_ids,test_input_masks,test_segment_ids,test_labels) =
    convert_examples_to_features(tokenizer, test_examples,
    max_seq_length=maxtokens)

model = build_model(maxtokens)

initialize_vars(sess)

history = model.fit([train_input_ids, train_input_masks, train_segment_ids],
train_labels,validation_data=([test_input_ids, test_input_masks,
test_segment_ids],test_labels), epochs=5, batch_size=32)
```

Builds the model

Converts the InputExample format into triplet final BERT input format, using the function in the BERT source repository

Instantiates the variables

Trains the model

Input IDs, as discussed in the previous chapter, are simply integer IDs of the corresponding token in the vocabulary—for the WordPiece tokenization used by BERT, the vocabulary size is 30,000. Because the input to the transformer is of fixed length, which is defined by the hyperparameter `max_seq_length` in listing 3.8, shorter inputs need to be padded and longer inputs need to be truncated. Inputs masks are simply binary vectors of the same length, with 0s corresponding to pad tokens (`[PAD]`) and 1s corresponding to the actual input. Segment IDs are the same as described in figure 8.2. The positional encodings and input embeddings, on the other hand, are handled internally by the TensorFlow Hub model and were not exposed to the user. It may be beneficial for you to work through chapter 3 again to fully grasp this comparison.

Although TensorFlow and Keras remain a critical component of any NLP engineer's toolbox—with unmatched flexibility and efficiency—the *transformers* library has arguably made these models a lot more approachable and easier to use for many engineers and applications. In the following subsections, we apply BERT from this library instead to the critical applications of question answering, filling in the blanks, and next-sentence prediction.

8.1.2 *Application to question answering*

Question answering has captured the imaginations of computer scientists since the inception of the NLP field. It concerns having a computer automatically provide answers to questions posed by a human, given some specified context. Potential applications are limited only by the imagination. Prominent examples include medical diagnosis, fact checking, and chatbots for customer service. In fact, anytime you search on Google for something like "Who won the Super Bowl in 2010?" or "Who won the FIFA World Cup in 2006?" you are using question answering.

Let's define question answering a bit more carefully. More specifically, we will consider *extractive question answering*, defined as follows: given a context paragraph p and question q, the task of question answering is concerned with producing the start and end integer indices in p where the answer is located. If no plausible answer exists in p, the system needs to be able to indicate this as well. Jumping directly into trying a simple example, as we do next using a pretrained BERT model with the transformers pipelines API, will help you make this much more concrete.

We pick an article from the World Economic Forum[5] about the effectiveness of masks and other lockdown policies on the COVID-19 pandemic in the United States. We pick the article summary as the context paragraph. Note that if no article summary were available, we could quickly generate one using a summarization pipeline from the same library. The initialization of the question-answering pipeline and context is carried out by the following code. Note that we are using BERT LARGE in this case, which has been fine-tuned on the Stanford Question-Answering Dataset (SQuAD),[6] the most extensive question-answering dataset to date. Note also that this is the default model transformers uses for this task, and we did not need to specify it explicitly. However, we do so for transparency.

```
from transformers import pipeline
```

> These models would have been loaded by default, but we make it explicit for transparency. It is important to use a model that has been fine-tuned on SQuAD; otherwise, results will be poor.

```
qNa= pipeline('question-answering', model= 'bert-large-cased-whole-word-
masking-finetuned-squad', tokenizer='bert-large-cased-whole-word-masking-
finetuned-squad')
```

```
paragraph = 'A new study estimates that if the US had universally mandated
masks on 1 April, there could have been nearly 40% fewer deaths by the start
of June. Containment policies had a large impact on the number of COVID-19
cases and deaths, directly by reducing transmission rates and indirectly by
constraining people's behaviour. They account for roughly half the observed
change in the growth rates of cases and deaths.'
```

Having initialized the pipeline, let's first see if we can automatically extract the essence of the article by asking what it is about. We do that with the following code:

```
ans = qNa({'question': 'What is this article about?','context':
    f'{paragraph}'})
print(ans)
```

This produces the following output, which we can probably agree is a plausible response:

```
{'score': 0.47023460869354494, 'start': 148, 'end': 168, 'answer':
    'Containment policies'}
```

Note that the relatively low score of 0.47 is indicative that the answer is missing some context. Something like "Effect of containment policies on COVID-19" is probably a better response, but because we are doing extractive question answering and this sen-

---

[5] https://www.weforum.org/agenda/2020/07/mask-mandates-and-other-lockdown-policies-reduced-the-spread-of-covid-19-in-the-us.

[6] P. Rajpurkar et al., "SQuAD: 100,000+ Questions for Machine Comprehension of Text," *arXiv* (2016).

tence is not in the context paragraph, this is the best the model can do. The low score can help flag this response for double-checking and/or improvement by a human.

Why not ask some more questions? Let us see if the model knows what country is described in the article, using the following code:

```
ans = qNa({'question': 'Which country is this article about?',
           'context': f'{paragraph}'})
print(ans)
```

This produces the following output, which is exactly right, as indicated by the higher-than-before score of approximately 0.8:

```
{'score': 0.795254447990601, 'start': 34, 'end': 36, 'answer': 'US'}
```

How about the disease being discussed?

```
ans = qNa({'question': 'Which disease is discussed in this article?',
           'context': f'{paragraph}'})
print(ans)
```

The output is spot-on, and the confidence is even higher than before at 0.98, as shown here:

```
{'score': 0.9761025334558902, 'start': 205, 'end': 213, 'answer': 'COVID-19'}
```

How about the time period?

```
ans = qNa({'question': 'What time period is discussed in the article?',
           'context': f'{paragraph}'})
print(ans)
```

The low score of 0.22 associated with the output is indicative of the poor quality of the result, because a time range of April to June is discussed in the article but never in a contiguous chunk of text that can be extracted for a high-quality answer, as shown next:

```
{'score': 0.21781831588181433, 'start': 71, 'end': 79, 'answer': '1 April,'}
```

However, the ability to pick out just one end point of the range is arguably already a useful outcome. The low score here can alert a human to double-check this result. In an automated system, the goal is for such lower-quality answers to be the minority, requiring little human intervention overall.

Having introduced question answering, in the next subsection we address the BERT training tasks of filling in the blanks and next-sentence prediction.

8.1.3   *Application to fill in the blanks and next-sentence prediction tasks*

We use the article from the previous subsection for the exercises in this one. Let's immediately proceed to defining a pipeline for filling in the blanks using the following code:

```
from transformers import pipeline

fill_mask = pipeline("fill-mask",model="bert-base-cased",tokenizer="bert-
    base-cased")
```

Note that we are using the BERT BASE model here. These tasks are fundamental to the training of any BERT model, so this is a reasonable choice, and no special fine-tuned models are needed. Having initialized the appropriate pipeline, we can now apply it to the first sentence of the article in the previous subsection. We drop the word "cases" by replacing it with the appropriate masking token, [MASK], and ask the model to predict the dropped word, using the following code:

```
fill_mask("A new study estimates that if the US had universally mandated
masks on 1 April, there could have been nearly 40% fewer [MASK] by the start
of June")
```

The output shows with the top one being "deaths" and being an arguably plausible completion. Even the remaining suggestions could work in different contexts!

```
[{'sequence': '[CLS] A new study estimates that if the US had universally
    mandated masks on 1 April, there could have been nearly 40% fewer deaths
    by the start of June [SEP]',
  'score': 0.19625532627105713,
  'token': 6209},
 {'sequence': '[CLS] A new study estimates that if the US had universally
    mandated masks on 1 April, there could have been nearly 40% fewer
    executions by the start of June [SEP]',
  'score': 0.11479416489601135,
  'token': 26107},
 {'sequence': '[CLS] A new study estimates that if the US had universally
    mandated masks on 1 April, there could have been nearly 40% fewer
    victims by the start of June [SEP]',
  'score': 0.0846652239561081,
  'token': 5256},
 {'sequence': '[CLS] A new study estimates that if the US had universally
    mandated masks on 1 April, there could have been nearly 40% fewer masks
    by the start of June [SEP]',
  'score': 0.0419488325715065,
  'token': 17944},
 {'sequence': '[CLS] A new study estimates that if the US had universally
    mandated masks on 1 April, there could have been nearly 40% fewer
    arrests by the start of June [SEP]',
  'score': 0.02742016687989235,
  'token': 19189}]
```

We encourage you to play around by dropping various words from various sentences to convince yourself that this almost always works quite well. Our companion notebook does this for several more sentences, but we do not print those results here in the interest of brevity.

Let's then proceed to the next-sentence prediction (NSP) task. At the time of writing, this task is not included in the pipelines API. We will thus use the transformers API directly, which will also give you more experience with it. The first thing we will need to do is make sure that a version of transformers greater than 3.0.0 is installed, because this task was included only in the library at that stage. We do this using the following code; Kaggle comes installed with an earlier version by default, at the time of writing:

```
!pip install transformers==3.0.1 # upgrade transformers for NSP
```

With the version upgraded, we can load an NSP-specific BERT using the following code:

```
from transformers import BertTokenizer, BertForNextSentencePrediction     ◁──┐   NSP-specific BERT
import torch
from torch.nn.functional import softmax     ◁──┤   Computes the final probabilities
                                                 from raw outputs

tokenizer = BertTokenizer.from_pretrained('bert-base-cased')
model = BertForNextSentencePrediction.from_pretrained('bert-base-cased')
model.eval()     ◁──┐   PyTorch models are trainable by default. For cheaper inference and
                        execution repeatability, set to "eval" mode as shown here. Set back to
                        "train" mode via model.train(). Not applicable to TensorFlow models!
```

First, as a sanity check, we determine whether the first and second sentences are plausible completions as far as the model is concerned. We do that using the following code:

```
prompt = "A new study estimates that if the US had universally mandated masks
    on 1 April, there could have been nearly 40% fewer deaths by the start
    of June."
next_sentence = "Containment policies had a large impact on the number of
    COVID-19 cases and deaths, directly by reducing transmission rates and
    indirectly by constraining people's behavior."
encoding = tokenizer.encode(prompt, next_sentence, return_tensors='pt')
logits = model(encoding)[0]     ◁────────────┐   The output is a tuple; the
probs = softmax(logits)     ◁────────────┐        first item describes the
print("Probabilities: [not plausible, plausible]")   relationship between the
print(probs)          Computes the probability      two sentences we are after.
                          from raw numbers
```

Note the term `logits` in the code. This is a term for the raw input to the softmax. Passing `logits` through the softmax yields probabilities. The output from the code confirms that the correct relationship was found, as shown here:

```
Probabilities: [not plausible, plausible]
tensor([[0.1725, 0.8275]], grad_fn=<SoftmaxBackward>)
```

Now, let's replace the second sentence with a somewhat random "Cats are independent." This produces the following outcome:

```
Probabilities: [not plausible, plausible]
tensor([0.7666, 0.2334], grad_fn=<SoftmaxBackward>)
```

It appears that things work as expected!

You should now have a very good sense of which tasks BERT is solving during training. Note that so far in this chapter we have not fine-tuned BERT on any new domain or task-specific data. This was done on purpose to help you understand the model architecture without any distractions. In the following section, we demonstrate how fine-tuning can be carried out, by working on a cross-lingual transfer learning experiment. Transfer learning for all the other tasks we have already presented can be carried out analogously, and by completing the exercise in the next section, you will be in a good position to do so on your own.

8.2   *Cross-lingual learning with multilingual BERT (mBERT)*

In this section, we carry out the second overall, and the first major, cross-lingual experiment of the book. More specifically, we are working on a transfer learning experiment that involves transferring knowledge from a multilingual BERT model to a language it was not originally trained to include. As before, the language we are using for our experiments will be Twi, a language considered "low-resource" due to a relative lack of availability of quality training data for a variety of tasks.

Multilingual BERT (mBERT) is essentially BERT, as described in the previous section, applied to a multilingual corpus of about 100 concatenated language Wikipedias.[7] The language set was initially the top 100 largest Wikipedias and has been expanded to the top 104 languages. The language set does not include Twi but does include a handful of African languages such as Swahili and Yoruba. Because the sizes of the various language corpora differ widely, an "exponential smoothing" procedure is applied to undersample high-resource languages such as English and oversample low-resource languages such as Yoruba. As before, WordPiece tokenization is used. For our purposes, it suffices to remind you that this tokenization procedure is subword, as we saw in the previous sections. The only exceptions are Chinese, Japanese kanji, and Korean hanja, which are converted into effective character-tokenization by surrounding every character with whitespace. Moreover, the vocabulary is reduced by eliminating accents—a trade-off choice between accuracy and a more efficient model made by the mBERT authors.

We can intuitively believe that a BERT model trained on over 100 languages contains knowledge that could transfer to a language that was not originally included in the training set. Simply put, such a model is likely to learn common features of the languages that are common across all of them. One simple example of such a common

---

[7] https://github.com/google-research/bert/blob/master/multilingual.md

feature is the concept of words and verb-noun relationships. If we frame the proposed experiment as a multitask learning problem, as we discussed in chapter 4, we expect improved generalizability to new previously unseen scenarios. In this section, we will essentially prove that this is the case. We first transfer from mBERT to monolingual Twi data using the pretrained tokenizer. We then repeat the experiment by training the same mBERT/BERT architecture from scratch and training a suitable tokenizer as well. Comparing these two experiments will allow us to qualitatively evaluate the effectiveness of the multilingual transfer. We use a Twi subset of the JW300 dataset[8] for our purposes.

The exercise in this section has implications reaching beyond multilingual transfer for your skill set. This exercise will teach you how to train your own tokenizer and transformer-based model from scratch. It will also demonstrate how to transfer from one checkpoint to new domain/language data for such a model. The previous sections and a bit of adventure/imagination will arm you with transformer-based transfer learning superpowers, be it for domain adaptation, cross-lingual transfer, or multitask learning.

In the next subsection, we briefly overview the JW300 dataset, followed by subsections performing cross-lingual transfer and then training from scratch.

8.2.1 *Brief JW300 dataset overview*

The JW300 dataset is a wide-coverage parallel corpus for low-resource languages. As previously mentioned, it is an arguably biased sample, being composed of religious text translated by the Jehovah's Witnesses. However, for a lot of low-resource language research, it serves as a starting point and is often the only open source of parallel data available. It is important to remember the bias, though, and couple any training on this corpus with a second stage during which the model from the first stage can be transferred to a less biased and more representative sample of the language and/or task at hand.

Although it is inherently a parallel corpus, we need only the monolingual corpus of Twi data for our experiments. The Python package opustools-pkg can be used to obtain a parallel corpus for a given language pair. To make things easier for you, we already did this for the English-Twi language pair and hosted it on Kaggle.[9] To repeat our experiment for some other low-resource language, you will need to tinker a bit with the opustools-pkg and obtain an equivalent corpus (please share with the community if you do). We use only the Twi part of the parallel corpus for our experiments and ignore the English part.

Let's proceed to transferring mBERT to the monolingual low-resource language corpus.

---

[8] http://opus.nlpl.eu/JW300.php
[9] https://www.kaggle.com/azunre/jw300entw

8.2.2 Transfer mBERT to monolingual Twi data with the pretrained tokenizer

The first thing to do is to initialize a BERT tokenizer to the pretrained checkpoint from one of the mBERT models. We use the cased version this time, as shown by the following code:

```
from transformers import BertTokenizerFast          ◁──┘  This is just a faster version
                                                           of BertTokenizer, which you
tokenizer = BertTokenizerFast.from_pretrained("bert-base-multilingual-cased")  ◁──┐
                                                                  could use instead.
```

This is just a faster version of BertTokenizer, which you could use instead.

Uses the pretrained mBERT tokenizer

Having prepared the tokenizer, let's load the mBERT checkpoint into a BERT masked language model, and display the number of parameters as follows:

```
from transformers import BertForMaskedLM            ◁──┤  Uses masked
                                                        language modeling
model = BertForMaskedLM.from_pretrained("bert-base-multilingual-cased")  ◁──┐

print("Number of parameters in mBERT model:")
print(model.num_parameters())
```

Uses masked language modeling

Initializes to the mBERT checkpoint

The output indicates that the model has 178.6 million parameters.

Next, we build the dataset using the tokenizer from the monolingual Twi text, using the convenient LineByLineTextDataset method included with transformers as follows:

```
from transformers import LineByLineTextDataset

dataset = LineByLineTextDataset(
    tokenizer=tokenizer,
    file_path="../input/jw300entw/jw300.en-tw.tw",
    block_size=128)                                ◁──┘
```

Indicates how many lines to read at a time

As shown in the following code, we will next need to define a "data collator"—a helper method that creates a special object out of a batch of sample data lines (of length block_size). This special object is consummable by PyTorch for neural network training:

```
from transformers import DataCollatorForLanguageModeling

data_collator = DataCollatorForLanguageModeling(
    tokenizer=tokenizer,
    mlm=True, mlm_probability=0.15)                ◁──┘
```

Uses masked language modeling, and masks words with a probability of 0.15

Here we used masked language modeling, as described in the previous section. In our input data, 15% of words are randomly masked, and the model is asked to predict them during training.

Define standard training arguments, such as output directory and training batch size, as shown next:

```
from transformers import TrainingArguments

training_args = TrainingArguments(
    output_dir="twimbert",
    overwrite_output_dir=True,
    num_train_epochs=1,
    per_gpu_train_batch_size=16,
    save_total_limit=1,
)
```

Then use training arguments with the previously defined dataset and collator to define a "trainer" for one training epoch across the data as follows. Note that the data contains over 600,000 lines, so one pass across all of it is a significant amount of training!

```
trainer = Trainer(
    model=model,
    args=training_args,
    data_collator=data_collator,
    train_dataset=dataset,
    prediction_loss_only=True)
```

Train and time how long training takes, as shown here:

```
import time
start = time.time()
trainer.train()
end = time.time()
print("Number of seconds for training:")
print((end-start))
```

The model takes about three hours to complete the epoch at the hyperparameters shown and reaches a loss of about 0.77.

Save the model as follows:

```
trainer.save_model("twimbert")
```

Finally, we take the following sentence from the corpus—"Eyi de ɔhaw kɛse baa sukuu hɔ"—which translates to "This presented a big problem at school." We mask one word, sukuu (which means "school" in Twi), and then apply the pipelines API to predict the dropped word as follows:

```
from transformers import pipeline

fill_mask = pipeline(        ◁─┐  Defines the fill-in-
    "fill-mask",               │  the-blanks pipeline
    model="twimbert",
    tokenizer=tokenizer)
                                               ┐ Predicts
print(fill_mask("Eyi de ɔhaw kɛse baa [MASK] hɔ."))  ◁─┘ the masked
                                                 token
```

This yields the following output:

```
[{'sequence': '[CLS] Eyi de ɔhaw kɛse baa me hɔ. [SEP]', 'score':
0.13256989419460297, 'token': 10911}, {'sequence': '[CLS] Eyi de ɔhaw kɛse
baa Israel hɔ. [SEP]', 'score': 0.06816119700670242, 'token': 12991},
{'sequence': '[CLS] Eyi de ɔhaw kɛse baa ne hɔ. [SEP]', 'score':
0.06106790155172348, 'token': 10554}, {'sequence': '[CLS] Eyi de ɔhaw kɛse
baa Europa hɔ. [SEP]', 'score': 0.05116277188062668, 'token': 11313},
{'sequence': '[CLS] Eyi de ɔhaw kɛse baa Eden hɔ. [SEP]', 'score':
0.033920999616384506, 'token': 35409}]
```

You can immediately see the religious bias in the outcome. "Israel" and "Eden" are suggested as among the top five completions. That said, these are somewhat plausible completions—for one thing, they are nouns. Overall, the performance is arguably decent.

If you do not speak the language, do not worry. In the next section, we will train BERT from scratch and compare the loss value to the one we obtained here to confirm the efficacy of the transfer learning experiment we just performed. We hope you get to try the steps outlined here on other low-resource languages you are interested in.

8.2.3 mBERT and tokenizer trained from scratch on monolingual Twi data

To train BERT from scratch, we first need to train a tokenizer. We can initialize, train, and save our own tokenizer to disk using the code in the next listing.

> **Listing 8.1   Initialize, train, and save our own Twi tokenizer from scratch**

```
from tokenizers import BertWordPieceTokenizer

paths = ['../input/jw300entw/jw300.en-tw.tw']

tokenizer = BertWordPieceTokenizer()          ⟵  Initializes the
                                                  tokenizer

tokenizer.train(          ⟵  Customizes the
    paths,                   training, and
    vocab_size=10000,        carries it out
    min_frequency=2,
    show_progress=True,
    special_tokens=["[PAD]", "[UNK]", "[CLS]", "[SEP]", "[MASK]"],   ⟵
    limit_alphabet=1000,
    wordpieces_prefix="##")
                                                  Standard BERT
                                                  special tokens
!mkdir twibert          ⟵  Saves the
                           tokenizer to disk

tokenizer.save("twibert")
```

To load the tokenizer from what we just saved, we just need to execute the following:

> Uses the language-specific tokenizer we just
> trained with max_len=512, to be consistent
> with previous subsection

```
from transformers import BertTokenizerFast
tokenizer = BertTokenizerFast.from_pretrained("twibert", max_len=512)   ⟵
```

Note that we use a maximum sequence length of 512 to be consistent with the previous subsection—this is what the pretrained mBERT uses as well. Also note that saving the tokenizer creates the vocabulary file vocab.txt file in the specified folder.

From here we just need to initialize a fresh BERT model for masked language modeling as follows:

```
from transformers import BertForMaskedLM, BertConfig       Don't initialize to pretrained;
model = BertForMaskedLM(BertConfig())                      create a fresh one.
```

Otherwise, the steps are the same as the previous subsection, and we do not repeat the code here. Repeating the same steps yields a loss of about 2.8 in about 1.5 hours after one epoch, and 2.5 in about 3 hours after two epochs. This is clearly not as good a loss as the previous subsection value of 0.77 after one epoch, confirming the efficacy of the transfer learning in that case. Note that this experiment took a shorter time per epoch because the tokenizer we built is fully focused on Twi and so has a smaller vocabulary than the 104-language pretrained mBERT vocabulary.

Go forth and transform!

Summary

- The transformer architecture uses self-attention to build bidirectional context for understanding text. This has enabled it to become a dominant language model in NLP recently.
- The transformer allows tokens in a sequence to be processed independently of each other. This achieves greater parallelizability than bi-LSTMs, which process tokens in order.
- The transformer is a good choice for translation applications.
- BERT is a transformer-based architecture that is a good choice for other tasks, such as classification.
- BERT can be trained on multiple languages at once, producing the multilingual model mBERT. This model captures knowledge transferable even to languages not originally included in the training.

ULMFiT and
knowledge distillation
adaptation strategies

> ### This chapter covers
>
> - Implementing the strategies of *discriminative fine-tuning* and *gradual unfreezing*
> - Executing *knowledge distillation* between *teacher* and *student* BERT models

In this chapter and the following chapter, we will cover some adaptation strategies for the deep NLP transfer learning modeling architectures that we have covered so far. In other words, given a pretrained architecture such as ELMo, BERT, or GPT, how can we carry out transfer learning more efficiently? We can employ several measures of efficiency here. We choose to focus on *parameter efficiency*, where the goal is to yield a model with the fewest parameters possible while suffering minimal reduction in performance. The purpose of this is to make the model smaller and easier to store, which would make it easier to deploy on smartphone devices, for instance. Alternatively, smart adaptation strategies may be required just to get to an acceptable level of performance in some difficult transfer cases.

In chapter 6, we described the method ULMFiT,[1] which stands for Universal Language Model Fine-Tuning. This method introduced the concepts of *discriminative*

---

[1] http://nlp.fast.ai/ulmfit

fine-tuning and *gradual unfreezing.* As a brief reminder, gradual unfreezing progressively increases the number of sublayers of the network that are *unfrozen,* or fine-tuned. Discriminative fine-tuning, on the other hand, specifies a variable learning rate for each layer in the network, also leading to more effective transfer. We did not implement these methods in the code in chapter 6 because, as adaptation strategies, we felt that they would best fit in this chapter. In this chapter, we employ the *fast.ai* library, written by the ULMFiT authors, to demonstrate the concepts on a pretrained recurrent neural network (RNN)–based language model.

A few model-compression methods have been employed generally on large neural networks to decrease their size. Some prominent methods include weight pruning and quantizing. Here, we will focus on the adaptation strategy knows as *knowledge distillation,* due to its recent prominence in the NLP field. This process essentially attempts to mimic the output from the larger *teacher* model using the significantly smaller *student* model. In particular, we use an implementation of the method DistilBERT[2] in the transformers library to demonstrate that the size of a BERT can be more than halved by this approach.

Let's begin with ULMFiT in the next section.

9.1 Gradual unfreezing and discriminative fine-tuning

In this section, we will implement in code the ULMFiT method for adapting language models to new data domains and tasks. We first discussed this method conceptually at the end of chapter 6 because, historically, it was first introduced in the context of recurrent neural networks (RNNs). However, we delayed the actual coding exercise until now, to underscore that at its core, ULMFiT is an architecture-agnostic set of adaptation techniques. This means that they could also be applied to transformer-based models. We carry out the exercise in the context of an RNN-based language model, however, for consistency with the source material. We focus the coding exercise on the fake news detection example we looked at in chapter 6.

As a reminder, discriminative fine-tuning specifies a variable learning rate for each layer in the network. Additionally, the learning rates are not constant during learning. Instead they are *slanted triangular*—linearly increasing in the beginning up to a point and then linearly decaying. In other words, this involves increasing the learning rate rapidly until it reaches the maximum rate and then decreasing it at a slower pace. This concept was illustrated in figure 6.8, and we duplicate it here for your convenience.

Note that the point in the figure labeled as "maximum learning rate" will be something different in our case (not 0.01). The total number of iterations will also be different from the 10,000 cases shown in the figure. This schedule results in more effective transfer and a more generalizable model.

Gradual unfreezing, on the other hand, progressively increases the number of sublayers of the network that are *unfrozen,* which reduces overfitting and also results in a

---

[2] V. Sanh et al., "DistilBERT, a Distilled Version of BERT: Smaller, Faster, Cheaper and Lighter," EMC^2: 5th Edition Co-located with NeurIPS (2019).

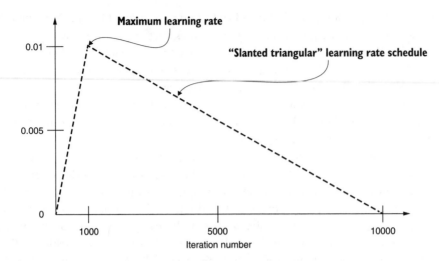

Figure 6.8 (Duplicated from Chapter 6) Suggested slanted triangular ULMFiT rate schedule for the case of 10,000 total iterations. The rate increases linearly for 10% of the total number of iterations (i.e., 1,000) up to a maximum of 0.01 and then decreases linearly afterward to 0.

more effective transfer and a more generalizable model. All these techniques were discussed in detail in the final section of chapter 6, and it may be beneficial to review that discussion briefly before tackling the rest of this section.

We will use the illustrative example from section 5.2—the fact-checking example—here as well. Recall that this dataset contains more than 40,000 articles divided into two categories: "fake" and "true." The true articles were collected from reuters.com, a reputable news website. The fake articles, on the other hand, were collected from a variety of sources flagged by PolitiFact—a fact-checking organization—as unreliable. In section 6.2, we trained a binary classifier on top of feature vectors derived from a pretrained ELMo model. This classifier predicts whether a given article is true (1) or fake (0). An accuracy of 98%+ was achieved with a dataset composed of 2,000 articles, 1,000 from each category. Here, we will see if we can do better with the ULMFiT method.

In this section, we split the method into two subsections. The first subsection addresses the first ULMFiT stage of fine-tuning a pretrained language model on the target task data. The slanted triangular learning rates come into play here, as well as the idea of discriminative fine-tuning. Some data preprocessing and model architecture discussions are naturally woven into this first subsection as well. The second subsection covers the second stage, involving fine-tuning the target task classifier—which sits on top of the fine-tuned language model—on the target task data. The effectiveness of the gradual unfreezing procedure is thereby demonstrated.

Please note that the code presented in this section is written in version 1 syntax of fast.ai. The reason for this choice is that version 2 of the library changed the handling of input data, providing internal functions to split it into train and validation sets, rather than allowing you to specify your own. For consistency with our work in the previous chapters, where we split the data ourselves, we stick to version 1 here. We also provide an equivalent fast.ai version 2 syntax code in a Kaggle notebook,[3] which you should also run and compare with the version 1 code presented here. Finally, note that version 1 documentation is hosted at https://fastai1.fast.ai/ whereas version 2 documentation is hosted at https://docs.fast.ai/.

9.1.1 *Pretrained language model fine-tuning*

Section 5.2 already described the initial data preprocessing steps that we need to carry out on the fact-checking example dataset. In particular, we shuffle the article text data and load it into the NumPy arrays `train_x` and `test_x`. We also construct the corresponding label NumPy arrays `train_y` and `test_y`, containing 1 whenever the corresponding article is true and 0 otherwise. Sticking with 1,000 samples and a test/validation ratio of 30%, as in section 5.2, yields train arrays—`train_x`, `train_y`—of length 1,400 and test arrays—`test_x`, `test_y`—of length 600.

The first thing we need to do is prepare data in the form that the fast.ai library expects. One such data format is a two-column Pandas DataFrame, with the first column containing labels and the second column containing the data. We can construct training and testing/validation DataFrames accordingly as follows:

```
train_df = pd.DataFrame(data=[train_y,train_x]).T
test_df = pd.DataFrame(data=[test_y,test_x]).T
```

These DataFrames should have 1,400 rows and 600 rows, respectively—one for each article in the corresponding data sample—and it is a good idea to check this with the usual `.shape` command before continuing, as shown here:

```
train_df.shape
test_df.shape
```

The expected outputs are `(1400, 2)` and `(600, 2)`, respectively.

Data in fast.ai is consumed by language models using the `TextLMDataBunch` class, instances of which can be constructed from the DataFrame format we just prepared using the following command:

```
data_lm = TextLMDataBunch.from_df(train_df = train_df, valid_df = test_df,
    path = "")
```

On the other hand, data in fast.ai is consumed by a task-specific classifier using the `TextClasDataBunch` class. We construct an instance of this class, in preparation for the next subsection, from our DataFrames using the following analogous command:

```
data_clas = TextClasDataBunch.from_df(path = "", train_df = train_df,
    valid_df = test_df, vocab=data_lm.train_ds.vocab)
```

---

[3] https://www.kaggle.com/azunre/tlfornlp-chapter9-ulmfit-adaptation-fast-aiv2

We are now ready to fine-tune our language model on the target data! To do this, we need to create an instance of the `language_model_learner` fast.ai class with the following command:

```
learn = language_model_learner(data_lm, AWD_LSTM, drop_mult=0.3)
```

Initializes a pretrained weight-dropped LSTM with a weight drop probability of 30%. This is pretrained on the WikiText-103 benchmark dataset.

Here, `AWD_LSTM` stands for *ASGD weight-dropped LSTM*.[4] This is just the usual LSTM architecture in which some weights have been randomly dropped, like what the usual dropout layer does with neural network activations, as opposed to weights. It is the most similar architecture choice to what was done in the original ULMFiT paper[5] in the fast.ai library. Also, if you check the execution log of the previous command, you should be able to confirm that it is also loading pretrained weights from a checkpoint trained on the WikiText-103 benchmark.[6] This dataset, officially called the "WikiText long-term dependency language modeling dataset," is a collection of Wikipedia articles judged to be "good" by humans. It is a nice, clean source of unsupervised data that has been used by a large number of NLP papers for benchmarking.

Now that we have loaded an instance of the model and some pretrained weights, we are going to try to determine the best or optimal learning rate for fine-tuning our language model. A nifty utility method in fast.ai called `lr_find` can do this for us automatically. It iterates through a number of learning rates and detects the point at which the loss function is dropping the fastest on the resulting loss versus learning rate curve. Equivalently, this is where the loss gradient is the smallest.[7] We can carry it out quickly using our language model learner `learn` as follows:

```
learn.lr_find()
learn.recorder.plot(suggestion=True)
```

Finds best/optimal learning rate

Plots it

The resulting loss versus learning rate curve, with the optimal rate highlighted, is shown in figure 9.1.

We can programmatically retrieve this learning rate and display it using the following commands:

```
rate = learn.recorder.min_grad_lr
print(rate)
```

Retrieves the best/optimal rate

Displays it

---

[4] S. Merity et al., "Regularizing and Optimizing LSTM Language Models," ICLR (2018).

[5] http://nlp.fast.ai/ulmfit

[6] https://www.salesforce.com/ca/products/einstein/ai-research/the-wikitext-dependency-language-modeling-dataset/

[7] L. Smith et al., "A Disciplined Approach to Neural Network Hyper-Parameters: Part 1—Learning Rate, Batch Size, Momentum, and Weight Decay," *arXiv* (2018).

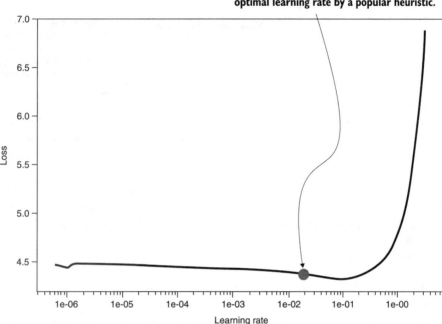

The loss is dropping the fastest at this point, and this is the point that is selected as the optimal learning rate by a popular heuristic.

Figure 9.1   **The result of the optimal learning rate–finding procedure from the fast.ai library for the language model fine-tuning step on the fake news detection example. Several learning rates are iterated through, and the optimal one is selected as the point where the loss is dropping fastest on the curve.**

In our execution of the code, the optimal learning rate returned was approximately 4.0e-2.

Having found the optimal rate, we can now fine-tune our pretrained weight-dropped LSTM model with a slanted triangular learning rate using the fit_one_cycle fast.ai command as shown next:

```
learn.fit_one_cycle(1, rate)
```

This command uses the slanted triangular learning rate under the hood. It takes the number of epochs and the desired maximum learning rate as inputs.

Executing the command yields an accuracy of 0.334 in about 26 seconds of fine-tuning on a single Kaggle GPU.

Having obtained that baseline value, we would like to find out whether discriminative fine-tuning can lead to an improvement. We do this by first unfreezing all layers with the unfreeze command and then using the slice method to specify the upper and lower bounds for the learning rate range. This command sets the maximum learning rate of the layer closest to the output to the upper bound and geometrically decreases—via division by a constant factor—each subsequent layer's maximum learning rate toward the lower bound. The exact code for doing this is shown next:

Makes sure all layers are unfrozen for fine-tuning

Varies the maximum learning rate geometrically between the optimal rate in the final layer and a value that is two orders of magnitude smaller

```
learn.unfreeze()
learn.fit_one_cycle(1, slice(rate/100,rate))
```

As can be seen from the code, we arbitrarily chose to vary the learning rate from the maximum optimal value down to a value that is two orders of magnitude smaller. The intuition behind this schedule is that the subsequent layers contain information that is more general and less task-specific, and thus it should learn less from this target-specific dataset than the layers closest to the output.

Executing the discriminative fine-tuning code presented yields an accuracy score of 0.353, a clear improvement over the 0.334 value we obtained without it. Save the fine-tuned language model for later use with the following command:

```
learn.save_encoder('fine-tuned_language_model')
```

Having tuned our pretrained language model via slanted triangular learning rates and discriminative fine-tuning, let's see how good a target task classifier—that is, a fake news detector—we can get. We fine-tune a classifier on top of the fine-tuned language model in the next subsection.

9.1.2 *Target task classifier fine-tuning*

Recall that in the previous subsection, we created an object for consumption of data by the target task classifier. We called this variable data_clas. As a next step for fine-tuning our target task classifier, we need to instantiate an instance of a classifier learner, with the method aptly named text_classifier_learner in fast.ai. This is done with the following code:

Instantiates an instance of the target task classifier learning. Uses the same settings as the language model we fine-tuned, so we can load without problems.

```
learn = text_classifier_learner(data_clas, AWD_LSTM, drop_mult=0.3)
learn.load_encoder('fine-tuned_language_model')
```

Loads our fine-tuned language model

As the next step, we again employ the utility fast.ai method lr_find to find the optimal learning rate, with the following code:

Finds the best rate

```
learn.lr_find()
learn.recorder.plot(suggestion=True)
```

Plots it

Executing the code yields the loss versus learning rate curve shown in figure 9.2.

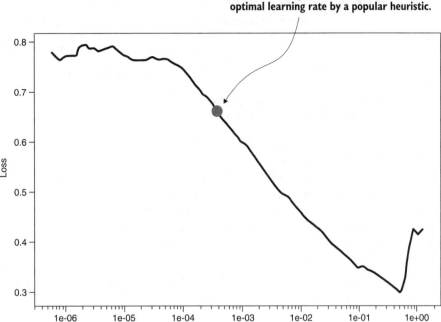

The loss is dropping the fastest at this point, and this is the point that is selected as the optimal learning rate by a popular heuristic.

Figure 9.2   The result of the optimal learning rate–finding procedure from the fast.ai library for the target task classifier fine-tuning step on the fake news detection example. Several learning rates are iterated through, and the optimal one is selected as the point where the loss is dropping fastest on the curve.

We see that the optimal rate is about 7e-4. We train the classifier learner for one epoch, using slanted triangular learning rates, via the following code:

```
rate = learn.recorder.min_grad_lr
learn.fit_one_cycle(1, rate)
```

Extracts the optimal maximum learning rate

Fine-tunes the target task classifier using the determined maximum learning rate in the slanted triangular learning rate schedule

Executing the code yields an accuracy of about 99.5%. This is already better than the result of 98%+ we obtained by training a classifier on top of the ELMo embedding in chapter 6 (section 6.2). Is there anything else we can do to improve it even further?

Luckily, we have one more trick up our sleeve: gradual unfreezing. As yet another reminder, this is when we unfreeze just one layer, fine-tune it, unfreeze an additional lower layer, fine-tune it, and repeat this process for a fixed number of steps. The ULM-FiT authors found that applying this method during the fine-tuning of the target task classifier stage significantly improves results. As a simple illustration, to execute this procedure up to a layer depth of 2, we would need the following bit of code:

We execute gradual unfreezing up to two unfrozen layers only.

Unfreezes progressively more layers, first one and then two, training for one epoch each time with slanted triangular learning rates

```
depth = 2
for i in range(1,depth+1):
    learn.freeze_to(-i)
    learn.fit_one_cycle(1, rate)
```

This command unfreezes the top i layers.

Slanted triangular learning rate execution for one epoch, as already introduced

Note that the command `learn.freeze_to(-i)` unfreezes the top i layers and is critical for the recipe. When we executed the code on our fake news detection example, we found the accuracy reached 99.8% in the first step, hitting the stunning score of 100% at the second step when the top two layers were unfrozen. These results speak for themselves and appear to suggest that the ULMFiT method is an extremely useful set of techniques to have in one's toolbox. Note that we could have continued unfreezing layers to greater depths—3, 4, and so on—if we found it necessary.

Fascinating stuff! It appears that being clever about how we adapt models to new scenarios can lead to significant benefits! In the next section, we will touch on another method for doing this—knowledge distillation.

9.2   *Knowledge distillation*

Knowledge distillation is a neural network compression method that seeks to teach a smaller student model the knowledge contained within a larger teacher model. This strategy, which has become popular recently in the NLP community, essentially attempts to mimic the output from the teacher by the student. This approach is also model-agnostic—the teacher and student could be transformer-based, RNN-based, or some other architecture, and can be completely different from each other.

Initial applications of this method in NLP were driven by questions about the representation power of bidirectional LSTMs (bi-LSTMs) compared to transformer-based architectures.[8] The authors wanted to know how much of BERT's information could be captured by a single bi-LSTM layer. Surprisingly, researchers found that in some cases, pretrained transformer-based language models could be reduced in parameter size by a factor of 100, with an inference time lower by a factor of 15, while not sacrificing in the standard performance metrics. This is a huge reduction in size and time that can make the difference between whether or not these methods can be practically deployed! The process of knowledge distillation is briefly summarized in figure 9.3.

As can be seen in the figure, traditionally, labels produced by the teacher are used to compute "soft" labels, which determine the distillation loss by comparison with the student output. This loss encourages the student model to track the teacher model

---

[8] R. Tang et al., "Distilling Task-Specific Knowledge from BERT into Simple Neural Networks," *arXiv* (2018).

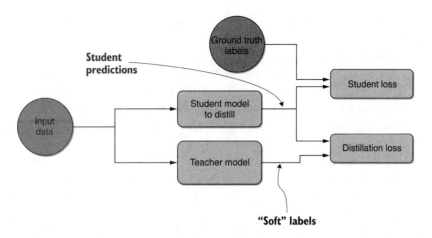

Figure 9.3 An illustration of the general process of knowledge distillation. "Soft" labels produced by the teacher model are used to encourage the student model to behave similarly via the distillation loss. At the same time, the student loss is trained to behave similarly to ground truth via the student loss.

output. Additionally, the student is simultaneously taught the "hard" ground truth labels via the student loss. We will show you how to use this idea quickly via an implementation in the transformers library by Hugging Face.

Several architectures have been proposed to reduce the size of pretrained NLP language models, including TinyBERT[9] and DistilBERT.[10] We choose to focus on DistilBERT due to its ready availability within the transformers library. DistilBERT was developed by Hugging Face, which is the same team that wrote the transformers library. As before, our coverage of this topic is not meant to be exhaustive but rather illustrative. Keeping up with further development and literature in a fast-moving field like this one remains important. It is our hope that the coverage presented here will set you up to do that.

The goal of the DistilBERT study was to generate a smaller version of the BERT model specifically. The student architecture was chosen to be the same as BERT— stacked transformer encoders as described in chapters 7 and 8. The number of the layers in the student was reduced by a factor of two, yielding a model of just six layers. This is where most of the size savings comes from. The authors found variations in internal hidden dimensions to have little impact on efficiency in this framework, and as such, those are all similar between the teacher and the student. An important part of the process is student initialization to an appropriate set of weights from which convergence will be reasonably quick. Because the dimensions of all the layers are similar between the teacher and the student, the authors could simply use the pretrained

---

[9] X. Jiao et al., "TinyBERT: Distilling BERT for Natural Language Understanding," *arXiv* (2020).

[10] V. Sanh et al., "DistilBERT, a Distilled Version of BERT: Smaller, Faster, Cheaper and Lighter," EMC^2: 5th Edition Co-located with NeurIPS (2019).

teacher weights in corresponding layers to initialize the student and found that to work well.

The authors did extensive experiments on benchmarks such as GLUE, which we will look at later in the next chapter, and SQuAD. They found that performance on the GLUE benchmark by the resulting DistilBERT model retained 97% of the performance of the BERT teacher with 40% of the number of parameters. It is also 60% faster, in terms of inference time on a CPU, and 71% faster on mobile devices such as the iPhone. As you can see, the improvement is significant.

Scripts for performing the actual distillation are available in the official transformers repository.[11] To train your own DistilBERT model, you create a file with one text sample per line and execute a sequence of commands provided on that page, which prepare the data and distill the model. Because the authors already made a variety of checkpoints available for direct loading—all of the checkpoints are listed on that page—and our focus here is on transfer learning, we do not repeat the training from scratch steps here. Instead, we work with a checkpoint analogous to the mBERT checkpoint we used in chapter 8 for our cross-lingual transfer learning experiment. This allows us to directly compare the performance and benefits of using the distilled architecture over the original mBERT, while also teaching you how to start using this architecture in your own projects. It also gives you another opportunity to work on fine-tuning a pretrained transformer-based model on a custom corpus—directly modifying the code with a different architecture, pretrained checkpoint, and custom dataset should work for your own use cases.

More specifically, we will be repeating the experiment we carried out in section 8.2.2, where we transferred the knowledge contained in mBERT—trained on over 100 languages simultaneously—to a monolingual Twi scenario by fine-tuning on a corpus from the JW300 dataset. We perform the variant of the experiment that uses the pretrained tokenizer included with the checkpoint, rather than training a new one from scratch, for simplicity.

9.2.1   Transfer DistilmBERT to monolingual Twi data with pretrained tokenizer

Our goal in this subsection is to generate a DistilBERT model for the Ghanaian language Twi from a model trained on more than 100 languages, not including Twi, simultaneously. The multilingual equivalent of BERT is called mBERT; therefore, the multilingual equivalent of DistilBERT is predictably called DistilmBERT. This DistilmBERT model is directly analogous to the mBERT model we experimented with in chapter 8. We found then that starting with this checkpoint was beneficial, even though Twi was not included in the original training. Here, we will essentially replicate the same sequence of steps, replacing every instance of mBERT with DistilmBERT. This allows us to compare the two directly and thereby get an intuition for the

---

[11] https://github.com/huggingface/transformers/blob/master/examples/research_projects/distillation

benefits of knowledge distillation, while also learning how to use DistilBERT in your own projects. As before, we fine-tune the model on the monolingual Twi subset of the JW300 datatset.[12]

We start by initializing a DistilBERT tokenizer to the pretrained checkpoint from the DistilmBERT model. We use the cased version this time, as shown by the following code:

This is just a faster version of DistilBertTokenizer, which you could use instead.

```
from transformers import DistilBertTokenizerFast
tokenizer = DistilBertTokenizerFast.from_pretrained("distilbert-base-
    multilingual-cased")
```

Uses the pretrained DistilmBERT tokenizer

Having prepared the tokenizer, load the DistilmBERT checkpoint into a DistilBERT masked language model, and display the number of parameters as follows:

```
from transformers import DistilBertForMaskedLM
```

Uses masked language modeling

```
model = DistilBertForMaskedLM.from_pretrained("distilbert-base-multilingual-
    cased")
```

Initializes to an mBERT checkpoint

```
print("Number of parameters in DistilmBERT model:")
print(model.num_parameters())
```

The output indicates that the model has 135.5 million parameters versus the 178.6 million parameters we found BERT has in chapter 8. Thus, our DistilBERT model is just 76% the size of the equivalent BERT model.

Next, build the dataset from the monolingual Twi text, using the convenient Line-ByLineTextDataset method included with transformers, shown next:

```
from transformers import LineByLineTextDataset

dataset = LineByLineTextDataset(
    tokenizer=tokenizer,
    file_path="../input/jw300entw/jw300.en-tw.tw",
    block_size=128)
```

The English to Twi JW300 dataset we introduced in section 8.2.1

How many lines to read at a time

Subsequently, define a "data collator"—a helper method that creates a special object out of a batch of sample data lines (of length block_size)—as shown in the next code snippet. This special object is consummable by PyTorch for neural network training:

```
from transformers import DataCollatorForLanguageModeling

data_collator = DataCollatorForLanguageModeling(
    tokenizer=tokenizer,
    mlm=True, mlm_probability=0.15)
```

Uses masked language modeling, and masks words with a probability of 0.15

---

[12] http://opus.nlpl.eu/JW300.php

Here, we used masked language modeling—15% of the words are randomly masked in our input data, and the model is asked to predict them during training.

Next, define standard training arguments, such as the output directory (which we select to be `twidistilmbert`) and training batch size, as follows:

```
from transformers import TrainingArguments

training_args = TrainingArguments(
    output_dir="twidistilmbert",
    overwrite_output_dir=True,
    num_train_epochs=1,
    per_gpu_train_batch_size=16,
    save_total_limit=1,
)
```

Then, use training arguments with the previously defined dataset and collator to define a "trainer" for one training epoch across the data, as shown here. Remember the Twi data contains over 600,000 lines, so one pass across all of it is a significant amount of training!

```
trainer = Trainer(
    model=model,
    args=training_args,
    data_collator=data_collator,
    train_dataset=dataset,
    prediction_loss_only=True)
```

Finally, train and time how long training takes as follows:

```
import time
start = time.time()
trainer.train()
end = time.time()
print("Number of seconds for training:")
print((end-start))
```

As always, be sure to save the model:

```
trainer.save_model("twidistilmbert")
```

We found that the model takes about 2 hours and 15 minutes to complete the epoch, versus the 3 hours it took for the equivalent teacher to complete the epoch in chapter 8. Thus, the student training time is just 75% of the teacher. Significant improvement!

Moreover, the loss reaches a value of about 0.81, whereas the mBERT equivalent reached a loss of about 0.77 in chapter 8. In absolute terms, the difference in performance can then be roughly quantified as approximately 5%—we see DistilBERT reach 95% of the performance of BERT. This is pretty close to the benchmark number of 97% reported by the DistilBERT authors in their paper.

As the last step, take the following sentence from the corpus: "Eyi de ɔhaw kɛse baa sukuu hɔ." Drop/mask one word, sukuu (which means "school" in Twi), and then apply the pipelines API to predict the dropped word as follows:

```
from transformers import pipeline

fill_mask = pipeline(
    "fill-mask",
    model="twidistilmbert",
    tokenizer=tokenizer)

print(fill_mask("Eyi de ɔhaw kɛse baa [MASK] hɔ."))
```

Defines the fill-in-the-blanks pipeline

Predicts the masked token

This yields the following output:

```
[{'sequence': '[CLS] Eyi de ɔhaw kɛse baa fie hɔ. [SEP]', 'score':
0.31311026215553284, 'token': 29959}, {'sequence': '[CLS] Eyi de ɔhaw kɛse
baa me hɔ. [SEP]', 'score': 0.09322386980056763, 'token': 10911},
{'sequence': '[CLS] Eyi de ɔhaw kɛse baa ne hɔ. [SEP]', 'score':
0.05879712104797363, 'token': 10554}, {'sequence': '[CLS] Eyi de ɔhaw kɛse
baa too hɔ. [SEP]', 'score': 0.052420321851968765, 'token': 16683},
{'sequence': '[CLS] Eyi de ɔhaw kɛse baa no hɔ. [SEP]', 'score':
0.04025224596261978, 'token': 10192}]
```

These are indeed plausible completions. What is interesting to note here is that the religious bias in the outcome that we saw in section 8.2.2 appears to have been alleviated in the model. Completions such as "Israel" and "Eden," which were suggested by the mBERT equivalent model in section 8.2.2, are no longer present. This can be explained, in retrospect, by the significant difference in the number of parameters between the two. DistilBERT is less likely to overfit due to this, whereas BERT is much more likely to do so.

And now you know how to use DistilBERT in your own projects! We again stress that the exercise you just carried out taught you how to fine-tune a pretrained transformerbased model on a custom corpus—simply modify the code with a different architecture, pretrained checkpoint, and custom dataset to apply it to your own use cases.

In the first section of the next chapter, we will get another opportunity to fine-tune a transformer-based model on a custom corpus, this time in English! We will discuss the adaptation ideas behind the architecture ALBERT—A Lite BERT—and fine-tune it on some reviews from the Multi-Domain Sentiment Dataset.[13] Recall that we played with this dataset in chapter 4. It is a dataset of reviews of 25 product categories on Amazon, of which we will focus on book reviews, as in chapter 4.

---

[13] https://www.cs.jhu.edu/~mdredze/datasets/sentiment/

Summary

- ULMFiT strategies of slanted triangular learning rates, discriminative fine-tuning, and gradual unfreezing can lead to noticeably more effective transfer.
- Executing knowledge distillation of a larger teacher BERT model yields a significantly smaller student BERT model with minimal sacrifice of performance.

ALBERT, adapters, and multitask adaptation strategies

This chapter covers

- Applying embedding factorization and parameter sharing across layers
- Fine-tuning a model from the BERT family on multiple tasks
- Splitting a transfer learning experiment into multiple steps
- Applying adapters to a model from the BERT family

In the previous chapter, we began our coverage of some adaptation strategies for the deep NLP transfer learning modeling architectures that we have covered so far. In other words, given a pretrained architecture such as ELMo, BERT, or GPT, how can transfer learning be carried out more efficiently? We covered two critical ideas behind the method ULMFiT, namely the concepts of *discriminative fine-tuning* and *gradual unfreezing*.

The first adaptation strategy we will touch on in this chapter revolves around two ideas aimed at creating transformer-based language models that scale more favorably with a bigger vocabulary and longer input length. The first idea essentially involves clever factorization, or splitting up a larger matrix of weights into two

177

smaller matrices, allowing you to increase the dimensions of one without affecting the dimensions of the other. The second idea involves sharing parameters across all layers. These two strategies are the bedrock of the method known as ALBERT, A Lite BERT.[1] We use the implementation in the transformers library to get some hands-on experience with the method.

In chapter 4, we introduced the idea of multitask learning, where a model is trained to perform a variety of tasks at once. The resulting model is usually more generalizable to new scenarios and can result in better transfer. Unsurprisingly, this idea reappears in the context of adaptation strategies for pretrained NLP language models. When faced with a transfer scenario where there is insufficient training data to fine-tune on a given task, why not fine-tune on multiple tasks? Discussing this idea provides a great opportunity to introduce the (GLUE) dataset:[2] a collection of data for several tasks representative of human language reasoning. These tasks include detecting similarity between sentences, similarity between questions, paraphrasing, sentiment analysis, and question answering. We show how to quickly leverage the transformers library for multitask fine-tuning using this dataset. This exercise also demonstrates how to similarly fine-tune a model from the BERT family on a custom dataset from one of these important classes of problems.

In chapter 4, where we also discussed domain adaptation, we found that the similarity of the source and target domains plays a crucial role in the effectiveness of transfer learning. Greater similarity implies an easier transfer learning process in general. When the source and target are too dissimilar, you may find it impossible to carry out the process in a single step. In those circumstances, the idea of *sequential adaptation* may be used to break the overall desired transfer into simpler, more manageable steps. A language-based tool that fails to transfer between West and East Africa, for instance, may transfer successfully first between West Africa and Central Africa, and then between Central Africa and East Africa. In this chapter, we sequentially adapt "fill-in-the-blanks" objective pretrained BERT to a low-resource sentence similarity-detection scenario, by first adapting to a data-rich question similarity scenario.

The final adaptation strategy we will explore is the use of so-called *adaptation modules* or *adapters*. These are newly introduced modules of only a few parameters between layers of a pretrained neural network. Fine-tuning this modified model for new tasks requires training only these few additional parameters. The weights of the original network are kept the same. Virtually no loss in performance, compared to fine-tuning the entire model, is often observed when adding just 3–4% additional parameters per task.[3] These adapters are also modular and easily shared between researchers.

---

[1] Z. Lan et al., "ALBERT: A Lite BERT for Self-Supervised Learning of Language Representations," ICLR (2020).

[2] A. Wang et al., "Glue: A Multi-Task Benchmark and Analysis Platform for Natural Language Understanding," ICLR (2019).

[3] N. Houlsby et al., "Parameter-Efficient Transfer Learning for NLP," ICML (2019).

10.1 Embedding factorization and cross-layer parameter sharing

The adaptation strategies we discuss in this section revolve around two ideas aimed at creating transformer-based language models that scale more favorably with a bigger vocabulary and longer maximum input length. The first idea essentially involves clever factorization of a larger matrix of weights into two smaller matrices, allowing one to increase in dimension without affecting the dimensions of the other one. The second idea involves sharing parameters across all layers. These two strategies are the bedrock of the method known as ALBERT.[4] We again use the implementation in the transformers library to get some hands-on experience with the method. This serves both to give you a sense of what sorts of improvements are attained, as well as to arm you with the ability to use it in your own projects. We will be using the Amazon book reviews in the Multi-Domain Sentiment Dataset[5] from chapter 4 as our custom corpus for this experiment. This will allow you to gain further experience fine-tuning a pre-trained transformer-based language model on a custom corpus, this time in English!

The first strategy, namely embedding factorization, is motivated by the observation that in BERT, the size of the input embedding is intrinsically linked to the dimension of its hidden layers. The tokenizer creates a one-hot encoded vector for each token—this vector is equal to 1 in the dimension corresponding to the token and 0 otherwise. The dimension of this one-hot encoded vector is equal to the size of the vocabulary, V. The input embedding can be thought of as a matrix of dimension V by E, multiplying the one-hot encoded vector and projecting it into a dimension of size E. In earlier models such as BERT, this was equal to the hidden layer dimension H, so that this projection happened directly into the hidden layers.

This means that when the size of the hidden layer increases, the dimension of the input embedding must increase as well, which can be very inefficient. On the other hand, the ALBERT authors observed that the role for the input embedding is to learn context-independent representations, whereas that of the hidden layers is to learn context-dependent representations—a harder problem. Motivated by this, they propose splitting the single-input embedding matrix into two matrices: one of dimension V by E and the other E by H, allowing H and E to be completely independent. Said differently, the one-hot encoded vectors can be first projected into an intermediate embedding of a smaller size and only then fed into the hidden layers. This allows the input embedding to have a significantly smaller size, even when the hidden layer dimensions are large or need to be scaled up. This design decision alone leads to an 80% reduction in the size of the matrix/matrices projecting the one-hot embedded vector into the hidden layers.

The second strategy, cross-layer parameter sharing, is related to the *soft-parameter sharing multitask learning* scenario we discussed in chapter 4. Corresponding weights

---

[4] Z. Lan et al., "ALBERT: A Lite BERT for Self-Supervised Learning of Language Representations," ICLR (2020).
[5] https://www.cs.jhu.edu/~mdredze/datasets/sentiment/

across all layers are encouraged to be similar to each other by imposing appropriate constraints on them during learning. This serves as a regularization effect, reducing the risk of overfitting by reducing the number of degrees of available freedom. Taken together, the two techniques allowed the authors to build pretrained language models that outperformed both the GLUE and the SQuAD record performances at the time (February 2020). Compared to BERT, an approximately 90% reduction in parameter size was achieved with only a slight reduction in performance (less than 1% on SQuAD).

Again, because a variety of checkpoints have been made available for direct loading and our focus here is on transfer learning, we do not repeat the training steps from scratch here. Instead, we work with a checkpoint analogous to the "base" BERT checkpoint we used in the previous chapter and in chapter 8 for our cross-lingual transfer learning experiments. This allows us to directly compare the performance and benefits of using this architecture over the original BERT, while also teaching you how to start using this architecture in your own projects.

10.1.1 *Fine-tuning pretrained ALBERT on MDSD book reviews*

We prepare the data using the same steps as in section 4.4, which we will not repeat here. These are also repeated in the Kaggle notebooks made available with this book. We start with the variable `data` produced by listing 4.6. Assuming the same hyperparameter settings as section 4.4, this is a NumPy array of 2,000 book review texts.

Write this NumPy array to file using Pandas with the following code:

```
import pandas as pd

train_df = pd.DataFrame(data=data)
train_df.to_csv("albert_dataset.csv")
```

We start by initializing an Albert tokenizer to the pretrained checkpoint from the base ALBERT model as follows. We are using version 2 because it is the latest available version at the moment. You can find the list of all available ALBERT models at any point on the Hugging Face website.[6]

```
from transformers import AlbertTokenizer          ◁──  Loads the ALBERT
                                                        tokenizer
tokenizer = AlbertTokenizer.from_pretrained("albert-base-v2")   ◁──┐
                                                          Uses the pretrained
                                                          ALBERT tokenizer
```

Having prepared the tokenizer, load the base ALBERT checkpoint into an ALBERT masked language model, and display the number of parameters as follows:

```
from transformers import AlbertForMaskedLM        ◁──  Uses masked language
                                                        modeling

model = AlbertForMaskedLM.from_pretrained("albert-base-v2")   ◁──┐
                                                          Initializes to
                                                          the ALBERT
                                                          checkpoint
```

----

[6] https://huggingface.co/models?filter=albert

```
print("Number of parameters in ALBERT model:")
print(model.num_parameters())
```

The output indicates that the model has 11.8 million parameters—this is a huge reduction in size versus BERT's 178.6 million parameters from chapter 8 and Distil-BERT's 135.5 million parameters from the previous chapter. In fact, this is a reduction of 15 times from the BERT model. Wow!

Next, as before, build a dataset with the tokenizer from the monolingual Twi text, using the convenient `LineByLineTextDataset` method included with transformers, shown next:

```
from transformers import LineByLineTextDataset

dataset = LineByLineTextDataset(
    tokenizer=tokenizer,
    file_path="albert_dataset.csv",        How many lines
    block_size=128)          ◄──────       to read at a time
```

Define a "data collator"—a helper method that creates a special object out of a batch of sample data lines (of length `block_size`)—as shown next. This special object is consummable by PyTorch for neural network training:

```
from transformers import DataCollatorForLanguageModeling

data_collator = DataCollatorForLanguageModeling(      Uses masked language
    tokenizer=tokenizer,                              modeling, and masks words
    mlm=True, mlm_probability=0.15)    ◄──────        with a probability of 0.15
```

Here we use masked language modeling with 15% of the words to be randomly masked in our input data, and the model is asked to predict them during training.

Define standard training arguments, such as output directory and training batch size, as shown in the next code snippet. Note that we are training for 10 epochs this time, because the dataset is so much smaller than the monolingual Twi sample of over 600,000 used in the previous chapter:

```
from transformers import Trainer, TrainingArguments

training_args = TrainingArguments(
    output_dir="albert",
    overwrite_output_dir=True,
    num_train_epochs=10,
    per_gpu_train_batch_size=16,
    save_total_limit=1,
)
```

Then, use training arguments with the previously defined dataset and collator to define a "trainer" for one training epoch across the data as shown next:

```
trainer = Trainer(
    model=model,
    args=training_args,
    data_collator=data_collator,
    train_dataset=dataset,
    prediction_loss_only=True,
)
```

Train and time how long training takes as follows:

```
import time
start = time.time()
trainer.train()
end = time.time()
print("Number of seconds for training:")
print((end-start))
```

Over this small dataset, the 10 epochs take only approximately five minutes to finish training. The loss reaches a value of around 1.

Save the model as follows:

```
trainer.save_model("albert_fine-tuned")
```

Finally, let's apply the pipelines API to predict the masked word in a fictional book review as follows:

```
from transformers import pipeline

fill_mask = pipeline(          ◁──┤ Defines the fill-in-the-
    "fill-mask",                      blanks pipeline
    model="albert_fine-tuned",
    tokenizer=tokenizer
)
                                                    ┤ Predicts the
                                                      masked token
print(fill_mask("The author fails to [MASK] the plot."))   ◁──┘
```

This yields the following, very plausible, output:

```
[{'sequence': '[CLS] the author fails to describe the plot.[SEP]', 'score':
0.07632581889629364, 'token': 4996}, {'sequence': '[CLS] the author fails to
appreciate the plot.[SEP]', 'score': 0.03849967569112778, 'token': 8831},
{'sequence': '[CLS] the author fails to anticipate the plot.[SEP]', 'score':
0.03471902385354042, 'token': 27967}, {'sequence': '[CLS] the author fails to
demonstrate the plot.[SEP]', 'score': 0.03338927403092384, 'token': 10847},
{'sequence': '[CLS] the author fails to identify the plot.[SEP]', 'score':
0.032832834869623184, 'token': 5808}]
```

You may have observed by now that the sequence of steps we executed to fine-tune ALBERT on the custom book review corpus here is very similar to the sequence of steps we used with DistilBERT in the previous chapter. That sequence of steps is, in turn, quite similar to the sequence of steps we used with mBERT in chapter 8. We stress yet again that this recipe can be used as a blueprint with virtually any other architecture available in transformers. Although it is impossible for us to provide an example of fine-tuning on every possible type of application, this recipe should generalize, or at least serve as a good starting point, for many use cases. Consider, for instance, the scenario where you wanted to teach GPT-2 to write in some chosen style. Simply copy over the same code we have used here, point the dataset paths to a corpus of your chosen writing style, and change the tokenizer and model references from `AlbertTokenizer` / `AlbertForMaskedLM` to `GPT2Tokenizer` / `GPT2LMHeadModel`.

One thing to note is that all the PyTorch transformers models have all the layers unfrozen for training by default. To freeze all layers, you can execute the following code snippet:

```
for param in model.albert.parameters():
    param.requires_grad = False
```

You can freeze only some parameters using analogous code snippets.

In the next section, where we will discuss multitask fine-tuning, we will have yet another opportunity to look at fine-tuning of these types of models, this time for various tasks.

10.2 *Multitask fine-tuning*

In section 3 of chapter 4, we introduced the idea of multitask learning, where a model is trained to perform a variety of tasks instead of just one. The resulting model is usually more generalizable to new scenarios and can result in better transfer and performance. Unsurprisingly, this idea reappears in the context of adaptation strategies for pretrained NLP language models, where models fine-tuned on multiple tasks have been observed to be more robust and performant.[7]

Our discussion of this idea here provides a great opportunity to introduce the *General Language Understanding Evaluation* (GLUE) dataset,[8] a collection of data for several tasks representative of human language reasoning. This dataset includes tasks such as detecting similarity between sentences, similarity between questions, paraphrasing, sentiment analysis, and question answering. In this section, we demonstrate how to quickly leverage the transformers library to fine-tune the various transformer-based pretrained models we have discussed on various tasks from the GLUE dataset. This exercise also demonstrates how to analogously fine-tune a model from the BERT family on a custom dataset from one of the important classes of problems included in GLUE.

We also demonstrate *sequential adaptation*—the process of breaking up an overall desired transfer experiment into simpler, more manageable steps. Consider a hypothetical scenario where a language-based tool fails to transfer between West and East

---

[7] X. Liu et al., "Multi-Task Deep Neural Networks for Natural Language Understanding," ACL Proceedings (2019).

[8] A. Wang et al., "GLUE: A Multi-Task Benchmark and Analysis Platform for Natural Language Understanding," ICLR (2019).

Africa—it still may transfer successfully first between West Africa and Central Africa, and then between Central Africa and East Africa. This is related to the idea of multitask fine-tuning in the sense that it is essentially that carried out sequentially, one after the other. Instead of fine-tuning the model on several tasks simultaneously—which is how multitask fine-tuning is typically conceptualized—sequential adaptation fine-tunes on one task first, and then the other.

In this section, we demo multitask fine-tuning and sequential adaptation by fine-tuning some pretrained transformer-based language models on several tasks from the GLUE dataset. Specifically, we focus on a question similarity task known as the *Quora Question Pair* (QQP) task, as well as the *Semantic Textual Similarity Benchmark* (SST-B) task for measuring similarity between a pair of sentences.

10.2.1 General Language Understanding Dataset (GLUE)

The General Language Understanding Dataset (GLUE) was introduced to provide a challenging set of benchmark datasets for a diverse set of natural language understanding tasks. These tasks were selected to represent the implicit agreement among researchers in NLP over the years about what constitutes an interesting, challenging, and relevant set of problems. In table 10.1, we summarize the tasks available in the dataset and data counts for each task.

Table 10.1 List of tasks, descriptions, and data counts for each task made available in the original General Language Understanding Dataset (GLUE)

Task Name	Data Count	Description
The Corpus of Linguistic Acceptability (CoLA)	8,500 train, 1,000 test	Determines whether or not an English sentence is grammatical
The Stanford Sentiment Treebank (SST2)	67,000 train, 1,800 test	Detects the sentiment of a given sentence—positive or negative
Microsoft Research Paraphrase Corpus (MRPC)	3,700 train, 1,700 test	Determines whether one sentence is a paraphrase of another
Semantic Textual Similarity Benchmark (STS-B)	7,000 train, 1,400 test	On a scale of 1 to 5, predicts the similarity score between a pair of sentences
Quora Question Pairs (QQP)	3,640,000 train, 391,000 test	Determines whether a pair of Quora questions are semantically equivalent
Multi-Genre Natural Language Inference (MultiNLI)	393,000 train, 20,000 test	Determines whether a premise sentence implies/entails or contradicts a hypothesis sentence
Question-Answering Natural Language Inference (QNLI)	105,000 train, 5,400 test	Detects whether the context sentence contains an answer to the question
Recognizing Textual Entailment (RTE)	2,500 train, 3,000 test	Measures the textual entailment between the premise and the hypothesis, similarly to MultiNLI

Table 10.1   List of tasks, descriptions, and data counts for each task made available in the original General Language Understanding Dataset (GLUE) *(continued)*

Task Name	Data Count	Description
Winograd Schema Challenge (WNLI)	634 train, 146 test	Determines to which noun from a set of possible options an ambiguous pronoun refers

As can be seen from the table, the original GLUE dataset covered a variety of tasks with different amounts of data available. This is to encourage the sharing of knowledge between different tasks, which is the essence of the multitask fine-tuning idea we are exploring in this section of the chapter. We now briefly describe the various tasks in the table.

The first two tasks—the *Corpus of Linguistic Acceptability* (CoLA) and the *Stanford Sentiment Treebank* (SST2)—are single-sentence tasks. The former tries to determine if a given English sentence is grammatically correct, whereas the latter tries to detect whether the sentiment expressed in a sentence is positive or negative.

The following three tasks—*Microsoft Research Paraphrase Corpus* (MRPC), *Semantic Textual Similarity Benchmark* (STS-B), and *Quora Question Pairs* (QQP)—are classified as similarity tasks. These involve comparisons between two sentences in various ways. MRPC tries to detect if one sentence is a paraphrase of another, that is, if it expresses the same concepts. STS-B measures the similarity between a pair of sentences on a continuous scale between 1 and 5. QQP tries to detect if one Quora question is equivalent to another.

The remaining four tasks are classified as inference tasks. The *Multi-Genre Natural Language Inference* (MultiNLI) task attempts to determine if a given sentence implies another sentence or contradicts it—it measures *entailment.* The *Question-Answering Natural Language Inference* (QNLI) task is similar to the SQuAD[9] dataset we discussed and used in chapter 8 to illustrate question answering. As a reminder, that dataset is composed of a context paragraph, a question about it, and the start and end positional indicators of an answer to the question in the context paragraph, if one exists. QNLI essentially turns this idea into a sentence-pair task by pairing each context sentence with the question and attempting to predict if the answer is in that context sentence. The *Recognizing Textual Entailment* (RTE) task is similar to MultiNLI in that it measures entailment between a pair of sentences. Finally, the *Winograd Schema Challenge* (WNLI) dataset attempts to detect to which noun from a set of available options an ambiguous pronoun in a sentence refers.

Since the inception of GLUE, another dataset called SuperGLUE[10] has been introduced as well. This new version became necessary as modern methods recently began achieving close to perfect performances on many parts of GLUE. SuperGLUE was

---

[9] P. Rajpurkar et al., "SQuAD: 100,000+ Questions for Machine Comprehension of Text," *arXiv* (2016).

[10] A. Wang et al., "Glue: A Multi-Task Benchmark and Analysis Platform for Natural Language Understanding," ICLR (2019).

developed to be more challenging and thus to provide more "dynamic range" for comparing methods. We focus on GLUE here, but we do think it is important to keep the existence of SuperGLUE in mind as you become more of an expert on NLP.

We will do some experiments with QQP and STS-B GLUE tasks as illustrative examples in the rest of this section. To start off, in the next subsection we demonstrate how to fine-tune pretrained BERT on any one of the tasks we have presented. We underscore that while we use STS-B as the example fine-tuning task in this case, the same sequence of steps is directly applicable for any of the presented tasks. We also alert you that this exercise prepares you to fine-tune BERT on your own custom dataset from any of the task categories presented.

10.2.2 *Fine-tuning on a single GLUE task*

In this subsection, we see how we can quickly fine-tune a pretrained model from the transformers family on a task from the GLUE benchmark set. Recall that BERT was pretrained on the "fill-in-the-blanks" and "next-sentence prediction" objectives. Here, we further fine-tune this pretrained BERT on the STS-B similarity task GLUE data. This exercise serves as an example of how you could carry this out on any other task in GLUE, as well as on any of your own custom datasets belonging to one of these important classes of problems.

The first thing we do is clone the transformers repository and install the necessary requirements using the following code:

```
!git clone --branch v3.0.1 https://github.com/huggingface/transformers
!cd transformers
!pip install -r transformers/examples/requirements.txt
!pip install transformers==3.0.1
```

Clones the (specified version of) transformers repository

Installs the necessary requirements

Fixes the transformers version for reproducibility

Please ignore dependency conflict messages in our Kaggle notebook—they are irrelevant to the libraries we are using here, as long as you fork our notebook instead of starting a new one from scratch.

Next, download GLUE data as follows:

Downloads the GLUE data for all tasks

```
!mkdir GLUE
!python transformers/utils/download_glue_data.py --data_dir GLUE --tasks all
```

This creates a GLUE directory, with a subdirectory in it named after each GLUE task and containing the data for that task. We can take a look at what is contained in GLUE/STS-B as follows:

```
!ls GLUE/STS-B
```

This produced the following output:

```
LICENSE.txt  dev.tsv  original   readme.txt  test.tsv  train.tsv
```

Moreover, we can take a peek at a slice of the STS-B training data as follows:

```
!head GLUE/STS-B/train.tsv
```

This produces the following output:

```
index genre    filename year old_index source1 source2 sentence1 sentence2 score

0      main-captions    MSRvid    2012test    0001    none    none    A plane is taking off.
An air plane -is taking off.    5.000

1      main-captions    MSRvid    2012test    0004    none    none    A man is playing a large
flute.    A man is playing a flute.    3.800

2      main-captions    MSRvid    2012test    0005    none    none    A man is spreading shredded
cheese on a pizza.    A man is spreading shredded cheese on an uncooked pizza.    3.800

3      main-captions    MSRvid    2012test    0006    none    none    Three men are playing
chess.    Two men are playing chess.    2.600

4      main-captions    MSRvid    2012test    0009    none    none    A man is playing the cello.
A man seated is playing the cello.    4.250

5      main-captions    MSRvid    2012test    0011    none    none    Some men are fighting.
Two men are fighting.    4.250

6      main-captions    MSRvid    2012test    0012    none    none    A man is smoking.    A man
is skating.    0.500

7      main-captions    MSRvid    2012test    0013    none    none    The man is playing the
piano.    The man is playing the guitar.    1.600

8      main-captions    MSRvid    2012test    0014    none    none    A man is playing on a
guitar and singing.    A woman is playing an acoustic guitar and singing.    2.200
```

Before proceeding, we note that in order to use the scripts discussed here to fine-tune the model on your own custom data, you just need to convert your data into the format shown and point the scripts to its location!

To fine-tune the "vanilla" bert-base-cased BERT checkpoint on the STS-B GLUE task for three epochs—with a batch size of 32, a maximum input sequence length of 256, and a learning rate of 2e-5—we execute the following command:

> **This is a "magic" command for timing in a Jupyter notebook.**

```
%%time
!python transformers/examples/text-classification/run_glue.py
--model_name_or_path bert-base-cased --task_name STS-B --do_train --do_eval
--data_dir GLUE/STS-B/ --max_seq_length 256 --per_gpu_train_batch_size 32
--learning_rate 2e-5 --num_train_epochs 3.0 --output_dir /tmp/STS-B/
```

This takes under 10 minutes to execute. Note that in the code, we specified the output directory to be /tmp/STS-B/. This folder contains the fine-tuned model and evaluation results. Then, to see the performance that was attained, we simply execute the following to print the results to screen:

```
!cat /tmp/STS-B/eval_results_sts-b.txt
```

This yields the following output:

```
eval_loss = 0.493795601730334
eval_pearson = 0.8897041761974835
eval_spearmanr = 0.8877572577691144
eval_corr = 0.888730716983299
```

These represent the final figures for the metrics used on this problem, namely the Pearson and Spearman correlation coefficients. Without delving into too much detail, these coefficients measure the correlation between the ground truth similarities provided in the dataset and the similarities obtained by our fine-tuned model on the test set. Higher values for these coefficients indicate a better model due to greater correlation with the ground truth. We see that a performance approaching 89% is attained for both coefficients. A quick look at the current GLUE leaderboard[11] as of this writing (early October 2020) indicates that the top 20 performances recorded worldwide vary between approximately 87% at the low end and 93% at the high end. These top performances also perform well on the other tasks in GLUE, although we have only fine-tuned on a single task so far. It is nevertheless impressive that we can obtain a performance so close to the state of the art this quickly. Note from table 10.1 that the amount of training data for this task is only 7,000 samples.

In the next subsection, we will fine-tune the model further on an additional task—Quora Question Pairs (QQP)—and thereby further illustrate the concepts of multitask learning and sequential adaptation.

10.2.3 Sequential adaptation

In this subsection, we will see if fine-tuning on the Quora Question Pairs (QQP) task, before fine-tuning on the STS-B task, can yield a better performance. Recall from table 10.1 that QQP has 364,000 training samples whereas STS-B has 7,000 samples. Clearly, QQP has considerably more data. Training on QQP first can then be interpreted as applying a sequential adaptation multitask learning strategy to handle a low-resource scenario where the amount of training data is less than ideal: only 7,000 samples.

We start the exercise assuming the transformers repository has been cloned, necessary requirements have been installed, and the GLUE data has been downloaded, as shown in the previous subsection. Now, the next thing to do is to fine-tune the "vanilla" `bert-base-cased` BERT checkpoint on the QQP GLUE task for one epoch, with a batch size of 32, a maximum input sequence length of 256, and a learning rate of 2e-5. Note that we use just one epoch this time, instead of three as in the previous

---

[11] https://gluebenchmark.com/leaderboard

subsection, because the training data is now so much larger. Each epoch—which involves passing over the training set once—now covers 364,000 samples, which we gauge to be sufficient. We use the following code:

```
!python transformers/examples/text-classification/run_glue.py
--model_name_or_path bert-base-cased --task_name QQP --do_train --do_eval
--data_dir GLUE/QQP/ --max_seq_length 256 --per_gpu_train_batch_size 32
--learning_rate 2e-5 --num_train_epochs 1 --output_dir /tmp/QQP/
```

The training epoch takes about 2 hours and 40 minutes to execute. As before, we can check the attained performance on the QQP task as follows:

```
!cat /tmp/QQP/eval_results_qqp.txt
```

This attains the following performance:

```
eval_loss = 0.24864352908579548
eval_acc = 0.8936433341578036
eval_f1 = 0.8581700639883898
eval_acc_and_f1 = 0.8759066990730967
epoch = 1.0
```

We can then load the QQP-fine-tuned model as follows:

```
from transformers import BertForSequenceClassification, BertConfig

qqp_model = BertForSequenceClassification.from_pretrained("/tmp/QQP")
```

Initializes to our fine-tuned model checkpoint

Uses sequence classification this time, because it is the form of the problem

Having loaded the fine-tuned model, let's extract its encoder so that we can use it in a successive model that can then be further fine-tuned on the STS-B task. Note that this is similar to the hard-parameter sharing scenario we analyzed in chapter 4. We illustrate this scenario in figure 10.1.

The encoder shared between tasks is clearly shown in the figure. The encoder is extracted and used to initialize a model for fine-tuning on STS-B using the following code snippet:

STS-B is a regression problem and requires only one output; QQP is a binary classification task and thus has two outputs.

Gets the fine-tuned QQP model encoder

Makes sure the vocabulary and output sizes of an STS-B configuration are set to be consistent

```
shared_encoder = getattr(qqp_model, "bert")

configuration = BertConfig()
configuration.vocab_size = qqp_model.config.vocab_size
configuration.num_labels = 1

stsb_model = BertForSequenceClassification(configuration)

setattr(stsb_model, "bert", shared_encoder)
```

Initializes the STS-B model with similar settings to QQP

Set its encoder to the QQP encoder

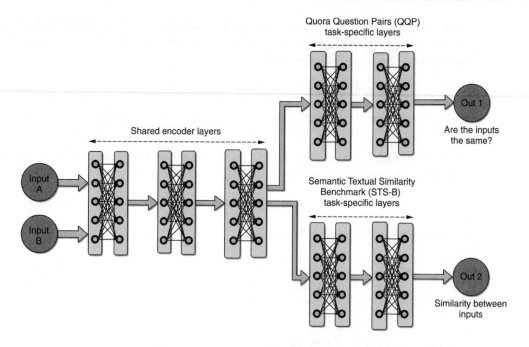

Figure 10.1   The hard-parameter sharing multitask learning scenario we are exploring in this section. The model is first fine-tuned on QQP, which is a data-rich scenario, and then STS-B, which is a low-resource scenario. The sequential nature of this experiment classifies it as sequential adaptation.

Save the initialized STS-B model for further fine-tuning as follows:

```
stsb_model.save_pretrained("/tmp/STSB_pre")
```

Make sure the vocabulary from the QQP model is available, as shown next:

```
!cp /tmp/QQP/vocab.txt /tmp/STSB_pre
```

Now fine-tune the previously QQP fine-tuned model on STS-B, using the same settings as in the previous subsection, as follows:

```
!python transformers/examples/text-classification/run_glue.py
--model_name_or_path /tmp/STSB_pre --task_name STS-B --do_train --do_eval
--data_dir GLUE/STS-B/ --max_seq_length 256 --per_gpu_train_batch_size 32
--learning_rate 2e-5 --num_train_epochs 3 --output_dir /tmp/STS-B/
```

The three training epochs take only about seven and half minutes to execute, given that the training set size is only 7,000. We check the attained performance as usual using the following:

```
!cat /tmp/STS-B/eval_results_sts-b.txt
```

The following performance is observed:

```
eval_loss = 0.49737201514158474
eval_pearson = 0.8931606380447263
eval_spearmanr = 0.8934618150816026
eval_corr = 0.8933112265631644
epoch = 3.0
```

We have attained an improvement over the previous subsection, where fine-tuning only on STS-B was carried out. The `eval_corr` attained there was about 88.9%, whereas we attain 89.3% here. The successive adaptation multitask learning experiment has thus been observed to be beneficial and to have resulted in a measurable improvement in performance.

In the next section, we will see if we can fine-tune similarly to new scenarios even more efficiently than we did here. We will investigate introducing so-called adaptation modules, or adapters, in between the layers of a pretrained language model to adapt to new scenarios. This approach holds promise because the number of introduced parameters is very small, and they can be pretrained and shared by the NLP community efficiently.

10.3 Adapters

The next adaptation strategy we explore is the use of so-called *adaptation modules* or *adapters*. The key idea behind them is shown in figure 10.2, which introduces them as additional layers in the vanilla transformer encoder from figure 7.6 in chapter 7.

As can be seen in the figure, these adapters are newly introduced modules of only a few parameters between layers of a pretrained neural network. Fine-tuning the modified model for new tasks requires training only these few additional parameters—the weights of the original network are kept the same. Virtually no loss in performance, compared to fine-tuning the entire model, is often observed when adding just 3–4% additional parameters per task.[12] In practice, this additional number of parameters is equivalent to the disk space of about 1 additional megabyte, which is very low by modern standards.

These adapters are modular, allowing for ready extendibility and easy sharing of experience among researchers. In fact, a project named AdapterHub,[13] which is built on the transformers library we have been using, aims to be the central repository for sharing such modules. In this section, we will use this project to build a BERT model fine-tuned on the Stanford Sentiment Treebank (SST2) task. This is equivalent to what we did in the previous section when fine-tuning on the STS-B subset of GLUE and will allow you to quickly gain an appreciation for the advantages afforded by the adapter framework versus what we did before.

---

[12] N. Houlsby et al., "Parameter-Efficient Transfer Learning for NLP," ICML (2019).
[13] https://adapterhub.ml/

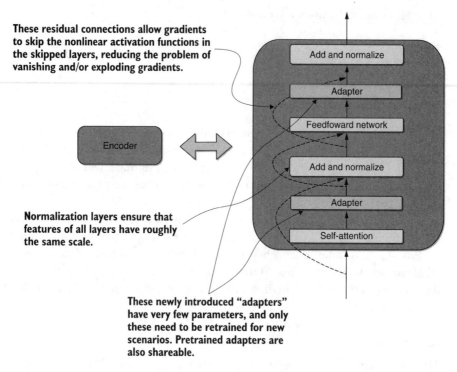

These residual connections allow gradients to skip the nonlinear activation functions in the skipped layers, reducing the problem of vanishing and/or exploding gradients.

Normalization layers ensure that features of all layers have roughly the same scale.

These newly introduced "adapters" have very few parameters, and only these need to be retrained for new scenarios. Pretrained adapters are also shareable.

Figure 10.2   Newly introduced adapter layers in the "vanilla" transformer encoder from figure 7.6

Let's install the AdapterHub library as follows:

```
pip install adapter-transformers
```

Import the required classes and load the required adapter with just three lines of code as follows:

Checkpoint to fine-tune

```
from transformers import BertForSequenceClassification, BertTokenizer
model = BertForSequenceClassification.from_pretrained("bert-base-uncased")
model.load_adapter("sentiment/sst-2@ukp")
```

Task-specific adapter selection specification

Available adapters and usage instructions are listed on the AdapterHub website.[14] That is literally all we had to do to adapt the BERT checkpoint to the SST2 sentiment-classification task. Comparing this with our fine-tuning steps from the previous section should make the utility of the adapter methodology obvious. Instead of fine-tuning, we just load additional modules and keep moving!

[14] https://adapterhub.ml/explore

Note that in our code we used the `bert-base-uncased` checkpoint, and the adapter we are loading was fine-tuned on the UKP Sentential Argument Mining Corpus,[15] due to the constraints of what is currently available in the AdapterHub repository. AdapterHub is an early-stage project, and we expect that significantly more adapters will be made available over time. At the time of writing in October of 2020, close to 200 adapters are available.[16]

As a final action of this section and the chapter, let's convince ourselves that the model we have built here is actually working as a sentiment-classification engine. We do this using the following code snippet, which compares the sentiment of two sentences: "That was an amazing contribution, good!" and "That is very bad for the environment."

Makes prediction B

Makes prediction A

Sentence B

Sentence A

```
import torch
```
Uses a regular pretrained tokenizer
```
tokenizer = BertTokenizer.from_pretrained("bert-base-uncased")
tokensA = tokenizer.tokenize("That was an amazing contribution, good!")
input_tensorA = torch.tensor([tokenizer.convert_tokens_to_ids(tokensA)])
tokensB = tokenizer.tokenize("That is bad for the environment.")
input_tensorB = torch.tensor([tokenizer.convert_tokens_to_ids(tokensB)])
outputsA = model(input_tensorA,adapter_names=['sst-2'])
outputsB = model(input_tensorB,adapter_names=['sst-2'])
print("The prediction for sentence A - That was an amazing contribution,
    good! - is:")
print(torch.nn.functional.softmax(outputsA[0][0]))
print("The prediction for sentence B - That is very bad for the environment.
    - is:")
print(torch.nn.functional.softmax(outputsB[0][0]))
```
Displays the prediction probabilities for sentence A

Displays the prediction probabilities for sentence B

This produces the following output:

```
The prediction for sentence A - That was an amazing contribution, good! - is:
tensor([0.0010, 0.9990], grad_fn=<SoftmaxBackward>)
The prediction for sentence B - That is very bad for the environment. - is:
tensor([0.8156, 0.1844], grad_fn=<SoftmaxBackward>)
```

The shown predictions can be interpreted as a pair of probabilities, the first of which indicates the probability of the input being "negative" and the second, the probability of being "positive." We see that the sentence "That was an amazing contribution, good!" is strongly positive with a probability of 99.9%. The sentence "That is very bad for the environment," on the other hand, is negative, with a probability of 81.6%. That certainly makes sense and validates our experiment.

---

[15] http://mng.bz/7j0e
[16] https://adapterhub.ml/explore

Summary

- Applying embedding factorization and parameter sharing across layers yields a more parameter-efficient model.
- Fine-tuning a model from the BERT family on multiple tasks simultaneously, that is, multitask fine-tuning, yields a more generalizable model.
- Employing adapters on a model from the BERT family can simplify fine-tuning.

Conclusions

11

This chapter covers

- Summarizing important concepts covered by this book
- Summarizing related important emerging concepts
- Considering limitations and environmental and ethical considerations around transfer learning methods for NLP
- Envisioning the future of transfer learning in NLP
- Keeping up with latest developments in the field

We've covered a great deal of material in the preceding chapters—we hope they were informative and engaging. This concluding chapter attempts to provide a meaningful summary of everything we did and looks to the future of the field and emerging research trends. Due to the prolific output and the quick-moving nature of the field, we certainly have not covered every single influential architecture or promising research direction. To mitigate this, we include a brief discussion of various research trends we did not get a chance to cover in this book, making connections to, and framing in the context of, covered material as much as possible.

In this chapter, we also try to provide a broader context by touching on emerging questions that have not traditionally been given much attention, such as ethical considerations and the environmental impact of the various models. These are closely tied to the awareness of the limitations of these models, which we try to highlight as much as possible in this chapter.

Crucially, we discuss various tips for staying up-to-date in a rapidly moving field such as this one. It is important to stress that having mastered the content of the book, you are only now beginning your journey in the field. The tools and skills presented will change over time, and each unique application of them may require creativity on your part or new techniques yet to be developed. Retaining a competitive edge in a rapidly moving field such as this is truly a journey, not a destination. We encourage readers to keep an inquisitive attitude toward ongoing research and to continue to contribute in some capacity to its development.

Let's begin this final chapter by overviewing the key concepts.

11.1 Overview of key concepts

Transfer learning aims to leverage prior knowledge from different settings—be it a different task, language, or domain—to help solve a problem at hand. It is inspired by the way in which humans learn, because we typically do not learn things from scratch for any given problem, but rather build on prior knowledge that may be related. Allowing a practitioner without substantial computing resources to achieve state-of-the-art performance is considered an important step toward democratizing access to the fruits of the ongoing technological revolution. As a more concrete motivation, consider the representative costs of training various sizes of the BERT model, as shown in figure 11.1.[1]

As can be seen in the figure, the largest-sized BERT training cost can reach into millions of dollars. Transfer learning literally enables you to reuse this precious knowledge on your personal computing projects within a few hours and, at worst, a few dollars for fine-tuning.

Transfer learning was popularized in computer vision before it recently came to be used heavily by the natural language processing (NLP) community. Whereas computer vision deals with teaching computers how to understand and act on images and videos, NLP considers how to do the same with human speech, be it text or speech audio. In this book, we focused on text. Some NLP tasks of particular interest to us include document classification, machine translation, and question answering.

Although historically such tasks were initially solved by attempting to specify fixed rules for every scenario—a paradigm now known as symbolic AI—machine learning has now become the dominant trend. Instead of explicitly programming a computer for every possible scenario, the computer is *trained* to associate input to output signals by seeing many examples of such corresponding input-output pairs. The methods used to *learn* appropriate input-output associations have traditionally included decision

---

[1] Sharir O. et al., "The Cost of Training NLP Models: A Concise Overview," *arXiv* (2020).

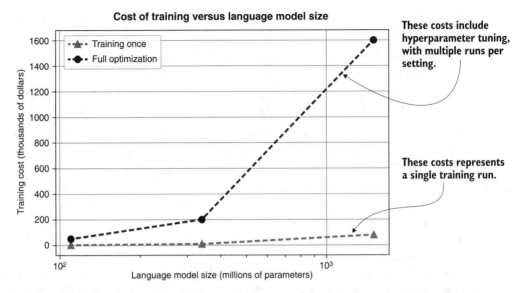

Figure 11.1   Training costs for various sizes of BERT. Two representative costs are shown—for a single run and for an entire training process that includes hyperparameter tuning. The largest size of 1.5 billion parameters costs $80k for single run, and $1.6 million when all optimization steps are accounted for!

trees, random forests, kernel methods such as SVM, and neural networks. Neural networks have recently become the clear favorite for learning such representations for perceptual problems, that is, computer vision and NLP. As such, this is the most important class of methods we explored in this book.

Before diving into modern transfer learning method for NLP, we conducted a review experiment with some traditional machine learning methods. Specifically, we employed the following:

- Logistic regression
- Support vector machines
- Random forests
- Gradient-boosting machines

to look at two important problems: email spam detection and Internet Movie Database (IMDB) movie review classification. To turn text into numbers for this experiment, we used the bag-of-words model. This model simply counts the frequency of word tokens contained in each email and thereby represents it as a vector of such frequency counts.

Modern NLP methodologies have focused on vectorizing sections of text—words, subwords, sentences, and so on—via techniques such as word2vec and sent2vec. The resulting numerical vectors are then further processed as features of a traditional machine learning approach, such as being used for classification with random forests.

As was outlined in the first chapter of this book, this important subarea of NLP research has a rich history originating with the *term-vector model of information retrieval* in the 1960s. This culminated with pretrained shallow neural-network-based techniques such as the following:

- fastText
- GloVe
- word2vec, which came in several variants in the mid-2010s including Continuous Bag of Words (CBOW) and Skip-Gram

Both CBOW and Skip-Gram are extracted from shallow neural networks that were trained for various goals. Skip-Gram attempts to predict words neighboring any target word in a sliding window, whereas CBOW attempts to predict the target word given the neighbors. GloVe, which stands for "Global Vectors," attempts to extend word2vec by incorporating global information into the embeddings. It optimizes the embeddings such that the cosine product between words reflects the number of times they co-occur, with the goal of making the resulting vectors more interpretable. The fastText technique attempts to enhance word2vec by repeating the Skip-Gram methods on character n-grams (versus word n-grams), thereby able to handle previously unseen words. Each of these variants of pretrained embeddings has its strengths and weaknesses. As a numerical demonstration of this class of methods, we used fastText word embeddings to revisit the IMDB movie classification example, where the bag-of-words method was replaced with fastText for converting the text into numbers.

Several techniques were inspired by word2vec to try to embed larger section of text into vector spaces in such a way that sections of text with similar meanings would be closer to each other in the induced vector space. This enables arithmetic to be performed on these sections of text to make inference with regards to analogies, combined meanings, and so forth. Such methods include the following:

- Paragraph vectors, or *doc2vec*, which exploits the concatenation (versus averaging) of words from pretrained word embeddings in summarizing them
- *Sent2vec*, which extends the classic Continuous Bag of Words (CBOW) of word2vec—where a shallow network is trained to predict a word in a sliding window from its context—to sentences by optimizing word and word n-gram embeddings for an accurate averaged representation

As a numerical demonstration of this class of methods, we used an implementation of sent2vec that builds on fastText, instead of bag-of-words, to perform the IMDB movie classification experiment.

Several authors[2, 3, 4] have suggested various classification systems for categorizing transfer learning methods into groups. Roughly speaking, categorization is based on

---

[2] S.J. Pan and Q. Yang, "A Survey on Transfer Learning," IEEE Transactions on Knowledge and Data Engineering (2009).

[3] S. Ruder, "Neural Transfer Learning for Natural Language Processing," National University of Ireland, Galway, Ireland (2019).

[4] D. Wang and T. F. Zheng, "Transfer Learning for Speech and Language Processing," Proceedings of 2015 Asia-Pacific Signal and Information Processing Association Annual Summit and Conference (APSIPA).

whether transfer occurs among different languages, tasks, or data domains. Each of these types of categorization is usually correspondingly referred to as the following:

- *Cross-lingual learning*
- *Multitask learning*
- *Domain adaptation*

We performed a multitask transfer learning experiments using the familiar tasks of IMDB classification and email spam detection to illustrate the concept. To illustrate domain adaptation via example, we used an autoencoder to adapt a model trained for IMDB movie review classification to the domain of Amazon book reviews. This exercise also allowed us to illustrate an instance of zero-shot transfer learning, where no fine-tuning in the Amazon book review domain was necessary to begin providing valuable results.

Advances in sequence-to-sequence modeling brought forth a revolution for tasks such as machine translation. The encoder and decoder in this setup were initially recurrent neural networks (RNNs). Due to problems with long input sequences, the technique known as attention was developed to allow output to focus only on relevant sections of the input. Although initially this was combined with RNNs, it evolved into the technique of self-attention being used to build out both the encoder and decoder. Self-attention differs from the original attention formulation in that associations are sought between parts of a sequence and other parts of the same sequence, rather than between parts of two distinct input and output sequences. The architecture in which self-attention replaced attention came to be known as *the transformer*, and it scales better than earlier RNN-based sequence-to-sequence models on parallel computing architecture. This improved scalability drove its wide adoption over the competing architectures. We used a pretrained translation transformer model between English and the Ghanaian language Twi to probe the efficacy and other characteristics of this important architecture.

Early explorations of transfer learning for NLP focused on analogies to computer vision, where it has been used successfully for a while. One such model—SIMOn— employed character-level convolutional neural networks (CNNs) combined with bidirectional LSTMs for structural semantic text classification. SIMOn stands for *Semantic Inference for the Modeling of Ontologies*. It was developed during DARPA's Data-Driven Discovery of Models (D3M)[5] program,[6] which was an attempt to automate some typical tasks faced by data scientists. It demonstrated NLP transfer learning methods directly analogous to those that have been used in computer vision. The features learned by this model were shown to also be useful for unsupervised learning tasks and to work well on social media language data, which can be somewhat idiosyncratic and very different

---

[5] Lipmann Richard et al., "An Overview of the DARPA Data-Driven Discovery of Models (D3M) Program," Proceedings of the 29th Conference on Neural Information Processing Systems (NeurIPS) (2016).

[6] https://datadrivendiscovery.org/

from the kind of language on Wikipedia and other large book-based datasets. Column-type classification was used as an illustrative example for this modeling framework.

By way of reminder, the heuristics for fine-tuning in computer vision go roughly as follows:

- A threshold is moved away from the output (and toward the input) as more data becomes available in the target domain. Parameters between the threshold and output are *unfrozen* and trained while the rest are kept the same. This is motivated by the fact that an increased amount of data can be used to train more parameters effectively than could be done otherwise.

- Additionally, movement of the threshold must happen away from the output and toward the input, because this allows us to retain parameters encoding general features that are close to the input, while retraining layers closer to the output that encode features specific to the source domain.

- Moreover, when the source and the target are highly dissimilar, some of the more specific parameters/layers can be fully discarded.

One major weakness of the early embedding methods such as word2vec was disambiguation—distinguishing between various uses of a word that may have different meanings depending on context. These words are technically referred to as homographs, for example, duck (posture) versus duck (bird) and fair (a gathering) versus fair (just). *Embeddings from Language Models*—abbreviated as ELMo after the popular *Sesame Street* character—is one of the earliest attempts to develop contextualized embeddings of words, using bidirectional *long short-term memory networks* (bi-LSTMs). ELMo is arguably the most popular early pretrained language model associated with the ongoing NLP transfer learning revolution. It shares a lot of architectural similarities with SIMOn, also being composed of character-level CNNs followed by bi-LSTMs. The embedding of a word in this model depends on its context, which ELMo achieves by being trained to predict the next word in a sequence of words. Huge datasets, such as Wikipedia and various datasets of books, were used to train this model. We applied ELMo to an illustrative example problem, namely fake news detection, as a practical demonstration.

Universal Language Model Fine-Tuning (ULMFiT) took this a step further by formalizing a method to fine-tune any neural network–based language model for any particular task. This framework introduces and demonstrates some key techniques and concepts enabling adapting a pretrained language model for new settings more effectively. These include discriminative fine-tuning and gradual unfreezing. Discriminative fine-tuning stipulates that because the different layers of a language model contain different type of information, they should be tuned at different rates. Gradual unfreezing describes a procedure for fine-tuning progressively more parameters in a gradual manner with the aim of reducing the risks of overfitting. The ULMFiT framework also includes innovations in varying the learning rate in a unique way during the adaptation process. We illustrated these concepts numerically using the fast.ai library.

The OpenAI *Generative Pretrained Transformer* (GPT) modified the encoder-decoder architecture of the transformer to achieve a fine-tunable language model for NLP. It discarded the encoders, retaining the decoders and their self-attention sublayers. It is trained with a *causal modeling objective*—to predict the next word in a sequence. It is particularly suited for text generation. We demonstrated how you can quickly use the pretrained GPT-2 model for text generation using the transformers library by Hugging Face, which we introduced earlier in the book.

Bidirectional Encoder Representations from Transformers (BERT) did arguably the opposite, modifying the transformer architecture by preserving the encoders and discarding the decoders, also relying on *masking* of words, which would then need to be predicted accurately as the training metric. More specifically, it is trained with the *masked modeling objective*—to fill in the blanks. Additionally, it is trained with the *next sentence prediction* task—to determine whether a given sentence is a plausible following sentence after a target sentence. Although not suited for text generation, this model performs very well on other general language tasks such as classification and question answering. We applied it to the two important applications of question answering and document classification. The document classification use case was spam detection. We also demonstrated its application to filling in the blanks and detecting whether one sentence is a plausible next sentence for another one.

The model mBERT, which stands for "multilingual BERT," is effectively BERT pretrained on over 100 languages simultaneously. Naturally, this model is particularly well-suited for cross-lingual transfer learning. We showed how the multilingual pretrained weights checkpoint could facilitate creating BERT embeddings for languages that were not even originally included in the multilingual training corpus. Both BERT and mBERT were created at Google.

In all of these language-model-based methods—ELMo, ULMFiT, GPT, and BERT—it was shown that embeddings generated could be fine-tuned for specific downstream NLP tasks with relatively few labeled data points. This explains the focus the NLP community has paid to language models: it validates the conjecture that the hypothesis set induced by them would be generally useful.

We also covered some adaptation strategies for the deep NLP transfer learning modeling architectures that were covered. In other words, given a pretrained architecture such as ELMo, BERT, or GPT, how can transfer learning be carried out more efficiently? We focused on *parameter efficiency* for this purpose, where the goal is to yield a model with the fewest parameters possible while suffering minimal reduction in performance. The purpose of this is to make the model smaller and easier to store, which would make it easier to deploy on smartphone devices, for instance. Alternatively, smart adaptation strategies may be required just to get to an acceptable level of performance in some difficult transfer cases. The adaptation strategies we covered follow:

- The first adaptation strategies we explored were the aforementioned ULMFiT techniques of *gradual unfreezing* and *discriminative fine-tuning* with the fast.ai library.

- We then explored the model compression method known as *knowledge distillation*, due to its recent prominence in the NLP field. This process essentially attempts to mimic the output from the larger *teacher* model by the significantly smaller *student* model. In particular, we use an implementation of the method DistilBERT in the transformers library to demonstrate that the size of a BERT model can be more than halved by this approach.

- The next adaptation strategy we touched on revolves around two ideas aimed at creating transformer-based language models that scale more favorably with a bigger vocabulary and longer input length. The first involves clever factorization, or splitting up of a larger matrix of weights into two smaller matrices, allowing you to increase the dimensions of one without affecting the dimensions of the other. The second idea involves sharing parameters across all layers. These two strategies are the bedrock of the method known as ALBERT (A Lite BERT). We used the implementation in the transformers library to get some hands-on experience with the method.

Consequently, we built on the idea of multitask learning, where a model is trained to perform a variety of tasks at once and yields a more generalizable model. When faced with a transfer scenario where we have insufficient training data to fine-tune on a given task, why not fine-tune on multiple tasks? Discussing this idea provided a great opportunity to introduce the *General Language Understanding Evaluation* (GLUE) dataset, a collection of data for several tasks representative of human language reasoning, such as detecting similarity between sentences, similarity between questions, paraphrasing, sentiment analysis, and question answering. We showed how to quickly leverage the transformers library for multitask fine-tuning using this dataset. This exercise also demonstrated how to similarly fine-tune a model from the BERT family on a custom dataset from one of these important classes of problems.

We also built on the idea of domain adaptation, particularly the fact that the similarity of the source and target domains plays a crucial role in the effectiveness of transfer learning. Greater similarity implies an easier transfer learning process in general. When the source and target are too dissimilar, it may be impossible to carry out the process in a single step. In those circumstances, the idea of *sequential adaptation* may be used to break the overall desired transfer into simpler, more manageable steps. By way of example, we sequentially adapted a "fill-in-the-blanks" objective pretrained BERT to a low-resource sentence similarity-detection scenario, by first adapting to a data-rich question-similarity scenario. Data for both scenarios in the experiment came from the GLUE dataset.

The final adaptation strategy we explored was the use of so-called *adaptation modules* or *adapters*. These are newly introduced modules of only a few parameters between layers of a pretrained neural network. Fine-tuning this modified model for new tasks requires training only these few additional parameters. The weights of the original network are kept the same. Virtually no loss in performance, compared to fine-tuning the entire model, is often observed when adding just 3–4% additional parameters per task. These adapters are also modular and easily shared between researchers. We used the AdapterHub framework to load some of these adapters and show how they can be used to adapt a general BERT model to one expected to do well on a sentiment classification task.

11.2 Other emerging research trends

Throughout the book, we have tried to emphasize that in a fast-moving field such as transfer learning for NLP, it would be impossible for a single book like this one to fully cover every architecture or innovation. Instead, we have taken the approach of focusing on the architectures and techniques we think are fundamental. Future innovations are likely to be in some sense derived from such architectures and techniques, so readers can possibly pick them up by doing a little bit of their own legwork. To facilitate this even further, we focus this section on a brief discussion of various research trends we did not get a chance to cover in this book but which have become somewhat influential in the field. We frame these in the context of what we did cover as much as possible to ease your picking up of those topics if needed.

We begin the exercise by overviewing RoBERTa[7]—Robustly Optimized BERT Approach—which employs some optimization tricks to improve BERT efficiency.

11.2.1 RoBERTa

The study in question attempted to replicate BERT while paying extra attention to various training hyperparameters and settings and their effect on the outcome. In general, it was observed that the performance of the original BERT could be improved significantly via careful design choices. One such choice is removing the next-sentence prediction (NSP) task while maintaining the masked language modeling (MLM)— fill-in-the-blanks—task. In other words, they found NSP degraded performance on downstream tasks and showed that removing it was beneficial. Additional design choices included large learning rates and mini-batches during training. It is implemented in the transformers library by Hugging Face that we introduced earlier in the book.

Next, we look at one of the largest language model developed yet—GPT-3[8]—which has gathered much buzz lately, culminating in it winning the Best Paper Award at the NeurIPS 2020 virtual research conference (December 2020).

11.2.2 GPT-3

You may recall from our coverage of it that the GPT model has undergone several iterations—GPT, GPT-2, and, more recently, GPT-3. At the time of writing, GPT-3 happens to be one of the largest pretrained language models at 175 billion parameters. Its predecessor GPT-2 stands at 1.5 billion parameters and was also considered the largest when it was released just a year prior. Prior to the release of GPT-3 in June 2020, the largest model was Microsoft's Turing NLG, which stands at 17 billion parameters and

---

[7] Yinhan Liu et al., "RoBERTa: A Robustly Optimized BERT Pretraining Approach," *arXiv* (2019).
[8] Tom B. Brown et al., "Language Models Are Few-Shot Learners," NeurIPS (2020).

was released in February 2020. The sheer speed of progress on some of these metrics has been mind-blowing, and these records tend to be broken very quickly. For comparison, this explosion in parameters is illustrated in figure 11.2.

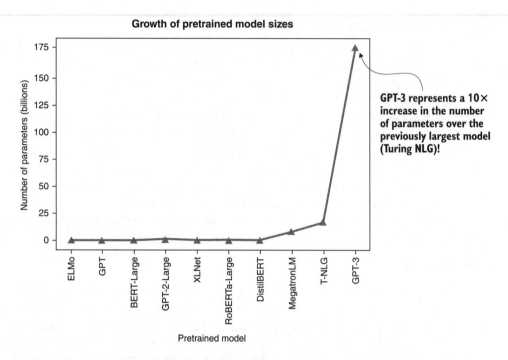

Figure 11.2   The growth in the number of parameters for the largest models over time. As can be seen in the diagram, the explosion in the size of the models appears to be accelerating, with one of the most recent advances—GPT-3—representing a growth factor of 10×.

As can be seen in the figure, GPT-3 represents an increase of more than 10x over the previously largest Turing NLG, a leap eclipsing prior progresses. Indeed, an architecture called the Switch Transformer,[9] which leverages sparsity by assigning separate transformer block sections to different inputs, claimed to have achieved a trillion parameter size in January 2021. We did not include this architecture in figure 11.2 because it is still undergoing peer review at the time of writing. It is abundantly clear, however, that this trend of growing model sizes appears to be accelerating.

In the GPT-3 paper, the authors show that this huge model can perform a broad range of tasks with very few examples. For instance, it can be primed to translate one language to another by seeing only a few example translations or to detect spam email by seeing only a few example spam emails. In fact, some unexpected applications,

---

[9] W. Fedus et al., "Switch Transformers: Scaling to Trillion Parameter Models with Simple and Efficient Sparsity," *arXiv* (2021).

such as writing code from a description of it, have been widely reported. At the moment, the model has not been released to the public by the OpenAI authors, only to a few early adopters by invitation and via a paid API. The stated reason by OpenAI for restricting access is monitoring use and thereby limiting any potential harmful applications of this technology. An early adopter of GPT-3 is an app called Shortly, which provides access to GPT-3 for creative writing purposes and which anyone can try for a small fee.

Additionally, a recent smaller but powerful open source alternative to GPT-3 is already available in the transformers library: GPT-Neo from EleutherAI. This organization aims to build a model equivalent to the full-size GPT-3 and make it available to the public under an open license.[10] Different models of varying sizes are available in their repository,[11] where you can also test-run the models using the Hugging Face–hosted inference API in the browser. We also provide a companion Kaggle notebook[12] showing it in action for the exercise we performed in chapter 7. Upon inspection, you should find its performance better but, naturally, at a significantly higher cost. (The weights are more than 10 GB in size for the largest model!)

An important thing to note about the GPT-3 work is that the authors themselves recognized in the paper that the benefits from making language models bigger has approached a limit. And even at that limit, performance on certain types of tasks, such as text generation concerning an understanding of common-sense physics, remains poor. Thus, although it does represent an important technological breakthrough, innovation in modeling approaches (versus simply scaling up models) has to be the path forward.

Next we look at a set of methods aimed at improving the performance of transformer-based models on longer input sequences. This is important because vanilla transformer models scale quadratically in run time and memory usage with input length.

11.2.3 XLNet

XLNet,[13] which builds on a similar earlier model Transformer-XL,[14] was designed to work better for longer input sequences. One of its critical component ideas is causal language modeling (CLM), which we discussed when covering GPT and which involves the classical language modeling task of predicting the next word in a sequence. Recall that future tokens are masked in this approach. The authors of the XLNet paper refer to this equivalently as autoregressive language modeling. The other critical component of XLNet is performing CLM over all possible permutations of the words in the input sequence. This idea is sometimes referred to as permutation language modeling (PLM). By combining

---

[10] https://www.eleuther.ai/projects/gpt-neo/
[11] https://huggingface.co/EleutherAI
[12] https://www.kaggle.com/azunre/tlfornlp-chapter7-gpt-neo
[13] Z. Yang et al., "XLNet: Generalized Autoregressive Pretraining for Language Understanding," NeurIPS (2019).
[14] Z. Dai et al., "Transformer-XL: Attentive Language Models beyond a Fixed-Length Context," ACL (2019).

PLM and CLM, bidirectionality is achieved because all tokens get to be included as past tokens in some permutation. Both XLNet and Transformer-XL have no sequence length limit and are implemented in the transformers library by Hugging Face.

With that view of XLNet in mind, let's move on to consider BigBird,[15] an innovation introducing the idea of a *sparse attention mechanism* for greater computational efficiency.

11.2.4 BigBird

BigBird reduces the quadratic dependency of traditional transformer-based models to linear by introducing a sparse attention mechanism that is shown to approximate and maintain the properties of the original full attention. Instead of applying the full attention to the entire input sequence at once, sparse attention looks at the sequence token by token, allowing it to be more intelligent and drop some connections. Sequences with a length up to eight times as long as what could be handled with traditional transformer-based models can be handled on similar hardware. It is implemented in the transformers library by Hugging Face.

Next, we touch on Longformer,[16] another innovation on the traditional full self-attention of the transformer that scales better with input length.

11.2.5 Longformer

Longformer is yet another attempt at battling the quadratic scaling of the traditional transformer attention. The innovation here is to combine a local windowed attention with a global task-oriented attention. The local attention is used for contextual representation whereas the global attention is used to build a full-sequence representation that is used in prediction. The scaling achieved is linear in the input sequence length, similar to BigBird. Longformer is implemented in the transformers library by Hugging Face.

We introduce the Reformer[17] next, which is another approach to alleviating the quadratic scaling of the original self-attention.

11.2.6 Reformer

The Reformer introduces two techniques for combating the quadratic scaling in computing time and memory with the input length of the original transformer. Replacing the original full self-attention with one that employs locally sensitive hashing reduces redundant computations and time complexity from quadratic to $O(L\log L)$ (where L is the input sequence length). A technique known as *reversible layers* allows storing activations only once. In practice, this means that instead of storing activations N times for a model with N layers, only a small fraction of the memory is used.

[15] M. Zaheer et al., "BigBird: Transformers for Longer Sequences," *arXiv* (2020).
[16] I. Beltagy et al., "Longformer: The Long-Document Transformer," *arXiv* (2020).
[17] N. Kitaev et al., "Reformer: The Efficient Transformer," *arXiv* (2020).

Depending on the value of N, the memory savings can be huge. Reformer is implemented in the transformers library by Hugging Face.

Clearly, making transformer-based models work better with longer input lengths has emerged as a meta research trend. We have likely not included all the great research on the subject here, and you will likely find much more if you do some of your own digging.

Next, we will touch on recently reemerging sequence-to-sequence modeling approaches. These attempt to cast the various problems we have encountered in this book into a text-to-text modeling framework.

11.2.7 T5

You may recall in our discussion in this book that sequence-to-sequence models have played an important role in NLP. First appearing in the context of recurrent neural network (RNN) models, they were also explored notably by the translation application area in the context of the original transformer architecture. T5, the "Text-to-Text Transfer Transformer,"[18] is an attempt to cast a broad range of NLP problems into a unifying sequence-to-sequence framework. It allows for the application of the same model, objective, training procedure, and decoding process for every task. Handled problem classes vary from summarization to sentiment analysis and question answering, among many others. Translation for the language pairs between English and each of Romanian, German, and French is included in training. Some representative data transformations, which make it possible to train a single model on diverse tasks, are shown in figure 11.3 for translation and summarization (it is inspired by figure 1 from the T5 paper).

As can be seen in the figure, task data is transformed by prepending a standard task descriptor to the original text data. Training data included the datasets GLUE and SuperGLUE, CNN/Daily Mail dataset for abstractive summarization, and so on. The goal was to handle the included diverse set of natural language understanding tasks without modifying the model. In that sense, it can be thought of as an interesting variant or iteration of the multitask learning idea that we have been bringing up throughout the book. The inclusion of such a variety of tasks for simultaneous learning is likely to enable parameter sharing and better generalizability of the resulting model. Crucially, the model is initially trained on a dataset the authors call the Colossal Clean Crawled Corpus (C4) using a masked language modeling or autoencoding objective, before fine-tuning on the aforementioned variety of tasks. Basically, 15% of all tokens are dropped, and the result is fed to the input, while the uncorrupted input is fed to the output for prediction. Note that the C4 corpus is essentially the internet for the target language (English) with pornographic material, code, and other "garbage data" filtered out. The model architecture used for training is similar to the transformer

---

[18] C. Raffel et al., "Exploring the Limits of Transfer Learning with a Unified Text-to-Text Transformer," *arXiv* (2020).

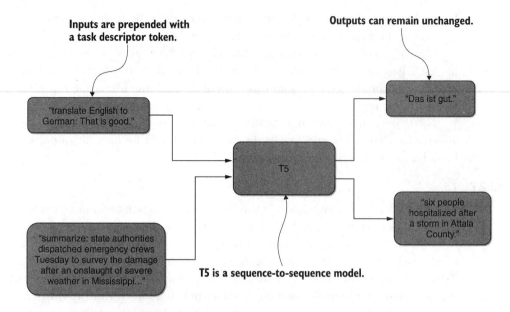

Inputs are prepended with a task descriptor token.

Outputs can remain unchanged.

"translate English to German: That is good."

"Das ist gut."

T5

"six people hospitalized after a storm in Attala County."

"summarize: state authorities dispatched emergency crews Tuesday to survey the damage after an onslaught of severe weather in Mississippi..."

T5 is a sequence-to-sequence model.

Figure 11.3   T5 is a sequence-to-sequence model that employs a number of transformations to enable a single model, decoding procedure, and objective to be trained on a variety of tasks simultaneously. It can be thought of as an interesting variation of multitask learning.

architecture we used in chapter 7 for translation. State-of-the-art results were achieved by the resulting model on many of the included tasks.

In addition to the original T5 model, a multilingual version, unsurprisingly called mT5, was also developed[19] by training on 101 languages simultaneously. Both T5 and mT5 are implemented in the transformers library by Hugging Face.

In what follows, we briefly introduce BART, which is similar to T5 in that it is a transformer-based sequence-to-sequence modeling framework.

11.2.8   *BART*

BART,[20] which stands for Bidirectional and Autoregressive Transformers, can be thought of as T5 minus the single unifying transformation to enable an unmodified model to be applied to a variety of tasks. Instead, a standard transformer encoder-decoder architecture is first pretrained to reproduce corrupted input via a variety of noising approaches. This ranges from masked language modeling, as in BERT and T5, to permutation language modeling as in XLNet, among others. The model is then modified for a variety of tasks, such as SQuAD, summarization, and so on, and fine-tuned separately for each such task similar to what we did with the traditional BERT.

---

[19] L. Xue et al., "mT5: A Massively Multilingual Pre-Trained Text-to-Text Transformer," *arXiv* (2019).

[20] M. Lewis et al., "BART: Denoising Sequence-to-Sequence Pre-training for Natural Language Generation, Translation, and Comprehension," *arXiv* (2020).

This model performs particularly well in language-generation tasks, such as summarization, translation, and dialogue. A multilingual version—mBART[21]—obtained by training on 25 languages simultaneously, has also been developed. Both BART and mBART are also implemented in the transformers library by Hugging Face.

In the following subsection, we look at a recent cross-lingual model that goes beyond merely training on multiple languages simultaneously, by modeling cross-lingual transfer explicitly via a modified language modeling objective when parallel data is available.

11.2.9 XLM

XLM,[22] which the authors use to mean a "cross-lingual language model," is a modeling framework that combines both monolingual and parallel data cross-lingual learning approaches. Monolingual embeddings learned on different languages can be *aligned* using a small vocabulary of words with known numerical representation. If parallel data is available, the authors introduce an approach they call *translation language modeling* (TLM) and exploit it for cross-lingual learning simultaneously. Essentially, this applies masked language modeling to a concatenated sequence of parallel data in both languages, with words dropped and asked to be predicted in both parts of the concatenated sequence.

Significant improvements were observed in cross-lingual learning tasks. It also spurred a number of similar models, notably XLM-R,[23] which combines the ideas of XLM with those of RoBERTa for improved performance. Both XLM and XLM-R are implemented in the transformers library by Hugging Face.

Finally, we briefly touch on a model specializing in an important class of problem data we encountered in the book—tabular data.

11.2.10 TAPAS

In chapters 5 and 6, we discussed the method SIMOn and its handling of tabular data type classification—an important class of problem data typically encountered by data scientists. TAPAS[24] is an attempt to extend the modeling benefits of transformer-based models to this important class of problems, by modeling and specializing for question answering in tabular data explicitly. TAPAS stands for Table Parser. In chapter 8, we discussed applying BERT to the task of question answering. The output of the resulting specialized model was the beginning and end positions of a potential answer to the question of interest in the input context paragraph. In addition to this, TAPAS learns to detect which cell in a table might contain the context paragraph from which the answer can be extracted with similar start and end indices. Like most of the other models discussed in this section, this model is implemented in the transformers library by Hugging Face.

---

[21] Y. Liu et al., "Multilingual Denoising Pre-Training for Neural Machine Translation," *arXiv* (2020).
[22] G. Lample and A. Conneau, "Cross-Lingual Language Model Pretraining," *arXiv* (2019).
[23] A. Conneau et al., "Unsupervised Cross-Lingual Representation Learning at Scale," *arXiv* (2019).
[24] J. Herzig et al., "TaPas: Weakly Supervised Table Parsing via Pre-Training," *arXiv* (2020).

This brings us to the end of this overview tour of recent work that we have not had an opportunity to analyze in detail in this book. Most of these model architectures can be used via code very similar to what we have used to work with BERT and DistilBERT in the transformers library.

In the next section, we try to make an educated guess on where we can expect the field to move next—what sorts of topics might remain and/or become popular given current and emerging research trends.

11.3   *Future of transfer learning in NLP*

In this section, we attempt to extrapolate the trends described in the previous two sections by anticipating what the immediate future of the field is likely to look like.

Critical analysis of the past two sections reveals two arguably orthogonal meta-trends—a push to make the models as large as possible, as well as a push to develop more efficient versions of larger models.

GPT-3, one of the largest leaps in the number of parameters we have observed yet—10 times—initially raised some concerns among researchers that top research companies would begin to focus on size over clever modeling. However, as we discussed in the previous section, the limitations of scaling up models quickly became apparent, with the authors of the GPT-3 paper admitting to limits that have likely been reached. Given that GPT-3 is currently available only via a limited paid API, we can expect the other players in the space to attempt to build even larger models soon as they have a monetary incentive to do so (we already mentioned the trillion-parameter Switch Transformer undergoing peer review). This race will likely culminate in a similar model from Google and/or Facebook being released, which will likely push GPT-3 to be fully open sourced (a similar scenario historically played out with GPT-2). Beyond that, we expect more resources to begin to be dedicated to more efficient methods of achieving similar performance.

Most of the interesting problems remaining in the immediate future of NLP transfer learning likely lie in the movement some have termed *TinyML*. This can be defined as a general goal to shrink the size of models so that they can fit on smaller hardware. We saw an instance of this when we demonstrated that the size of BERT can be roughly halved with little loss in performance via an approach such as DistilBERT in chapter 9. Another approach that accomplished this for us was ALBERT in chapter 10, achieving a 90% reduction in model size. A large fraction of the world's population now owns a smartphone, which can run these smaller versions of cutting-edge models. The opportunities this opens for a field such as the Internet of Things (IoT), where devices form smart networks with each node executing complex functions independently, cannot be overstated. Although many phone apps featuring translation and other tools today probably feature a server backend where the actual translation and other computation happens, the ability to run such algorithms locally on smartphone devices without an internet connection is becoming a more feasible and prevalent paradigm. We expect the drive to make models such as BERT and its derivatives smaller and more parameter-efficient to continue at a fever pitch over the next couple years.

Another trend you may have picked up from the previous section is the increasing focus on cross-lingual models. In fact, the past year has seen an increase in global investment in methods for so-called "low-resource" languages. We alluded to this via an example in chapter 7, when we used a transformer architecture to translate a low-resource West African language, Twi, into English. Many popular economic models project that an increasingly important class of consumers is emerging in the African market, which is likely at least one driver behind sudden interest and investment in this space. For many low-resource languages, the initial barrier to the applicability of all the methods that we discussed tends to be data availability. Therefore, we can expect appropriate multilingual data development to receive much attention over the upcoming year or so, followed by intense research into language-specific methodology enhancements in the subsequent years. Notable places to keep an eye on for these developments, specifically as they pertain to African languages, include NLP Ghana,[25] Masakhane,[26] EthioNLP,[27] Zindi Africa,[28] AfricaNLP,[29] and Black in AI.[30]

Speech is another NLP research frontier that is poised for a watershed moment. Until recently, automatic speech recognition models, which transcribe speech into text, required many hours of parallel speech-text data to achieve good results. A recent architecture, Wav2Vec2[31] from Facebook, demonstrated that pretraining on speech in many languages simultaneously dramatically reduced how much parallel data is required. This is similar to the functionality of mBERT we explored in this book for text. The Wav2Vec2 model is available in the transformers library and can be fine-tuned on new languages with just a few hours of annotated speech data. We expect this to spur the development of speech-recognition tools for many languages for the first time over the next year. Moreover, we anticipate that something similar is on the horizon for the reverse direction: text-to-speech, that is, the generation of speech from text.

In chapter 1, we described how transfer learning in NLP was inspired by its advances in computer vision. Interestingly enough, recent advances in NLP transfer learning seem to be inspiring further advances in computer vision. One specific example is DALL-E,[32] a version of GPT-3 trained on text description–image pairs, which has learned to generate images from text prompts. A wider trend is to build contextual

---

[25] https://ghananlp.org/
[26] https://www.masakhane.io/
[27] https://ethionlp.github.io/
[28] https://zindi.africa/
[29] https://www.k4all.org/project/language-dataset-fellowship/
[30] https://blackinai.github.io/
[31] https://huggingface.co/facebook/wav2vec2-large-xlsr-53
[32] https://openai.com/blog/dall-e/

scene-based object embeddings,[33] which try to predict missing objects from other observable objects in the scene, analogously to the fill-in-the-blanks objective for words utilized by BERT and similar masked language models.

Another research question that seems to be gaining more attention recently is this: What are the environmental and ethical impacts of these models? At the outset of the recent research spike, researchers seemed content with releasing models that improved technical metrics only, but over time, the field has come to value detailed explorations of any potential ethical impacts. Of related increased interest are questions around explainability: Can we actually explain how a model came to its decisions, so we know for sure that it is not discriminating? We dive into these ethical questions further in the next section.

11.4   *Ethical and environmental considerations*

You may recall that when we looked at the problem of fake news detection in chapters 5 and 6, we raised the point that what can be called fake is debatable. If care is not taken with the quality of the data labels, the biases ingrained in whoever prepared the labels for the training data will likely just transfer to the classification system. This was our first encounter with the important need to be fully aware of any potential limitations of these models before deploying them in circumstances which can significantly impact human lives.

When we fine-tuned mBERT on the JW300 dataset prepared by Jehovah's Witnesses in chapter 8, we found that it filled in the blanks in a biased way. When we tried to predict a basic noun "school," it would offer words such as Eden as plausible completions. This indicated strong religious bias, and it was the second time during our journey that we were alerted of the fact that blindly applying these models to some data can have biased and unforeseen outcomes.

In this section, we will discuss this on a broader level, considering potential ethical and environmental considerations that should probably be kept at the back of the mind of any practitioner working on deploying these models. This is a topic that is receiving increasing attention recently, but it is far from new in the machine learning field in general.

Early high-profile machine learning studies of bias predictably happened in computer vision. The landmark work, "Gender Shades,"[34] studied the accuracy of commercial gender-classification systems along racial and gender dimensions. It found that these systems underperformed for dark-skinned women as compared to lighter-skinned males by up to 35 absolute percentage points. This has an immense practical impact on minority communities, which may be policed by some of these automatic computer vision systems in some regions. An incorrect classification or detection can

---

[33] A. Dosovitskiy et al, "An Image Is Worth 16x16 Words: Transformers for Image Recognition at Scale," *arXiv* (2020).

[34] J. Buitamwini and T. Gebru, "Gender Shades: Intersectional Accuracy Disparities in Commercial Gender Classification," Journal of Machine Learning Research 81 (2018).

mean wrongful arrest, which even if cleared can mean job loss in the most vulnerable communities. There have been multiple widespread reports of this happening to real people. A cynical power imbalance was uncovered behind systems parading as "objective" and "scientific," where the richer communities where these systems were developed and their economic benefits were mostly reaped did not suffer the harm inflicted on the poorer communities. The impact of this work and related studies was significant, with the US Congress recently taking up related mitigating regulation arguably as a direct consequence. Companies such as IBM and Amazon have also been forced to review how they share these technologies with law enforcement authorities, with IBM completely discontinuing the service.

Concerns about bias of pretrained NLP language models has also been high recently. In fact, the GPT-3 paper[35] includes a dedicated section for a study along several dimensions, namely race, sex, and religion. It has become more and more common to see academic articles do this recently, which is quite encouraging to see. The GPT-3 study in particular probes the association the model learned from the training data for the various dimensions of interest. For instance, they discovered that occupations usually associated with a higher level of education were more closely associated with male pronouns when filling in the blanks. Similarly, prompts implying professional competence were more likely to be completed by male pronouns and specifiers. This is likely gender bias directly learned by the model from the internet, which we probably can't expect to be an unbiased source. On the other hand, positive descriptors were assigned to nouns primed with "Asian" and "White" at a significantly higher rate than for "Black" personas. Again, a racial bias was clearly learned by the model from the internet, and blind application of the model would simply propagate this bias. On the religious dimension, the word "Islam" was associated with the word "terrorism" among the most likely completions. As a direct real-world impact of this bias, consider the case of the Palestinian man whose benign "good morning" Facebook post was incorrectly translated as "attack them" and led to significant unfair consequences.[36]

Another way pretrained NLP language models could inadvertently affect poor communities is via climate change. In fact, these models have recently been shown to have quite the carbon footprint.[37, 38] Although the carbon footprint of training a single BERT model once was found to be equivalent to a single average roundtrip flight between New York and San Francisco, during fine-tuning and hyperparameter optimization, the model is actually trained many times. If the model was to be deployed via *neural architecture search*, where various architecture hyperparameters are exhaustively varied and the best-performing model selected, the researchers found a single model deployment to cost the footprint of up to five average cars

[35] Tom B. Brown et al., "Language Models Are Few-Shot Learners," NeurIPS (2020).
[36] http://mng.bz/w0V2
[37] E. Strubell et al., "Energy and Policy Considerations for Deep Learning in NLP," ACL (2019).
[38] E. Bender et al., "On the Dangers of Stochastic Parrots: Can Language Models Be Too Big?" FAccT (2021).

over their entire lifetime. Again, this is serious and particularly egregious, because the effects of climate change, directly linked to these carbon footprints, hit hardest in the poorest communities, which do not experience the direct benefits of these models. It is clear that these costs need to be taken into account when evaluating these models. This realization is arguably one of the forces driving the field toward more parameter-efficient models.

A lingering criticism of pretrained language models, and deep learning in general, is that the models tend to be not very *explainable*—it is hard to explain how a model arrived at its predictions for any particular scenario. This is related to the earlier bias discussion we had in this section—having the model explain how it arrived at associations related to education, for instance, could help detect if such a decision was made based on the race or sex variable. Most notable recent approaches at achieving this, such as bertviz,[39] try to build on the attention visualization we explored in chapter 7. This still does not address the lack of training data transparency question that remains: the training of language models takes place at such a large data scale that it is virtually impossible for researchers to ensure that it is unbiased. Therefore, we expect to see an investment of time and effort into the development of methods that could perform comparably from significantly smaller, well-curated datasets.

With our brief discussion of some ethical issues that should be kept in mind complete, we provide some tips in the next section on how to stay up-to-date in this fast-moving field.

11.5   *Staying up-to-date*

As we have stressed throughout this chapter, the state of transfer learning methods in NLP updates very quickly. The material covered in this book should be viewed only as a platform from which to continue keeping yourself updated on latest developments. In this section, we present a few basic tips on how one might achieve this. To summarize, participating in various relevant competitions on the Kaggle and/or Zindi platforms can be a good way to work on realistic, yet sufficiently clean, trending relevant data and problems. Keeping track of latest papers on *arXiv* is a must, and although news and social media coverage can be sensationalist and otherwise unreliable, it can still help one spot impactful papers early on.

11.5.1   *Kaggle and Zindi competitions*

Throughout the book, we have encouraged you to use Kaggle to run the various code presented. Although the free GPU compute provided by the platform and ease of setup were immediately stated benefits, the biggest benefit may not have been explicitly stated until now. Arguably the most powerful aspect of the Kaggle platform is access to the numerous constantly ongoing and archived-for-posterity competitions on the platform.

---

[39] Jesse Vig, "A Multiscale Visualization of Attention in the Transformer Model," ACL (2019).

Top firms facing all sorts of technical challenges use the platform to stimulate research and development of solutions to said problems by offering cash prizes, sometimes into the thousands of dollars for top-place finishes. This means that by tracking these competitions, you are kept updated on what the most pressing problems in industry are, while having access to the representative data for immediate testing and experimentation. You could browse current and past competitions by topic to find data to test any ideas you might have—all you need to do is attach the dataset to the notebooks we have been using in this book, change some paths, and you likely will be ready to produce some preliminary insights. Winning the competitions is, of course, great, if you can do so, but the learning value you will get from experimenting, failing, and trying again is what is truly invaluable. Indeed, in my experience, a solution to a contest problem that may be considered mediocre by leaderboard placement may be the one that leads to a real-world impact, if it is easier to deploy and scale in practice, for instance. We provide some specific tips for using Kaggle in appendix A to help beginners get started with it.

We have also highlighted the recent increase in focus on low-resource languages in NLP. It is thus crucial to mention the Zindi Africa platform, which provides many of the same functionalities as Kaggle but focuses on African languages and problems. If you are a researcher who wants to see how your methods might perform on some of these types of languages, this platform would be a good place to find related contests and data for experimentation.

11.5.2 *arXiv*

Machine learning, and by extension NLP, is arguably the most open field of research today. With a few exceptions, results are typically published on the open platform *arXiv* immediately when they become available. This allows research teams to claim priority to any discovery, while going through refinements and paper publication formalities. This means that the most cutting-edge research is already available to you if you are able to find it. *arXiv* is archived by Google Scholar, so setting alerts there for keywords that are important to you can help you detect relevant papers early on.

The volume of paper uploads to the *arXiv* platform is huge, and it is hard to find the most important papers that might be relevant to you. To address this issue, I recommend following the authors of your favorite papers on social media—Twitter seems to be the platform preferred by researchers in this space. Keeping an eye on media coverage can also be helpful, as long as you treat all claims with a grain of salt. We say a few more words about that next.

11.5.3 *News and social media (Twitter)*

In general, it is good to treat news and social media coverage of scientific topics as potentially sensationalist and otherwise technically unreliable. This makes sense if one thinks about the incentives a media outlet might have related to covering the technology and the fact that often journalists may not have a technical background on the subject. However, vetted news can be a good indicator of excitement in the community about a particular paper or topic, and that is always a good thing to be aware of.

If you use a platform such as Google News, you can set alerts for topics such as "language models" in your feed. You will probably get a lot of hits, and not all of them might be worth your attention. I usually really dig into a paper deeply only after I see it come up in venues that I consider consistently "reliable" over a period of time, which gives me some confidence that the claims have withstood at least a short period of open review. The case of GPT-3 comes up when thinking about a recent example—this was one whose impact was immediately evident by following this heuristic on Google News.

With regard to social media, Twitter appears to be the platform of choice for machine learning research scientists. In fact, many are very open about their work and will gladly engage with you directly on the platform if you just ask them a question. This is one of the things I love most about working in this field. Please feel free to reach out to me at @pazunre. Your favorite author or scientist probably shares their latest favorite papers on their feed, and by just following them you could have these delivered to you directly. Some popular accounts you may find interesting in this space include @fchollet, @seb_ruder, and @huggingface.

Beyond competitions, reading papers on *arXiv*, and tracking news and social media, nothing is really a good substitute for working on real-world practical challenges with these tools. For many people, this might just mean holding a job in machine learning and/or NLP and working on a practical application of them daily. Practical experience is what is valued most by the majority of potential employers in this field. If you have yet to gain such practical experience in this area and are looking to break in, open source projects can be a great way to do that—check out TensorFlow, PyTorch, Hugging Face, NLP Ghana, Masakhane, and so on. The list is endless, and there is no shortage of interesting problems to solve and contribute to, while also potentially benefitting everyone.

I hope these tips will help guide you into your machine learning and NLP future, where you are empowered to make a significant positive impact on your society. It has been a privilege to share a part of your journey with you.

11.6 *Final words*

This is it! You have done it—you have read all of this book. I had an incredible time writing it, interacting with many researchers in the process to discuss ideas and working through the many challenges. I sincerely hope that you enjoyed the journey as much as I did. As you go forth and change the world with these tools, remember to be kind to those around you, do no harm to the ecosystem, and stay vigilant about the potential misuses of your tech. From my brief time interacting with some of the brilliant minds working in this field, I sincerely believe that most are excited about making these technological breakthroughs a source for good. Thus, I watch the research news with excitement day after day, impatient to see what our collective human mind will come up with next. I can only hope that you share some of this excitement.

Summary

- You are only at the beginning of your journey in this rapidly evolving field; retaining a competitive edge is a journey and not a destination.
- The skills you have picked up by working through this book have put you in a good position to enable you to stay up-to-date with continued effort.
- Some key fundamental pretrained transfer-learning-enabled language modeling architectures we covered include the Transformer, BERT, mBERT, ELMo, and GPT.
- The desire to make these larger models smaller and more efficient led to the development of architectures/techniques such as ALBERT, DistilBERT, and ULMFiT, which we covered as well.
- Emerging architectures that are the descendants of the aforementioned models, which are not covered by the book in detail but which you should be aware of, include BART, T5, Longformer, Reformer, XLNet, and many more.
- It is important to be aware of potential ethical and environmental impacts of these models when deploying them in practice.
- Recent concerns about ethical and environmental impacts, as well as the desire to put model capabilities on smartphones and IoT, will likely continue to fuel the development of increasingly more efficient transformer architectures in the near future.

appendix A
Kaggle primer

The Kaggle platform provides an excellent way for beginners in data science and machine learning to pick up basic skills. By appropriately leveraging the platform, you get the opportunity to practice a broad range of problems on a variety of datasets, as well as to present and discuss your work with fellow machine learning engineers. This can potentially help grow your professional network. Importantly, the platform allows you to run Python notebooks directly in the cloud, which can significantly remove system setup barriers for a beginner. It also provides a limited amount of free GPU computing per week. This further democratizes access to the tools and methods discussed in this book. Throughout the book, we encourage you to use Kaggle to run the code presented.

Another tool—Google Colab—similarly provides free GPU computing while integrating with the Google Drive. If you had to pick one tool, however, I would recommend Kaggle due to its social nature and the access to datasets, discussions, and competitions—which are all extremely valuable learning resources. In reality, of course, most engineers likely leverage both at some point, to increase their weekly free GPU quota, for instance.

In this appendix, we attempt to provide a brief primer that can help a beginner ease their way into the various features of Kaggle. We divide it into two sections. We first discuss the Kaggle kernel concept for running the notebooks and follow that with a look at competitions, related discussions, and Kaggle blog features.

A.1   Free GPUs with Kaggle kernels

As previously mentioned, you can run Python code directly in the cloud for free using Kaggle. These cloud notebooks are sometimes referred to as *Kaggle kernels*. At the time of writing this in January 2021, Kaggle provides about 36 weekly GPU hours, which you can enable for any notebooks that you think might need it. We will demonstrate how to get started by walking through a simple scenario a beginner in Python might find useful.

Let's say you were such a beginner and were interested in learning basic Python syntax with these kernels. A good place to start would be to go to https://www.kaggle .com/kernels and search for "Python tutorial." The search results for this might look as shown in figure A.1.

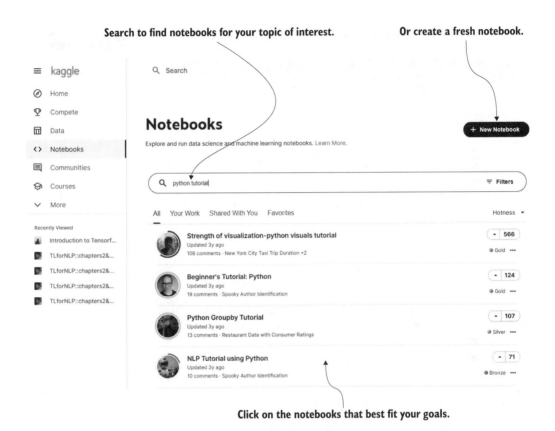

Figure A.1 The best place to start learning about Kaggle kernels and launching a relevant notebook to learn something new. Go to https://www.kaggle.com/kernels, and search for the topic you are interested in. In the diagram, we show the result list of such a query for a beginner starting out with Python. Select the best-fitting one to proceed. Or create a new notebook using the New Notebook button.

As can be seen in the figure, searching will return a list of results, and you can select one that best fits your needs. In this case, the beginner might want the tutorial to start with an NLP focus directly, given the content of the book, and might thus select the highlighted tutorial notebook. Clicking it brings up the relevant rendered notebook, with a representative view shown in figure A.2.

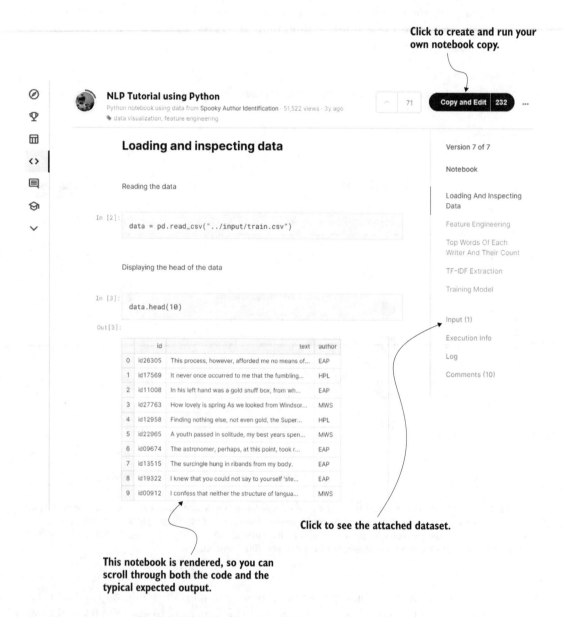

Click to create and run your own notebook copy.

Click to see the attached dataset.

This notebook is rendered, so you can scroll through both the code and the typical expected output.

Figure A.2   A view of the rendered notebook, with some key actions that can be performed highlighted

Note that the view shown is representative of the first view you will encounter when you click on one of our companion notebook links in the book repository.[1] As stated in the figure, the notebook is rendered, which means you can scroll and see representative output for all code even without running it.

To run the code, click the Copy and Edit button to create your own version of the notebook. The resulting notebook will have the same dependencies—Python library versions preinstalled in the Kaggle environment and those used to generate the representative notebook output. Note that if you clicked the New Notebook button in figure A.1 instead of opting to copy an existing notebook, the dependencies will be the latest ones specified by Kaggle. Thus, you may need to modify the original code to get it to work, which makes things harder. To complete the copy and edit, or forking, process, you will be asked for login information. You can either register with your email address or use a social account such as Google to log in directly.

To replicate exactly the Kaggle environment we used for the companion notebooks for this book, we have included requirement files in the companion book repository. Note that these requirement files are only for the purpose of replicating the Kaggle environment on a Kaggle notebook. If you tried to use them on your local machine, depending on local architecture, you might run into additional issues and may need to modify them. We do not support this mode, and if you are pursuing it, use the requirement files only as a guide. Also keep in mind that not every listed requirement will be needed for your local installation.

Clicking Copy and Edit will bring you to the main workspace, which is illustrated in figure A.3. As can be seen in the figure, you can either run the currently selected cell or run all the code in the notebook using buttons on the top left. On the right panel, you can enable or disable your internet connection. Internet connection might be required to download data or install packages. This right panel also houses the option to enable GPU acceleration in the current notebook, which you will need for training neural networks in reasonable time. You will also see the datasets currently attached to the notebook and be able to click on any one of them to be taken to the dataset's description. Clicking Add Data will open a search query box where you will be able to search for datasets of interest for adding to the current notebook, by keyword. For all of the companion notebooks for this book, necessary data has been attached to the notebook for you already.

On the top right, you can select the Share settings of the notebook—you can make notebooks private to just yourself, share them with other users privately, or make them public to the world, depending on your project needs. All of our companion notebooks are public so that anyone can access them, but you can make your forks of them

---

[1] https://github.com/azunre/transfer-learning-for-nlp

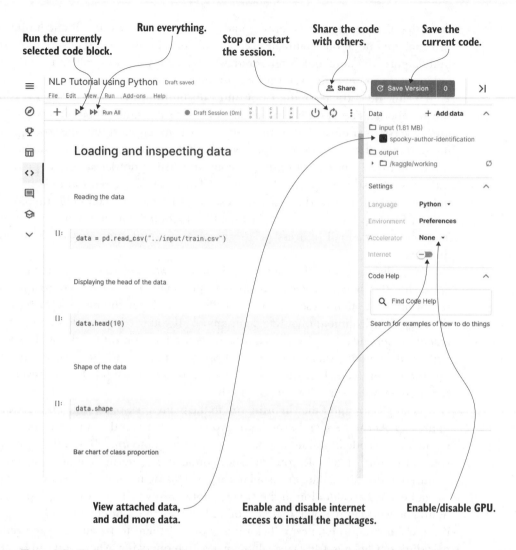

Run the currently selected code block.

Run everything.

Stop or restart the session.

Share the code with others.

Save the current code.

View attached data, and add more data.

Enable and disable internet access to install the packages.

Enable/disable GPU.

Figure A.3   The main workspace when using Kaggle kernels. In the top left corner, buttons for running the notebook. In the top right, options to share, save, restart, and turn off the notebook. The right panel houses options for connecting to the internet (for installing packages or downloading data), enabling/ disabling GPU acceleration for the current notebook, and adding data.

private. Importantly, also on the top right, selecting Save Version will bring up the dialog box to save your work, as shown in figure A.4.

As the figure demonstrates, there are two save modes. The Quick Save mode will save the current code and output under the name specified in the version name text blog. In the case that the current output took several hours to generate, this would be the right choice. The Save & Run All option will save the code and run it afresh in a

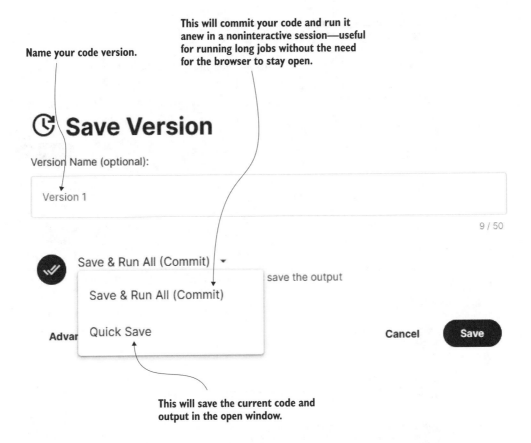

Name your code version.

This will commit your code and run it anew in a noninteractive session—useful for running long jobs without the need for the browser to stay open.

This will save the current code and output in the open window.

Figure A.4 Save options for notebook. You can either commit the code and have it run noninteractively for inspection later or quick-save the code and current output directly.

background, noninteractive process. This is particularly useful when running training jobs for long periods, such as for five or six hours. You can close the session and all windows and come back whenever you want to inspect the results. Inspection of the recent runs/saves can typically be carried out at the personalized URL www.kaggle .com/<username>/notebooks, where <username> is your username. For my username azunre, the view of this page is shown in figure A.5.

We have thus covered the main features you need to know about to get started with the exercises in this book. There are many other features that we have not covered, and many more continue to get added frequently by Kaggle. Usually, a quick Google search and some persistence and desire to experiment is enough to figure out how to use any such feature.

In the next section, we briefly discuss Kaggle competitions.

Go to www.kaggle.com/<<username>>/notebooks to inspect recent notebook runs after saving.

Recent notebook runs will be listed here.

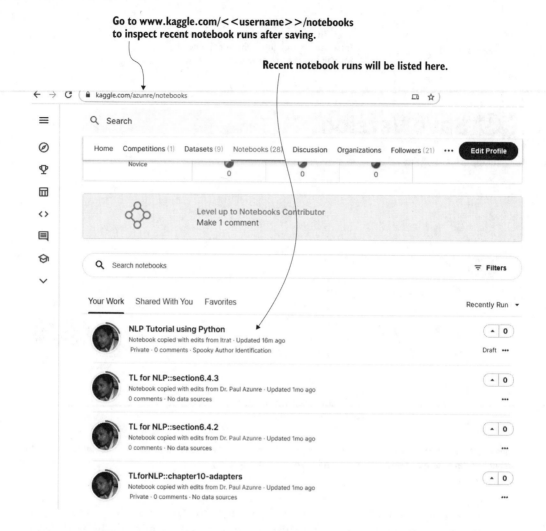

Figure A.5 Inspection of the recent runs/saves can typically be carried out at the personalized URL www.kaggle.com/<username>/notebooks, where <username> is your username (shown here for my username azunre**).**

A.2 Competitions, discussion, and blog

Leading enterprises facing technical challenges use Kaggle to stimulate research and development into solutions by offering significant cash prizes for top innovations. Let's inspect the Kaggle competition page by selecting the trophy icon visible on the left panel of any Kaggle page, as shown in figure A.6.

You can track these competitions to be updated on the most pressing problems in industry, while having access to the underlying data for immediate testing and experi-

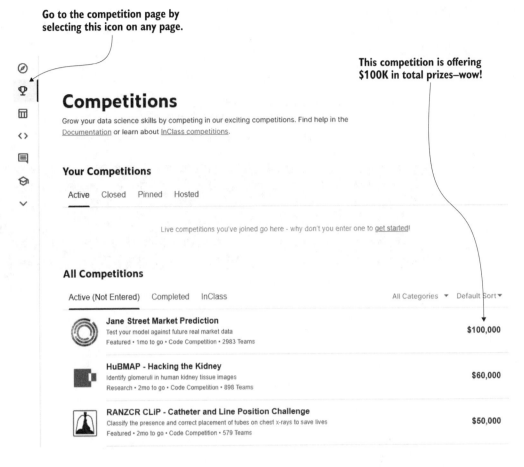

Go to the competition page by selecting this icon on any page.

This competition is offering $100K in total prizes—wow!

Competitions

Grow your data science skills by competing in our exciting competitions. Find help in the Documentation or learn about InClass competitions.

Your Competitions

Active   Closed   Pinned   Hosted

Live competitions you've joined go here - why don't you enter one to get started!

All Competitions

Active (Not Entered)   Completed   InClass   All Categories ▼   Default Sort ▼

Jane Street Market Prediction
Test your model against future real market data
Featured • 1mo to go • Code Competition • 2983 Teams $100,000

HuBMAP - Hacking the Kidney
Identify glomeruli in human kidney tissue images
Research • 2mo to go • Code Competition • 898 Teams $60,000

RANZCR CLiP - Catheter and Line Position Challenge
Classify the presence and correct placement of tubes on chest x-rays to save lives
Featured • 2mo to go • Code Competition • 579 Teams $50,000

Figure A.6   Go to the competitions page by selecting the trophy icon on the left panel of any Kaggle page. We can see that one competition is offering $100,000 in total prizes—that problem is likely quite valuable to that industry to motivate such an investment!

mentation. You could browse current and past competitions by topic to find data to test any ideas you might have. All you need to do is attach the dataset to the notebooks introduced in the previous section, change some paths, and likely you should be ready to produce some preliminary insights. Winning the competitions is, of course, great for the monetary reward, if you can do so, but the learning value you will get from experimenting, failing, and trying again is what is truly invaluable. Indeed, in my experience, a solution to a contest problem that may be considered mediocre by leaderboard placement may be the one that leads to a real-world impact, if it easier to deploy and scale in practice, for instance. This is what I personally care about, and so I tend to focus my efforts on working on problems most interesting to me that I know the least about, for the maximum learning value.

Clicking on any competition will bring up a dedicated page where you can browse its description, data, leaderboard, and, importantly, the "discussion" feature shown in figure A.7.

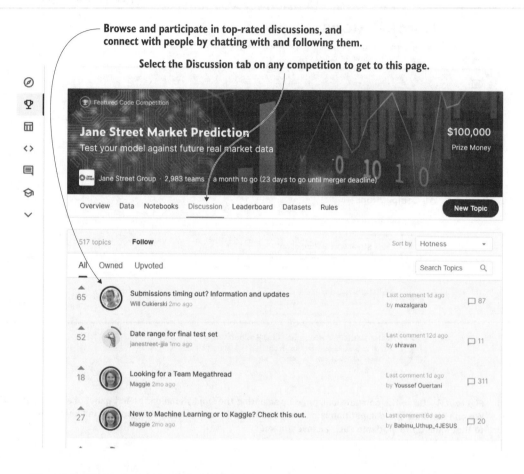

Browse and participate in top-rated discussions, and connect with people by chatting with and following them.

Select the Discussion tab on any competition to get to this page.

Figure A.7   The discussion feature enables you to engage with other members of the Kaggle community on specific topics of interest to you. Chat and build your network!

As you can probably see in figure A.7, this is a discussion forum relevant to the problem at hand. People post tips and starter notebooks, and ask important questions that might even be answered by competition organizers. If you run into any issues with a particular competition's data, for example, it is very likely you will find answers to your questions here. Many competitions provide prizes for the most valuable contributions—often measured by upvotes—which incentivizes folks to be quite helpful. Winners often post their solutions, sometimes even as notebooks that you can directly repurpose.

You might even strike up a friendship and build a team here for future challenges. Engage with the community, and give back some of what you take from it, and you will likely learn a lot more than you would otherwise. At the end of the day, science is still a social activity, which makes this feature of Kaggle particularly valuable.

Finally, Kaggle runs a blog at https://medium.com/kaggle-blog. Winners of big competitions are often interviewed here for tips they can share with others. Tutorials are frequently posted on various critical topics. Keep up-to-date with this to be sure to catch the latest emerging research trends in data science.

We hope this appendix was a useful exercise and brought you up to speed. Go forth and Kaggle!

appendix B
Introduction to
fundamental deep
learning tools

This appendix covers

- Introducing five fundamental algorithmic and software tools used in the book
- Overviewing stochastic gradient descent, the algorithm used to train neural networks
- Getting started with TensorFlow for neural network modeling
- Getting started with PyTorch for neural network modeling
- Overviewing higher-level neural network modeling frameworks Keras, fast.ai, and Hugging Face transformers

In this appendix, we attempt to provide a brief primer on a few fundamental tools and concepts that are used throughout the book. The brief introductions to these tools are not absolutely necessary to work through and fully benefit from the book. However, going through them can help one get oriented, and they are probably most useful to a new entrant into the field of deep learning.

Specifically, we first introduce the reader to the fundamental algorithm behind the deep learning revolution we are presently experiencing. This is, of course, the *stochastic gradient-descent algorithm*, which is used to train neural networks. We follow that up with introductions to two fundamental neural network modeling frameworks, PyTorch and TensorFlow. We then introduce three tools built on top of these modeling frameworks to provide a higher-level interface to them: Keras, fast.ai, and Hugging Face transformers. These tools all complement each other, and you are likely to use them all at some point in your career. Our exposition of the concepts is not exhaustive; it offers a "bird's-eye view" into why the various tools are needed and how they compare to and complement each other. We touch on introductory concepts and cite curated references to facilitate a deeper dive. If you feel your experience with these tools is minimal, you may benefit from diving deeper before beginning to work through this book.

Let's start with the algorithmic engine behind the deep learning revolution, the stochastic gradient-descent algorithm.

B.1   *Stochastic gradient descent*

A neural network has a set of parameters, called *weights*, which determine how it is going to transform input data into output data. Determining which set of weights allows the network to most closely approximate a set of training data is called *training* the network. Stochastic gradient descent is the method used to achieve this.

Let's denote the weights by W, the input data as x, and output data as y. Let's also denote the output data predicted by the neural network for the input x as y_pred. The loss function, which measures how close y is to y_pred, is denoted as the function f. Note that it is a function of x, y, and W. The stochastic gradient-descent algorithm is formulated as a procedure to find the minimum of f, that is, where the predictions are as close as possible to the training data. If the gradient for f, denoted by f', exists—if it is a *differentiable* function—we know f'=0 at such a point. The algorithm attempts to find such points using the following sequence of steps:

- Draw a random input-output batch x-y of data from the training set. This randomness is the reason the algorithm is qualified as *stochastic*.
- Pass inputs through the network with the current values of W to obtain y_pred.
- Compute the corresponding loss function value f.
- Compute corresponding gradient f' of the loss function with respect to W.
- Change W a bit in the opposite direction of the gradient to lower f. The size of the step is determined by picking the *learning rate* of the algorithm, a very important hyperparameter for convergence.

This process is illustrated for the overly simple case of a single weight, with the minimum found at step 2 of the algorithm in figure B.1. This figure is inspired by figure 2.11 of François Chollet's excellent book, *Deep Learning with Python* (Manning Publications, 2018), which you should also check out for a very intuitive explanation of the algorithm.

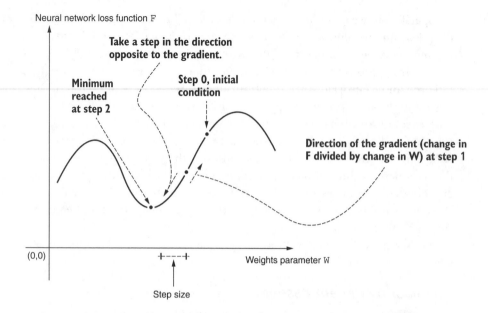

Figure B.1 Stochastic gradient descent illustrated in the overly simple case of a single weight. At each step, compute the gradient with respect to W, and take a step of a prespecified size, as determined by the learning rate, in the opposite direction of the gradient of the loss function. In this hypothetical scenario, the minimum is found at step 2.

A number of variants of this algorithm exist, including Adam, RMSprop, and Adagrad. These tend to focus on avoiding local minima and being adaptive in various ways (such as in learning rate) to converge faster. The concept of *momentum*—which manifests as an extra additive term in the W update at each step—is used by several such variants to avoid local minima. Some of the most popular variants, with brief descriptions, follow.

Adagrad adapts the learning rate in response to how often a parameter is encountered. Infrequent parameters are updated with larger steps to achieve a balance. This technique was used to train the GloVe static word embedding, described in chapter 4 of this book. It was needed in this case to appropriately handle rare words in language.

RMSprop was developed to address the observation that Adagrad's learning rate often decreased too quickly. We can partially alleviate the issue by scaling updates by an exponentially decaying average of squared gradients.

Adam, which stands for *Adaptive Moment Estimation,* also varies the learning rate for different parameters. It shares a similarity to RMSprop in that it uses the decaying squared gradient average to perform updates. Both the first and second moments of the decaying squared gradient average are estimated, updated, and then used to update the parameters at every step. This is a popular algorithm to try first for many problems.

Nadam, short for *Nesterov-accelerated Adam,* employs an innovation called the *Nesterov-accelerated gradient* to improve Adam convergence further.

Because the exposition here is meant to be only a brief introduction, and not a detailed treatment, we do not explore these variants further. This subject has been covered in detail by many excellent references,[1,2] and we encourage you to dive deeper to gain a better understanding. Even though you can use modern frameworks without a deep understanding of these variants, understanding them better can certainly help you tune hyperparameters and ultimately deploy better models.

B.2　*TensorFlow*

As described in the previous section, knowing the gradient of the loss function with respect to the neural network weights is critical to training the network. Because modern neural networks are huge, reaching into billions of parameters, this gradient function would be impossible to compute by hand. Instead, using a fundamental neural network modeling tool such as TensorFlow, the gradient is found automatically by applying the chain rule of taking derivatives to the functions composing the neural network model. This process is known as *automatic differentiation*.

The basic data structure within Tensorflow is a *tensor*, on which operations are performed by building a *graph*. In versions 1.x of the framework, the graph is put together with various `tf.*` API calls, and a `Session` object is used to compile and execute it to yield numerical values. An illustrative example of using this API to define a graph, and execute both it and its gradient, is shown in listing B.1. Specifically, we are interested in computing the matrix product z = x*y, where x is a simple column vector and y is a simple row vector. We are also interested in computing its gradient, with respect to both x and y, automatically.

Listing B.1　Computing the matrix product `z = x*y` and its gradient with TensorFlow 1

```
import tensorflow as tf          ←—   Always imports          Eager execution was introduced
                                       TensorFlow first        as the nondefault earlier than
                                                               2.0, so here we ensure it is off.
tf.compat.v1.disable_eager_execution()    ←—

x = tf.compat.v1.placeholder(tf.float32, name = "x")   ←—    Defines the placeholders
y = tf.compat.v1.placeholder(tf.float32, name = "y")         for vector variables to
                                                             assign values to later
z = tf.multiply(x, y) # Define vector product graph
gradient = tf.gradients(z,[x, y],grad_ys=tf.eye(2))          Executes the graph using
                                                             the Session object
with tf.compat.v1.Session() as session:       ←—
    z = session.run(z, feed_dict={x: [[1., 1.]], y: [[5.], [5.]]})   ←—
    zG = session.run(gradient,feed_dict={x: [[1.,1.]], y: [[5.],[5.]]})  ←—
```

Defines the vector derivative graph of the product, with respect to both x and y. Parameter grad_ys multiplies the output and can be used to take chain derivatives, so we set it to identity matrix for no effect.

Runs the gradient, specifying values for placeholders

Runs the function, specifying values for placeholders

---

[1] F. Chollet, *Deep Learning with Python* (Manning Publications, 2018).
[2] S. Ruder, "An Overview of Gradient Descent Optimization Algorithms," *arXiv* (2016).

```
print("Product:")          ⟵┐  Displays the
print(z)                      │  results
print("\n\n")
print("Gradient of Product:")
print(zG)
print("\n\n")
```

Executing this code yields the following output. You should be able to verify by hand that these values are correct, using your basic linear algebra knowledge, which is a pre-requisite for this book. We have also included a Kaggle kernel notebook executing these commands in the book's companion repository:[3]

```
Product:
[[5. 5.]
 [5. 5.]]

Gradient of Product:
[array([[5., 5.]], dtype=float32), array([[1.],
       [1.]], dtype=float32)]
```

Version 2.0 and later of the framework made the more "Pythonic" *eager execution* mode the default, which made the framework more accessible. It also now included Keras, making it easier to use a wide variety of higher-level functions. An illustrative example of using this API to define and execute the same graph from listing B.1 is shown in the next listing. The greater accessibility is immediately evident, with eager mode enabling execution right away instead of via a `Session` object on a graph.

Listing B.2 Computing the matrix product z = x*y and its gradient with TensorFlow 2

```
import tensorflow as tf
                                              Column vector
x = tf.convert_to_tensor([[1., 1.]])   ⟵┐  Row vector
y = tf.convert_to_tensor([[5.], [5.]])  ⟵┘

with tf.GradientTape() as g:
    g.watch(x)
    z = tf.multiply(x, y)
    dz_dx = g.gradient(z, x, output_gradients=tf.eye(2))

with tf.GradientTape() as g:           ⟵
    g.watch(y)
    z = tf.multiply(x, y)
    dz_dy = g.gradient(z, y, output_gradients=tf.eye(2))
```

This is how you would compute automatic derivatives with respect to x. The word "Tape" here means all states are "recorded" and can be played back to retrieve the info we need.

This is how you would compute automatic derivatives with respect to y. Parameter output_gradients multiplies the output and can be used to take chain derivatives, so we set it to identity matrix for no effect.

---

[3] https://github.com/azunre/transfer-learning-for-nlp

```
print("Dot Product:")          ◁──┐  Displays the
print(z)                           │  results
print("\n\n")
print("Gradient of Product (dz_dx):")
print(dz_dx)
print("\n\n")
print("Gradient of Product (dz_dy):")
print(dz_dy)
```

Executing this code should yield the same output values as before.

The framework is organized hierarchically, with both high-level and low-level APIs, as shown in figure B.2.

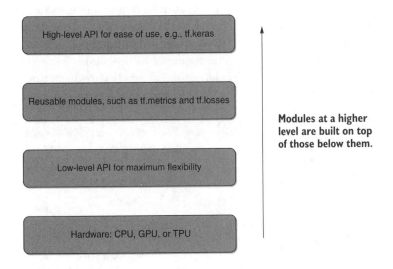

Figure B.2   Illustration of the hierarchical organization of the TensorFlow framework

This figure is heavily influenced by figure 1 of the official TensorFlow documentation.[4] If you are a beginner at using the framework, skimming through this reference in more detail can be helpful. The TensorFlow version of Keras, to be discussed further in the last section of this appendix, is also shown in the diagram.

The better way to pick up the ins and outs of the various features of TensorFlow is to get your hands dirty experimenting with relevant Kaggle kernel/notebook tutorials, as described in appendix A. In particular, just going to kaggle.com and searching for "TensorFlow tutorial" will bring up a myriad of wonderful tutorials, and you can choose something that works best for your learning style and experience level. The

---

[4] https://developers.google.com/machine-learning/crash-course/first-steps-with-tensorflow/toolkit

tutorial at https://www.kaggle.com/akashkr/tensorflow-tutorial seems to be a good one for beginners.

B.3   *PyTorch*

This framework was released by Facebook after TensorFlow (in 2016 versus 2015). However, it quickly became preferred by many researchers, as evidenced by declining relative popularity of TensorFlow to PyTorch in terms of academic paper citations.[5] This increased popularity has widely been attributed to the framework's ability to modify various PyTorch model objects programmatically at runtime, making for easier code optimization during the research process. Indeed, the introduction of eager mode in TensorFlow 2.0 is widely believed to have been influenced by PyTorch's success. Although the differences between the platforms became much smaller after the release of TensorFlow 2.0, the popular wisdom is that PyTorch is preferred by researchers whereas TensorFlow is preferred for deployment in production.

As an illustration, we perform the same sequence of operations from listings B.1. and B.2—vector multiplication and its derivative, which is core to neural network models—in PyTorch and show the corresponding code in the next listing.

Listing B.3   Computing the matrix product z = x*y and its gradient in PyTorch

```
import torch                                    ◁─── Always import PyTorch first.
from torch.autograd import grad                 ◁─── Imports the grad function for automatic differentiation
import numpy as np # tensors will be built from numpy arrays

x = torch.from_numpy(np.array([[1., 1.]]))      ◁─── Column vector
y = torch.from_numpy(np.array([[5.], [5.]]))    ◁─── Row vector

x.requires_grad = True                          ◁─── This ensures that gradients can be computed with respect to x.
y.requires_grad = True
z = torch.mul(x, y)                             ◁─── Computes the product

zGx = grad(outputs=z, inputs=x,grad_outputs=torch.eye(2),retain_graph=True) ◁───
zGy = grad(outputs=z, inputs=y,grad_outputs=torch.eye(2))

print("Dot Product")                            ◁─── Displays the results
print(z)
print("Gradient of Product(dz_dx)")
print(zGx)
print("\n\n")
print("Gradient of Product (dz_dy):")
print(zGy)
```

Computes automatic derivatives with respect to x. retain_graph ensures that we can keep taking derivatives; otherwise, the "Tape" is discarded and can't be played back.

Computes automatic derivatives with respect to y. The parameter grad_outputs multiplies the output and can be used to take chain derivatives, so we set it to identity matrix for no effect.

---

[5] https://en.wikipedia.org/wiki/TensorFlow

Executing this code should yield the same result as in the previous section. We have also included a Kaggle kernel notebook executing these commands in the book's companion repository.[6]

As before, we recommend working through some Kaggle kernels to pick up the ins and outs of PyTorch, if you are feel that you might need more experience. The tutorial at https://www.kaggle.com/kanncaa1/pytorch-tutorial-for-deep-learning-lovers seems to be a good one for beginners.

B.4   *Keras, fast.ai, and Transformers by Hugging Face*

As mentioned earlier in the appendix, the Keras library is a higher-level neural network modeling framework, which is also now included in TensorFlow versions 2.0 and later. By using it, you can specify neural network architectures in both TensorFlow and PyTorch from a single API—just change the backend as needed! It comes prepackaged with TensorFlow, as we illustrated in figure B.2. Its API is relatively simple compared to both TensorFlow and PyTorch, which has made it very popular. Many excellent resources exist for learning it, perhaps the best one being the author's own book.[7] This is also an excellent reference for learning TensorFlow, and about neural networks in general, and we highly recommend it if you feel you need to brush up on these topics. You can also work through some Kaggle kernels to pick up the basics, with the tutorial at https://www.kaggle.com/prashant111/keras-basics-for-beginners being just one good example.

Another popular higher-level modeling API in the field is fast.ai. This library was developed as a companion to the massive open online course (MOOC) of the same name and implements state-of-the-art methods in a way that makes them extremely easy to use. One of its motivations was democratizing these tools for the developing world. A popular feature of this library is its learning rate determination utility, which we use in chapter 9 of this book. The framework is used for both NLP and computer vision and runs on PyTorch. Naturally, the best reference for learning the library is the fast.ai MOOC[8] itself. The free course covers the basics of neural networks and deep learning and is another wonderful resource that we highly recommend. The library achieves simplicity by defining its own set of data structures that handle a lot of boilerplate stuff for the user. On the other hand, this might make it harder to customize for nonstandard use cases. In this author's experience, it is a wonderful tool to have in one's arsenal.

Finally, transformers by Hugging Face is a higher-level modeling framework specifically for transformer-based models. These have become arguably the most important architecture for modern NLP. You will learn exactly why that is the case throughout the book. The library might be the most popular library in the space today, due to the sheer ease of using it to deploy these models. Before this library existed, deploying

---

[6] https://github.com/azunre/transfer-learning-for-nlp
[7] F. Chollet, *Deep Learning with Python* (Manning Publications, 2018).
[8] https://www.fast.ai/

transformer models in Keras, TensorFlow, and/or PyTorch was quite tedious. The library simplified the process into a few lines of Python code in some cases, which led to an explosion in its popularity, and it is considered indispensable for the modern NLP practitioner. Due to the transparency and simplicity of the API, you can probably get away with just reading through the book and working through relevant examples, even without any prior experience with it. For further reference, check out the intro notebooks from the authors on GitHub[9] and their official quick start[10] documentation.

---

[9] https://github.com/huggingface/transformers/tree/master/notebooks
[10] https://huggingface.co/transformers/quicktour.html

index